PRIVATE LIVES/PUBLIC MOMENTS

READINGS IN AMERICAN HISTORY
VOLUME 1: BEFORE 1492 TO 1877

Dominick Cavallo, Editor
Adelphi University

Prentice Hall
Boston Columbus Indianapolis New York San Francisco
Upper Saddle River Amsterdam Cape Town Dubai London Madrid
Milan Munich Paris Montreal Toronto Delhi Mexico City Sao Paulo
Sydney Hong Kong Seoul Singapore Taipei Tokyo

Editorial Director: Leah Jewell
Publisher: Charlyce Jones Owen
Editorial Assistant: Maureen Diana
Director of Marketing: Brandy Dawson
Senior Managing Editor: Ann Marie McCarthy
Production Project Manager: Lynn Savino Wendel
Operations Specialist: Maura Zaldivar
Creative Director: Jayne Conte
Cover Designer: Bruce Kenselaar
Manager, Visual Research: Beth Brenzel
Manager, Rights and Permissions: Zina Arabia
Image Permission Coordinator: Silvana Attanasio
Manager, Cover Visual Research and Permissions: Karen Sanatar
Cover Art: The Gerlach-Barklow Col., Joliet, Ill., U.S.A./Library of Congress
Full-Service Project Management/Composition: Christian Holdener,
 S4Carlisle Publishing Services
Printer/Binder: R.R. Donnelley & Sons, Inc.
Cover Printer: R.R. Donnelley & Sons, Inc.

This book was set in 10/11 Palatino.

Library of Congress Cataloging-in-Publication Data
Private lives/public moments : readings in American history/Dominick Cavallo, editor.
 p. cm.
Includes bibliographical references.
ISBN 978-0-321-29856-0 (v. 1) — ISBN 978-0-205-72368-3 (v. 2) 1. United States—History.
I. Cavallo, Dominick,
 E178.1.P946 2010
 973—dc22   2009017441

10 9 8 7 6 5 4 3 2 1

Prentice Hall
is an imprint of

www.pearsonhighered.com   ISBN 13: 978-0-321-29856-0
                                 ISBN 10:   0-321-29856-X

For JoAnn

I pray thee, gentle mortal, sing again:
Mine ear is much enamour'd of thy note;
So is mine eye enthralled to thy shape;
And thy fair virtue's force, perforce, doth move me;
On the first view, to say, I swear, I love thee.

—William Shakespeare, *A Midsummer Night's Dream*

CONTENTS

Part 3   Social Reform, Slavery, and the Civil War

FOREWORD

Every generation must write a history that speaks to its own time. Today, many of the issues that preoccupy Americans involve private life. For more than a quarter-century, bitter political controversy has raged over abortion, dead-beat dads, domestic violence, gay rights, same-sex marriage, teenage pregnancy, and a host of other issues rooted in private life. This fascinating reader in American history provides essential historical context for understanding recent controversies over "traditional family values." It also helps us recognize that every major event in American history—from colonization to the Revolution, slavery to the Civil War—had a vital, but largely unrecognized, private dimension. It shows students the human meaning of public events—of how African Americans coped with slavery and racial discrimination, how immigrants adapted to new ways of life, how working families coped with the strains of industrialization and economic hardship, and how women have struggled to expand their roles and opportunities.

Equally important, *Private Lives/Public Moments* demonstrates that private choices have profound public consequences. Many of the most important historical developments were the result not of the actions of presidents, legislators, or judges, but of the cumulate decisions of millions of ordinary women and men. The decision to migrate, to protest discrimination, to raise or reduce the birthrate—these private choices have carried immense public implications.

By exploring the private side of American history, *Private Lives/Public Moments* shatters many myths and misconceptions that Americans take for granted. Sensationalized newspaper and television reports have led many Americans to conclude that divorce and family breakdown are recent phenomena. But readers of this volume will quickly learn that this view is wrong. Already, by the late nineteenth century, the United States had the Western world's highest divorce rate. The fact is that families in the past experienced many problems similar to those facing families today: desertion, child abuse, spousal battering, and alcohol and drug addiction.

Let's take another misconception. Many Americans mistakenly assume that the male-breadwinner family was always the traditional form in America. In fact, it was not until the 1920s that a majority of children lived in a home where the husband was the breadwinner, the wife was a full-time homemaker, and the kids could go to school instead of working for wages.

The history recounted in this volume decisively demonstrates that American family life has always been diverse, changing, and unstable. America's families have varied in structure and functioning across lines of social classes, ethnicity, and emotional and power dynamics over the course of American history. At the dawn of the twentieth century, single-parent households made up about 15 percent of urban families, as a result, largely, of abandonment and premature death. As recently as 1940, about 10 percent of children lived with neither of their biological parents.

Today, many Americans use the language of crisis and decline to describe private life. Many blame society's ills—including poverty, crime, violence, and substance abuse—on the decline of traditional family values. Many look at the rising age of those entering into marriage, and the high rates of divorce and nonmartial cohabitation, and fear that the marriage is disappearing, that family life is becoming more transient, that women and men are growing more selfishly independent.

Is family life less stable today than in the past? Not nearly as much as some assume. Divorce rates, lower today than a quarter-century ago, are much lower among better-educated and more affluent families than among the poor—suggesting that economic stress is a major contributor to marital instability. Are Americans abandoning marriage? The answer is clearly no. Young people delay marriage for multiple reasons—including the need to complete their education and to enter a satisfying career—but most eventually marry. About 90 percent of Americans marry at some point in their lives, and 75 percent of those who divorce eventually remarry. The overwhelming majority of today's children grow up in two-parent households—just as they have throughout American history.

By demonstrating that private decisions have public significance and that public events inevitably color private life, this volume offers a fresh way of thinking about American history. It also provides students with a new way of understanding our own time. Today, many families experience intense stress. This volume helps students understand that these strains cannot be understood apart from broader societal developments. For example, since the mid-1960s, our society has undergone a revolution in women's lives, but it is a revolution that remains incomplete. Even though our society is legally committed to gender equality, in many families responsibility for housework and child care remains unequal. This imbalance is a source of strain in many families.

Since the 1960s, our society has also experienced a revolution in the realm of work. The rapid influx of married women into the paid labor force not only gave women greater economic independence, it also spawned profound work–family conflicts. Professional child care is expensive and highly uneven in quality and is largely unavailable on weekends or during evenings. Many families find it difficult to provide the level of care that they would like for their children. As our population ages, many families are also hard-pressed to care for aging parents.

A "new," post-industrial service economy that began to emerge in the 1970s and 1980s has also carried profound consequences for private life. Today, many adults are on call 24/7, and very few Americans will work for a single employer throughout their work lives. Job insecurity and long work hours, in turn, have inflicted a great deal of stress on our personal lives.

Far from being two separate spheres, the private and public realms are inextricably interconnected. Changes in one domain inevitably affect the other. By showing students how public events have influenced private life and how private choices have altered society as a whole, *Private Lives/Public Moments* does something that is exceedingly rare: it encourages you to look at life, in the present as well as the past, differently.

Steven Mintz
Columbia University

ACKNOWLEDGMENTS

I owe an enormous debt to colleagues, friends, and experts in the field who guided me through the research and writing of this book. They include Mel Albin, David Burner, Jo Cavallo, Dennis Fagan, Dennis Hidalgo, Jeffrey Kane, Peter Katopes, Michael LaCombe, Alan Sadovnik, JoAnn Smith, Martin VanLith, Fred Weinstein, and Glen Zeitzer.

I also appreciated the wisdom, expertise, and insight of the editors and staff at Pearson: Vanessa Gennarelli, Rob DeRosa, and Lynn Savino Wendel. I especially want to thank my editor at Pearson, Charlyce Jones Owen: her focus, drive, creativity, and experience made working on this project a pleasure. Thanks as well to Christian Holdener and Jolynn Kilburg for their fine work in producing this book, and to Sue Nodine for her superlative copyediting.

Finally, I owe a special debt of gratitude to reviewers who read both manuscripts and provided both astute criticisms of their inadequacies and wise council about remedies. They include Sarah Knott, Indiana University; Mary Beth Emmerichs, University of Wisconsin; Don Palm, Sacramento City College; Rachel Standish, Menlo College; Donald C. Elder III, Eastern New Mexico University; Cornelia Sexauer, University of Wisconsin; James H. Williams, Middle Tennessee State University; Jeffrey C. Livingston, California State University; Paula Hinton, Tennessee Tech; David R. Novak, Purdue University; Shirley Teresa Wajda, Kent State University; Joseph Hawes, University of Memphis; Christy Snider, Berry College; Katherine Chavigny, Sweet Briar College; Nancy J. Rosenbloom, Canisius College; William Simons, SUNY Oneonta; Kathleen Carter, Highpoint University; Jacqueline M. Cavalier, Community College of Allegheny County; Peter Levy, York College of Pennsylvania; Jennifer L. Gross, Jacksonville State University; Randi Storch, SUNY Cortland; Leslie Heaphy, Kent State University; Mary Ann Bodayla, Southwest Tennessee State University; Julie L. Smith, Mt. Aloysius College; and Alison Parker, SUNY Brockport.

INTRODUCTION

The essays in this book examine the history of the United States by connecting the private lives of its people to the public issues that have had a major impact on the nation's destiny. Perhaps because of their traditions of personal freedom, economic individualism, and family privacy, Americans tend to think of "private" life and "public" concerns as distinct realms of experience. There are cultural and psychological barriers to thinking about the relationships between self and society, family life and public events, private desires and political conflicts. The premise of this book is that much of what we call "history" is the product of conflict or concord (or some combination of the two) between private aspirations, frustrations, and values on the one side and public issues, events, and policies on the other.

The essays in Volume 1 provide students with historical knowledge about significant *public* events in American history from 1492 to 1877. These include the encounter between Native American and European cultures, the colonization of North America, slavery, the American Revolution, westward expansion, and the Civil War. But they do so by exploring how those issues and events shaped—and were shaped by—Americans in determined pursuit of their *private* interests: their ambitions and frustrations, their values and fears, their hopes and disappointments.

For example, one advantage of linking private lives to public issues in American history is that it compels us to think about the interdependence of family and society. This interdependence has had a vital impact on the nation's fortunes. Despite the tendency to think of the family as a sanctuary from the pressures and stresses of the "outside" world (nineteenth-century Americans called the family a "haven in a heartless world"), the boundary between family and society has always been fluid. Public issues and events affect private lives. And decisions made privately within families often influence public policies and politics.

For instance, Chapter 10 ("A New Economy and a New American Family") describes how changes in the economy and the development of cities in the first half of the nineteenth century helped create a new middle-class family, especially in the Northeast. For a number of reasons, mostly economic, this new urban family required fewer children than traditional farm families. But just as public issues affected private lives in this example, the reverse was also true. The declining birthrate—which, after all, resulted from *private* decisions made by married couples to have fewer children—had an impact on *society*. It eventually caused a decrease in the rate of population growth, which, in turn, helped create the potential for a shortage of labor at precisely the time the American economy was undergoing rapid expansion. This was one of the reasons for the surge in immigration in these years, described in Chapter 11 ("Irish Immigrant Women and Their Men in New York

City"). The decline in the birthrate helped create a need for population increase by another means—immigration.

A different example of the interplay between private lives and public moments concerns religion. Most Americans probably consider religion a "private" matter. But Chapter 3 ("Religion in the Northern Colonies") describes the pivotal role played by religion in helping shape distinctive regional cultures in colonial America, and Chapter 14 ("A Religious Challenge to American Capitalism: The Oneida Community") portrays a nineteenth-century group of utopian evangelical Protestants who created a radical and controversial alternative to mainstream American society.

Still another illustration of the ways public moments and private values interact concerns gender and sexuality. Chapter 2 ("Columbus Meets Pocahontas: European Images of Native American Women") is a case in point. This chapter describes how European men imagined the sexuality of Native American women, and how those assumptions helped determine their views of Indian culture and life in general. In a very different setting, Chapter 15 ("Free Black Women, the Movement to Abolish Slavery, and the Struggle for Women's Rights") depicts the intimate relationship in the 1840s and 1850s among race, private beliefs about the "proper" role of women, and the movement to end slavery.

The important role played by personal ambition and private enterprise in the developing nation is displayed in a number of essays. The quests for wealth, economic opportunity, and status are described in a variety of settings: from the settlement of South Carolina (Chapter 4, "Settling South Carolina: Family Ties and the Quest for Wealth in the New World") and the opening of the western farming region (Chapter 8, "Pioneers on the Western Farming Frontier"), to the origin of the factory system (Chapter 9, "From Farm to Factory: The Beginning of Industrial Labor") and daily life in the male-dominated world of the California Gold Rush (Chapter 13, "After the Gold Rush: The Male World of California Mining Camps").

Finally, a number of articles focus on the assorted crises that confronted Americans during these years and how they affected—and were affected by—the private lives of its people. These include the development of slavery and its influence on the evolution of the African American family (Chapter 5, "From Africans to African Americans: Slavery, Women, and the Family"); the American Revolution and the dispute between patriot Benjamin Franklin and his son William, who remained loyal to England (Chapter 6, "Patriot Father, Loyalist Son: Benjamin and William Franklin"); and how the national "divided house" that led to the Civil War also created "divided homes" for hundreds of American families (Chapter 17, "Divided Houses: Rebel Sons in Union Families").

A brief introduction at the beginning of each essay provides students with a context for the issues raised in the article. At the end of each essay are "Questions for Discussion" and an extensive "For Further Reading" list on the topic.

1

Before 1492

Native Americans of the Southwest

David La Vere

When Europeans began their explorations of North America, they encountered a stunning variety of Native societies. For thousands of years before 1492, Native Americans created hundreds of distinct cultures. From the woodlands of the Northeast to the deserts of the Southwest, and from the tidewaters of the southeastern seaboard to the Great Plains of the continent's vast midsection, Indians developed numerous languages, economies, art forms, and religions. Despite important differences, however, many Native American tribes held similar views regarding important values. This was especially true of their attitudes toward religion, community, family, gender roles, sexuality, and child rearing. These "private" issues are crucial to how cultures regulate their economies, create order, and define social relationships.

Experts differ about the number of people who lived in the Americas in 1492. Most archaeologists and historians estimate that between 50 and 100 million people populated the hemisphere in that year; somewhere between 7 and 18 million of them dwelled in what is now the United States and Canada. (The combined population of all European countries at the time was about 70 million.) Most experts believe Indian people originated in Northeast Asia and migrated to North America through Beringia, a landmass (now submerged) that once connected Alaska to northeastern Asia. But other scholars claim Indians came from different parts of Asia at different times and traveled by boat from the Aleutian Islands to the Pacific Coast. Also open to question is when they arrived in the Americas: estimates range from 10,000 to 30,000 years ago.

Plains Indians perform the Bull Dance. According to the author, what role did animal dances play in Native American cultures?

What is not in dispute is that Native peoples created a wide variety of cultures that often shared important underlying values. Their myths of creation are one example. Tribes in the northeastern portion of North America believed that the world began when a female spirit fell from the sky and landed on the back of a giant turtle. But the Creeks of the Southeast, along with many other Native people, thought human beings originally sprang from beneath the earth.

Although their myths about the world's origins differed, Indian attitudes toward nature had much in common. They did not feel alienated from or superior to the world around them. Indians thought of themselves as a part of nature, not the center of it: they did not believe human beings were inherently superior to animals or other forms of life. This contrasted sharply with Christian-European attitudes toward nature. Their primary myth of creation centered on Adam and Eve, who sinned, were evicted from a blissful Garden of Eden, and were condemned to a painful exile on earth. In the Judeo-Christian worldview, life on earth was an alienating fall from grace. Europeans also believed human beings were superior to other forms of life.

Food gathering provides another example of how Indians had different ways of living but held similar values. Depending on their environment, tribes achieved subsistence in various ways. Some gathered most of their food by hunting, some mostly from fishing, others largely from agriculture, and still others from all three. But whatever their primary method of food gathering—and again, unlike Europeans—Native Americans did not believe in private, individual ownership of the land or of other vital natural resources. The resources that sustained life belonged in common to the tribe or clan.

In the following article, David La Vere describes the various Native cultures that existed before 1492 in the huge geographical area that eventually became Texas. Among other things, La Vere shows how various Indian tribes developed distinctive family structures, kinship networks and gender roles; equally important, and by contrast with Europeans of the time, he demonstrates that their "private" lives and "public" activities formed a unified whole, with no sharp boundaries between the two.

Because La Vere's work encompasses the enormous territory of Texas, it can help us understand both the varieties and similarities of Native cultures across North America before 1492. Much of Texas may be flat and plains-like, but it also possesses ocean coastlines, rivers, mountains, deserts, and forests. In other words, the different environments within Texas to some degree mirrored that of the entire North American continent. And according to La Vere, so did the various Indian cultures that evolved within those environments.

Source: David La Vere, *The Texas Indians* (College Station: Texas A&M Press, 2004), pp. 26–28, 31–37, 39–40, 44–50, 52–53.

When did any group of Indian people become a recognizable culture? When did the Caddo Indians of Northeast Texas actually come into being? How did the Tonkawas of Central Texas appear? At what point did the coastal Karankawas become Karankawas and the Rio Grande Coahuiltecans Coahuiltecans? Anthropologists and archeologists would say this happened when the people developed a language, religion, belief systems, and above all, a sense of themselves as a special, distinct people. It might also include the style of pottery they made, how they adorned themselves, how they married, how they went about hundreds of daily activities, from cooking breakfast to the lullabies they sing their children. While dates are rather nebulous, between A.D. 900 and 1500, most, but not all, of the Indians living in Texas had developed the distinct cultures that Europeans and Americans encountered and would write about.

With this comes a word of warning. Archeological digs can provide lots of information, particularly about the physical culture of a people: the tools they used, what they ate, how they designed their pottery, how they built their homes and laid out their villages. But archeology cannot tell what the Texas Indians called themselves, how they conducted their religious ceremonies, how they arranged marriages, why they did certain things, and what they felt was important and what was not. Not until Europeans arrived in Texas in the sixteenth century and recorded their interactions did these blank spaces begin to fill in.

Even here we must be careful, or at least be aware of several things. First, these Europeans, when they described the Indians they met, were taking a snapshot of them frozen in time. It does not show the changes

Indian culture underwent previously, or how it was to change in the future. Indian cultures were not static. The people migrated, united with other groups, and adopted outsiders. Communities might split apart, and through it all they constantly change the way they did things. . . .

Second, reading only European accounts gives the false impression that the Indians of Texas had no history until the Europeans arrived. Archeologists refer to these centuries prior to the coming of Europeans as "prehistoric" or "pre-Columbian"—before Columbus. These are unfortunate terms as they give the impression that only when Europeans arrived did the Indians of Texas spring to life. In reality, Texas Indians had a long history that shaped the way they reacted to Europeans.

The third point leads us to the question of how accurate these European observations were. Europeans had wholly different ways of looking at the universe, and they interpreted what they saw through the lenses of their own culture. They may have stressed things the Indians did not and overlooked what the Indians felt was important. . . .

Fourth, we must realize that the moment Columbus set foot in the Bahamas, the Indian societies of the Western Hemisphere began to undergo tremendous, rapid change. In many instances, long before Texas Indians ever saw a European, their cultures were already being affected by them. Some of this was change the Indians actively accepted and adopted; other times it was change forced upon them. . . .

TEXAS IN 1500

By 1500 a variety of distinct Indian cultures had developed in Texas. Some, such as those in East Texas and along the middle reaches of the Rio Grande, depended heavily on corn horticulture but supplemented it with hunting and gathering. Others along the Gulf Coast and in far South Texas were mainly hunters and gatherers. They used corn little, if at all, maybe growing small gardens when they could. Still, at the beginning of the sixteenth century, Indians lived in virtually every part of Texas. Exactly how many is not certain. There is no reliable way to calculate the past populations of people who did not write, took no censuses, and kept no written records; so counts given by scholars have varied widely. . . .

Years ago, when scholars tried to calculate the number of Indians living in the whole of North America, that is, the United States and Canada, they gave a figure somewhere between 1 and 2 million people. Now scholars believe North America held maybe 7 million, some say 9 million people, others say as many as 18 million and some may go even higher than that. So when it comes to Texas in 1500, there may have been anywhere from 50,000 to several hundred thousand to maybe a million living there. . . .

Essentially all the Indians of Texas could be divided into those who lived primarily by farming and those who lived mainly by hunting and gathering. Farmers usually lived in grass or adobe houses in villages and stayed tied to one place for long periods of time. Hunter-gatherers migrated with their food sources, living in camps of hide-covered shelters. Some of these might be the classic conical-shaped tepees, others just a hide stretched over a few bent branches. Farmers tended to have more earth-based and crop deities, such as the Corn Mother, while hunter-gatherers had more animal deities, such as the Tonkawa's Great Wolf. Farming tended to create larger populations and, therefore, one would think, more powerful nations, while hunter-gatherers normally had smaller populations. However, diseases hit settled populations harder. And the coming of Spanish horses to Texas during the seventeenth century added a new dynamic to Indian cultures and helped create potent horse-mounted buffalo-hunting societies.

Whether one was a hunter-gatherer or a farmer also shaped how one acted in society and even whom one considered as relatives. Hunter-gatherers tended to live in small bands, often migrating over a huge territory. Though women provided a large measure of food through foraging, hunter-gatherers depended heavily on meat, and since men did most of the hunting, it paid for fathers, sons, and brothers to hunt together. As they learned the terrain and the habits of the animals and as each hunter honed his own particular skills, these men formed an organized and efficient hunting team. Therefore, many hunter-gatherer societies were patrilocal, meaning that when it came time for a man to marry, he took a wife from outside his band and she moved in with his family. This way new blood came into the family while leaving the hunting team intact. Wives brought with them their own special skills in food, clothing, and tool preparation. Because of the importance placed on male hunters, and since women married into a man's family, most, but certainly not all, hunter-gatherer societies tended to be patrilineal, meaning that children traced their descent through their father and his family. They became members of their father's clan, if their societies possessed clans, and might have only weak relations to their mother's often-faraway family.

Once agriculture eclipsed hunting among some Indian peoples, and women provided more food than men, the rules of descent shifted toward women. Since women worked the fields, it profited mothers, daughters, and sisters to work together, forming a highly productive gang of farmers. The fields became part of the women's domain, and so did the household. With the fields providing most of the sustenance and the farm too productive to break up, agricultural societies tended to become matrilocal, meaning that when men married, they left their families and moved into the homes of their wives. Essentially "guests" in their wives' homes, men had little say in the actual running of the household, which was dominated by the matriarch. Most, but not all, farming societies became matrilineal, meaning that children became members of their mother's clan, were closely connected to the mother's family, and had only tenuous connections with their father and his family.

No matter what type of descent system a child lived in, she was surrounded by loving, caring people, often with several generations living in the same tepee or house. She lived not only among her own brothers and sisters but also among a host of cousins, referring to all of them as "older brother" or "younger brother" and "older sister" or "younger sister." In farming societies, her "aunts" might live in the same household, so she would refer to all her mother's sisters as "mother." Similarly, in a patrilineal household, her father was the most important male in her young life, but she would also call all her father's brothers "father." In matrilineal societies, the most important man in the child's life would be "mother's brother," her maternal uncle, who was from another clan and who often spent time with his own sister's children, took on something of the role of an older brother or an uncle whose main job was to spoil, not discipline, the child. While this sounds complicated, children knew who their parents were and quickly learned the proper conduct among people older and younger than themselves.

All Indian peoples of Texas, whether farmers or hunter-gatherers, divided labor in various ways. At the most basic, a division existed between women and men. There were things women did and things men did and rarely did these lines cross. A second division was that between seniors and juniors. Older men and women held certain offices and had certain duties and privileges that were not available to younger men and women. A division also existed between people with more prestige and status and those with less. Some men and women, whether through their own abilities, their family's reputation and connections, or the wealth they controlled, possessed a high degree of status, rank, and esteem. The more status one had, the more power one could wield. . . .

Regardless of whether a woman lived among agriculturalists or hunter-gatherers, her world revolved around hearth and home. In all early Texas Indian societies and on any given day, women spent much of their time gathering. They gathered firewood; clay for making pottery; cane, grass, or straw for weaving baskets and mats. They collected foods such as nuts, berries, roots, seeds, prickly pear tunas, grasses, whatever was in season. Much of this food was dried and stored. If her people were farmers, then during the warm growing season she tilled the fields with digging sticks or hoes made of walnut or buffalo shoulder blades and then planted the seeds. Once the corn and beans were high enough, she watched over them, often building small platforms where she sat to scare off birds, deer, and other hungry pests. When the corn was ripe, she and her sisters and daughters harvested their household's gardens and fields, often getting two crops of corn each season, and then stored it in baskets or on lines to dry. At home she scraped the dried corn off the cob, making it either into hominy for soups and stews, or grinding it into meal with a mortar and pestle, or a mano and metate. Corn meal might be fried, baked, or boiled into small loaves of bread. While small game—birds, squirrels, raccoons, and terrapins—might be dressed and eaten at the day's meal, excess meat from buffalo and deer would be cut into long strips a few inches wide, dried over a slow fire, and preserved for months. Coastal Indians prepared fish in similar ways. Bears were rendered for the great quantities of fat, which was then used for cooking or as a lotion for body and hair.

No matter the season, a woman always had to cook for her family. In cold weather, this might be done inside; in warm weather she moved outside to an open campfire or maybe to a small shaded brush arbor. Roasting meat and corn might be the easiest and most common way of cooking, but boiling was also prevalent. In fact, the Indians of Texas had an affinity for soups and stews. Depending on the people and what they had access to, these dishes might consist of a variety of meats, fish, nuts, seeds, berries, or corn, simmering all day in large clay pots. If a people lacked fireproof pottery, stews might be cooked in buffalo stomachs, heated by dropping hot stones into the mix. . . .

Women also made most of the utensils used by the family. Probably the most tiresome, backbreaking duty was processing buffalo, deer, and bear hides. Once a woman had cut the hide from the carcass using a flint knife, in later years replaced with one of metal, she pegged the hide to the ground and laboriously scraped away any remaining bits of flesh. If the hide was to be used for housing or warm-weather clothing, then she would also scrape off the hair. Hair would be left on for bedding or winter clothing. After scraping the hide, she periodically soaked it, pounded, it, and worked in a concoction of animal brains, which preserved the hide and made it supple. Once finished, the hide might be left as it was or maybe meticulously decorated with paint and beads in order to be used in trade. It might also be cut into pieces for tepees or ropes, or sewn into clothing, moccasins, containers, or any number of useful things. Besides processing hides and making decorating clothes and shoes, women also threw pottery, wove baskets and mats, made beads and other decorations, and did all the small jobs that allowed a household to run efficiently. . . .

Although a woman was supposed to be demure and retiring, she could be just as sexual as any man and make her wishes known without too much trouble. In fact, particularly in farming societies, women could initiate divorce and as a general rule throughout Texas, divorce was not too difficult to obtain by either sex. As a mother she could be both indulgent and practical. She made cradleboards to carry her babies, often using a wad of soft moss for a diaper and usually breast-feeding her children for the first few years. She taught her children what they needed to know to become good members of the community, and usually did so without resorting to spankings. . . .

A man's life revolved around politics, hunting, diplomacy, warfare, religion, and games. On any given day, a man might gather with his friends or other members of the camp or village to discuss issues facing the community. But just as often it was to loaf, smoke, eat, gamble, joke, and gossip. Nothing happened in the village or camp that was not known by almost everyone. Marital discord, extramarital affairs, and the failures and successes of any given individual were always of interest and might elicit admiration, jealousy, a wry comment, or an off-color joke. Tobacco smoking was ubiquitous among Texas Indian men. Virtually every man carried a pipe and a pouch of tobacco, sometimes mixed with sumac leaves, willow bark, or other herbs. . . . More than just a pastime, smoking, seen as an aspect of purification, was involved in virtually every ritual. So a man might have a larger, highly decorated pipe he kept at home and used when important visitors arrived and for serious ritual occasions. Communities might even have one or more special ritual pipes that were used in ceremonies, for greeting official visitors, in declaring war, or in making peace.

All men were essentially hunters and what they hunted depended on where they lived. In the forests, deer, bear, squirrels, raccoons, and a variety of birds predominated. The prairies and plains provided buffalo and antelope; on Texas' coast and estuaries, fish and shellfish were added to the diet. In East Texas, deer provided the main source of protein. . . .

Texas Indian men were very competitive. Whether hunter-gatherer or farmer, each man wanted to be considered the bravest warrior, most skillful hunter, or best shot. Men wrestled, ran races, and challenged each other to a variety of contests, using the outcomes as a way of attracting a woman's eye or of acquiring prestige. Indian men were also inveterate gamblers, often wagering everything they owned. Besides wagering on physical contests, men threw a crude sort of dice and played the "hand game," a sleight-of-hand game in which a person guessed who held a small object.

While men and women lived in two separate worlds, some people managed to blur the lines between the two. Homosexuality existed in all Texas Indian societies. There were some men and women who performed all the duties of their own gender but secretly found themselves attracted to people of the same sex. There were also male transvestites, who might dress as a woman and perform the work of a woman, but who remained heterosexual. Some homosexuals were very open about their lives. Some women took on the attributes of men, became hunters, even warriors; and some men became women, dressing as a woman, doing woman's work, refusing to take part in a man's world, maybe even becoming a man's "wife." The term *berdache* has been applied to these openly gay and lesbian Indians. Rather than being persecuted, berdaches were viewed as spiritually powerful. They were allowed, even encouraged, to participate in rituals and ceremonies and accepted in Indian societies. In some instances, since warriors on a raid were prohibited from consorting with women, berdaches went along to serve the men. This indicates that it was not celibacy that the men of a war party sought, but that a woman's spiritual power might overshadow and negate that of the war party.

All Indians were surrounded by a host of kin. How they interacted with their kin was determined by many things, including the person's gender, age, whether they lived in a patrilineal or matrilineal society, clan membership, family connections, and certain well-known demands and taboos. For example, it was taboo to have sex with one's kin. Naturally, members of a person's immediate family—fathers, mothers, brothers, sisters, aunts, uncles, cousins, and grandparents—were all taboo. For modern Anglo-Americans this taboo may extend to fourth, fifth, or sixth cousins, or may not extend beyond one's immediate nuclear family. For Indians of Texas, this taboo would include the immediate family but also extend to anyone associated with their mother's or father's family no matter how distantly related, and since everyone in a person's clan was considered kin, that meant there was a whole range of people a person was forbidden to marry. At the same time, virtually every Indian society in Texas demanded that kin take care of kin. Conversely, it was perfectly fine to cheat, rob, or even kill a stranger with no kin relationship to you or your people. . . .

Among Texas Indians, these reciprocal kinship obligations were extremely important because they could mean the difference between poverty and prosperity, even life and death. As with the early hunter-gatherers, each band hunted a certain territory, which was normally respected by other bands. Because of this, some bands might have access to more types of resources than did other bands. By forging kinships through marriages, obligations of reciprocity provided each band with a form of insurance. Since kin helped kin, when a band fell upon hard times, say during a drought that drove away the buffalo, they could turn for support to their kin in another band, in an area where the deer might still be plentiful. . . .

The role and power of kinship among Texas Indian peoples cannot be overstated. And much of what Indians said and did cannot be understood unless the rules and obligations of kinship are taken into account. Looking after kin obligated people to a vast number of commitments and strictures, obligations that non-Indian people often had difficulty understanding. A kinsperson might be called upon to provide food, shelter, assistance, protection, goods and commodities, physical and moral support, or give sage advice. In some instances, a man might even share his wife with his brother and a woman her husband with her sister. All this should be done willingly and with generosity. To refuse the request might break the relationship and even bring about violence. Conversely, the giving of these "gifts" created reciprocal obligations of their own.

In Indian societies, the welfare of the community took precedence over individual rights. Unlike capitalism, which stresses that an individual should accumulate as much personal capital as possible, reciprocity and kinship emphasized sharing, family, and community. A hunter shared his kill with his kin. A woman did not grow corn to sell on the open market but shared it with her family. A trader returning from a far-off place was expected to give some of his commodities to his kin. Rather than monetary profit, the sharer, or gift-giver, earned a favor, an obligation to reciprocate from the person who received the gift. Gift-givers also earned esteem through their generosity. This was essential if one wanted to acquire power in Indian societies. . . .

RELIGION

Virtually every Indian of Texas knew that she lived in a world filled not only with physical objects, but also with spirit powers. Anthropologists and historians call this animism, but no Indian ever used the term or had ever heard of it. For Indians, every physical thing possessed a spirit or essence. Mountains, plains, wind, forests, rivers all had spirits, as did every animal in the world. Each river and mountain and animal had its own individual spirit, and there was also a collective spirit of the rivers and mountains, as well as one of owls, sparrows, wolves, raccoons, and so on. Indians also might recognize a chief spirit, a sort of "master of animals," who regulated the animals as a whole. Celestial objects, such as the sun, stars, thunder, rain, and lightning, all possessed spirits as did some man-made items like bows and arrows, and pottery cups. Many Indians also believed in underworld spirits, such as ghosts, monsters, witches, and elf-type people. These spirits or powers were everywhere and had the potential to do both bad and good. Some were strong and one had to be careful around them. Some could be helpful; others, mischievous or downright deadly. And some were weak and could be safely ignored. That is not to say that Indians walked in constant fear of these spirits, but there was an awareness that powers were all around. . . .

Most Indians believed in a Creator, a very old entity that made the earth and universe. For the Apaches, it was Ussen, a power who lived before the universe came into being and who created two other important deities, White Painted Woman and Child of Water. White Painted Woman and Child of Water created the world, and it was Child of Water who created the Apaches. Child of Water is what anthropologists call a "culture hero," a spiritual being, often associated with the Creator, who helps bring about the creation of the people. The Kiowas viewed Sun Boy as their culture hero who rid the world of monsters and made it livable for the Kiowas. It was Neesh, also known as Moon, who led the Caddos from their underground world into this world. The Comanches have a similar hero, Kawus, made by the Creator, who brought the Comanches into being and taught them how to live. . . .

Beneath the Creator came the world of spirits. . . . While the Apaches might appeal to Ussen to provide them with power, it was these many spirits beneath the Creator that turned to for help. Since all animal spirits had power, an intelligent person tried to harness that power or at least appease the spirit so it would not harm him or her. The spirit of the buffalo could show the Comanches where to find food. A Comanche imbued with the spirit of the coyote could see the future. Eagle spirit helped a man in war, while deer spirit could both cause and cure disease. As seen among the painted caves along the Rio Grande, cougars were the best hunters, so if humans could curry the favor of the cougar spirit, they could become better hunters. Wolves could give a person the power to walk barefoot in the snow. Even small animals might have great power. Skunks gave men prowess in war, while mice imparted the ability to slip in and out of narrow places. Owls, seen as harbingers of death, were to be avoided. These traits applied to animal spirits were not universal and might change from people to people. Nevertheless, the kinship between humans and animals is seen in Indian dances, which often imitate the movements of animals. . . .

Indians always danced in a circle, as dance was the outward manifestation of the circle of life. And it was through dance that ceremonies were celebrated, deities honored, harmony preserved, war entered into, even the history of a nation recorded. The Indians of Texas had dances for most occasions. The Comanches, and other Indians as well, had a Hunting Dance before going on buffalo hunts and a Buffalo Tongue Dance when the hunt was over. There was a war dance before going on a raid and afterward a Scalp Dance, which celebrated a Comanche victory and the taking of an enemy's scalp. A Spanish visitor to the Karankawas in the 1760s reported that the Indians were much given to dances. Using tortoise shell tambourines and gourd rattles, the Karankawa dances could be happy or sad, with dancers circling a large fire for as many as three days. They dance, the Spaniard said, "for liberty and triumph over their enemies, or good success in their campaigns, or abundant harvests in their plantings, or abundance of deer, buffalo, or bear.". . .

WARFARE

Unlike European societies, rarely did Texas Indians mobilize a huge army, carry out chess-piece campaigns, and wage a prolonged all-out war, though these were not necessarily out of the question. During the mid-sixteenth century the Caddos and Wichitas were able to put hundreds of warriors into the field, all divided into regiments and battalions. But most warfare consisted of small-unit raids. Raiding parties could be composed of one or two men to several score, though a party of six to ten was probably the most common. Even then, when the fighting started, it usually developed into combat between individuals rather than bodies of disciplined troops. Most raids fell into two categories. They could be made to take revenge for an earlier attack or they could be economically motivated, essentially an effort to acquire resources from one's enemies. These motives might also be combined, so a strike for revenge might also gain the raiders hides, captives, and later on, horses.

While Indian war could be hell, there were strictures and rules to it. In 1500 Indians fought on foot, often in two opposing lines, armed with spears, bows and arrows, war clubs, tomahawks, and knives. By the eighteenth and nineteenth centuries, with the coming of horses and Europeans, Indian cavalry came into being, with metal weapons, lances, and firearms added to their arsenals. No matter what weapons they used, probably the most important rule of warfare was avoiding heavy casualties. The loss of too many men made a raid costly and defeated its purposes. Because camps and villages were not that large, heavy losses could devastate a family or band. To limit casualties, war parties relied on surprise and ambush. If surprise was lost or if the battle went badly, then it made sense to retreat and fight again another day. . . .

Nevertheless, Indian warfare could be terrible and terrifying. Warfare, particularly war for revenge, often resulted in the taking of captives. These captives, for the most part, would be taken back to their captors' villages, which might be a long hard road of several hundred miles or more. War parties often killed infants, the weak, and the feeble, knowing they would slow up the march because they were unable to stand up to the rigors of the journey. And if left alive, they would probably die a slow death of starvation or exposure. . . .

Indians also understood the value of terror, so scalping and torture played a role in warfare. Scalping, the taking of a piece of a person's scalp and hair, was done by Indians long before Columbus ever reached the Western Hemisphere. However, Europeans and Americans made it profitable. For Indians, a scalp was a war trophy, proof of their bravery and ability. It might be woven into their hair, attached to a shield, bow, or lance, or just hung on a wall. Dead enemies were scalped, if possible, but the wounded or captives might be also. While painful, scalping was rarely fatal, and so it was an ever-present badge of a person's inability to defend himself. Europeans and Americans often paid a bounty for Indian scalps.

Nevertheless, captives who did make it back to their captor's village might be enslaved or eventually adopted into families to replace members who had been killed in raids. Some, men and women alike, might undergo hours, even days, of beatings, stabbings, cuttings, and burning before finally being put to death. Torturing enemy captives was common to all Indians of Texas. The French scientist [Jean Louis] Berlandier reported that when he was in Texas in 1828 some Wichitas captured seven or eight Tonkawas and put them to death "by the slow and gradual tearing of the skin, first of their arms and legs, and finally of their trunks, while burning coals were pressed into the deep wounds cut in their flesh." On one level, torture was an act of revenge done to return balance and harmony; on another, it was pure retaliation. Indian life could be hard and children were taught to withstand pain, so it was just a short jump to inflicting pain. Virtually all Indians in Texas realized that if they were captured, they were going to suffer torture.

Questions for Discussion

1. Why are labels such as "pre-Columbian" and "prehistoric" misleading when applied to Native Americans? What are the major limitations to our knowledge about Indians and their ways of life before 1492? After 1492?
2. Some Texas tribes survived mainly by hunting, others primarily by farming. What were the major differences between each group in terms of tracing descent, housing, family life, and gender? In what ways were Indian men and women equal to one another? In what ways unequal? On both counts, how did they compare with European men and women?
3. How would you describe Indian attitudes toward homosexuals? How might it have differed from that of Europeans?
4. What role did kinship play in Indian culture? How did it affect the rights of the individual versus that of the community or tribe?
5. How would you describe Native American religion or spirituality? How might it have differed from that of Europeans?

For Further Reading

Gary Anderson, *The Indian Southwest, 1580–1830: Ethnogenesis and Reinvention* (1999); James Axtell, *After Columbus: Essays in the Ethnohistory of Colonial North America* (1988), *Beyond 1492: Encounters in Colonial North America* (1992), *The Invasion Within: The Contest of Cultures in Colonial North America* (1985); Colin Calloway, *New Worlds for All: Indians, Europeans, and the Remaking of Early America* (1997); Paul Carlson, *The Plains Indians* (1998); James Carson, *Searching for the Bright Path: The Mississippi Choctaws from Prehistory to Removal* (1999); Linda Cordell, *Prehistory of the Southwest* (1984); Michael Crawford, *The Origins of Native Americans: Evidence from Anthropological Genetics* (1998); William Cronon, *Changes in the Land: Indians, Colonists, and the Ecology of New England* (1983); Alfred Crosby, *The Columbian Exchange: Biological and Cultural Consequences of 1492* (1973), *Ecological Imperialism: The Biological Expansion of Europe, 900–1900* (1986); Bernal Diaz, *The Conquest of New Spain* (1963); Zvi Dor-Nor, *Columbus and the Age of Discovery* (1991); Thomas D. Hall, *Social Change in the Southwest, 1350–1880* (1989); Vance Holliday, *Paleoindian Geoarcheology of the Southern High Plains* (1997); Francis Jennings, *The Founders of America* (1993); David La Vere, *The Caddo Chiefdoms: Caddo Economics and Politics, 700–1835* (1998); Miguel Leon-Portilla, ed., *The Broken Spears: The Aztec Account of the Conquest of Mexico* (1962); Marvin Lunenfeld, *1492: Discovery, Invasion, Encounter* (1991); Lynda Shaffer, *Native Americans before 1492: The Moundbuilding Centers of the Eastern Woodlands* (1992); David Hurst Thomas, *Exploring Ancient Native America: An Archeological Guide* (1994); David Weber, *The Spanish Frontier in North America* (1992).

CHAPTER 2

Columbus Meets Pocahontas

European Images of Native American Women

Theda Perdue

Native American attitudes toward gender, family, sexuality, and the public activities of labor and warfare differed markedly from those of Europeans. For instance, as we saw in the previous chapter, many Indian tribes traced ancestral descent through the mother's line. When a couple from these tribes married, the husband usually moved into the dwelling of his wife's family. Their children were raised primarily by the wife and her male relatives, with fairly little input from her husband.

These practices indicate that an Indian wife, unlike her female counterparts in Europe, could have a social and, in effect, "legal" identity independent from that of her husband. Many Native women also possessed considerable economic clout and, in some cases, political influence. In many tribes, women did the farming and harvesting (tasks associated mainly with men in Europe), while Native men cleared fields, hunted, and fished. In other words, their *status* as farmers indicated that women were recognized for making a substantial and independent contribution to the Native American economy. A few might even exercise political power: for example, Iroquois women participated in choosing tribal leaders (who were, however, invariably male).

With regard to marriage, some Indian couples were monogamous and remained together for a lifetime. But, just as often, neither was the case. Divorce was relatively easy to obtain: the husband, the wife, or both simply

14

Native Americans engaged in a "Festival Dance" in sixteenth-century Virginia. At the center are three Native women. How does this engraving relate to the views about women presented in Chapter 2?

declared the marriage over. When a woman wanted a divorce and her husband refused, she placed his belongings outside their dwelling. That was a clear signal to both the tribe and her spouse that the marriage was over, and husbands normally complied with this custom. Most Native cultures condoned sexual experimentation among young, unmarried adolescents.

All of these values and practices scandalized Europeans when they encountered Native American cultures. European American women lacked both political rights and a legal identity apart from their husbands'. As Theda Perdue points out in the following article, these gender differences, along with certain Native customs regarding sexuality, created the basis for the general European perception of Indian women as sexually promiscuous, immoral, and "savage." In addition, Europeans were convinced that Native Americans did not value marriage or family. Perhaps more important, Europeans' view of these "private" elements of Native culture allowed them to denigrate the "public" qualities of Indian culture. From the white perspective, Native Americans were rootless, lazy, and disorderly.

But Perdue demonstrates that the shoe was often on the other foot. It was European men who longed to plunge into sexual promiscuity in the New World while they simultaneously plundered its material wealth. And it was Indian women and men who had stringent rules regarding sexual behavior, even though Europeans failed to understand or respect them.

Source: Theda Perdue, "Columbus Meets Pocahontas in the American South," *Southern Cultures* 3, no. 1 (1997), 4–21.

As icons of the European colonization of the Americas, Columbus and Pocahontas represent opposite sides of the experience—European and Native, invader and defender, man and woman. Biographies and other scholarly writings document their lives and deeds, but these feats pale in comparison to the encounter these two legendary figures symbolize. Columbus embodies European discovery, invasion, and conquest, while Pocahontas has become the "mother of us all," a nurturing, beckoning, seductive symbol of New World hospitality and opportunity. The two never actually met in the American South, of course, except metaphorically, but this symbolic encounter involved a sexual dynamic that was inherent in the process of European colonization, particularly that of the American South.

John Smith's tales of succor and salvation fixed the Pocahontas image forever in the American mind, and his autobiographical account of peaceful relations with her people, the Powhatans, has exempted Englishmen from the tarring Columbus has received as an international symbol of aggression. The Columbian encounter with Native women seemed, in fact, to be radically different from Smith's. On his initial voyage of discovery, Columbus had relatively little to report about Native women except that they, like men, went "naked as the day they were born." The loss of one of his ships on this voyage forced Columbus to leave about a third of his crew on Hispaniola. When he returned, he found the burned ruins of his settlement and the decomposing corpses of his men. Local Natives related that "soon after the Admiral's departure those men began to quarrel among themselves, each taking as many women and as much gold as he could." They dispersed throughout the island, and local caciques killed them. The men on Columbus's expedition had their revenge: "Incapable of moderation in the acts of injustice, they carried off the women of the islanders under the very eyes of their brothers and their husbands." Columbus personally presented a young woman to one of his men, Michele de Cuneo, who later wrote that when she resisted him with her fingernails, he "thrashed her well, for which she raised such unheard of screams that you would not have believed your ears." In the accounts of the conquistadores, Spaniards seized women as they seized other spoils of war. Such violence contributed to the "black legend" of Spanish inhumanity to Native peoples and stands in stark contrast to early English descriptions of their encounters with Native women.

John Smith, according to his own account, did not face the kind of resistance from Pocahontas and other Native women of the Virginia tidewater that the Spanish had met in the Caribbean. When Smith and a delegation from Jamestown called at the primary town of Powhatan, Pocahontas's father, they discovered that he was away, but the chief's daughter and other women invited the Englishmen to a "mascarado." "Thirtie young women," wrote Smith, "came naked out of the woods, only covered behind and before with a few green leaves, their bodies all painted." They sang and danced with "infernal passions" and then invited Smith to their lodgings. By his accounts, written with uncharacteristic modesty in the third person, "he was no sooner in the house, but all these Nymphes more tormented him than ever, with crowding, pressing, and hanging about him, most tediously crying, Love you not me? Love you not me?"

The contrast is obvious—the Spanish supposedly raped and pillaged while the English nobly resisted seduction. By focusing merely on the colonizing Europeans, however, we lose sight of the Native women who are central actors in this drama: they are, after all, both the victims of Columbus's barbarity and the seductive sirens luring Smith's party. Despite differences in the ways these women are portrayed in historical sources, their experiences suggest that conquest and colonization had their own sexual dynamic. One of the facts of colonization that rarely surfaces in polite conversation or scholarly writing is sex, yet we know from the written records left by Europeans and from the more obscure cultural traditions of Native people that European men had sexual relations with Native American women. What can the Columbian voyages, the Jamestown colonists, and the experiences of subsequent European immigrants to the American South tell us about the ways in which men and women crossed cultural and racial bounds in their sexual relations? What do these relationships reveal about European views of female sexuality? And how did these views shape European expansion?

THE EUROPEAN VIEW OF NATIVE SEXUALITY

One thing seems fairly certain: Native women were never far from the conscious thought of European men, be they Spanish or English. Nudity insured that this was so. Accustomed to enveloping clothes, Europeans marveled at the remarkably scant clothing of the Natives. De Cuneo described the Carib woman whom he raped as "naked according to their custom," and Smith noted that except for a few strategically placed leaves, his hostesses were "naked." De Cuneo and Smith were not alone in commenting on Native women's lack of clothing. The Lord Admiral himself noticed not only that the Caribbean women he encountered wore little but that they had "very pretty bodies." The Jamestown colonists first encountered the prepubescent Pocahontas frolicking naked with the cabin boys. The combination of her youthful enthusiasm as well as her nudity led William Strachey, official chronicler of the colony, to describe Pocahontas as "a well featured, but wanton young girl." Other Europeans also tended to link the absence of clothing to sexuality: Amerigo Vespucci, for whom America was named, noted that "the women . . . go about naked and are very libidinous."

While Native women frequently exposed breasts, particularly in warm weather, they normally kept pudenda covered. When women did bare all, Europeans had another shock in store: Native women in many societies plucked their public hair. While some evidence points to female singeing of pubic hair in ancient Greece and even early modern Spain, most Europeans recoiled from hairless female genitalia. Thomas Jefferson, whose interests extended far beyond politics, attempted to explain hair-plucking among Native Americans: "With them it is disgraceful to be hairy in the body. They say it likens them to hogs. They therefore pluck the hair as fast as it appears." Jefferson revealed both the reactions of non-Native men and the artificiality of the practice: "The traders who marry these women, and prevail on them to discontinue this practice say that nature is the same with them as with whites." However comfortable Euro-American men may have been with visible penises, depilation left female genitalia far more exposed than most could bear. Because women revealed their private parts intentionally, they seemed to be flaunting their sexuality. . . .

The arrangement and use of domestic space seemed to confirm a lack of modesty on the part of Native women. Native housing afforded little privacy for bathing, changing what little clothes women did wear, or engaging in sexual intercourse. Several generations, as well as visitors, usually slept in the same lodge. The essayist Samuel Stanhope Smith admitted that Indians were unjustly "represented as licentious because they are seen to lie promiscuously in the same wigwam." Nevertheless, few natives allowed the lack of privacy in their homes to become a barrier to sexual fulfillment. During early eighteenth-century explorations in Carolina, one of John Lawson's companions took a Native "wife" for the night, and the newlyweds consummated their "marriage" in the same room which other members of the exploration feasted and slept: "Our happy couple went to Bed together before us all as with as little Blushing, as if they had been Man and Wife for 7 Years."

Most European accounts of Native women in the South commented on their sexual freedom, particularly before they married. In the late eighteenth century, naturalist Bernard Romans observed: "Their women are handsome, well made, only wanting the colour and cleanliness of our ladies, to make them appear lovely in every eye; they are lascivious, and have no idea of chastity in a girl, but in married women, incontinence is severely punished; a savage never forgives that crime." John Lawson suggested that even married women "sometimes bestow their Favours also to some or others in their Husband's Absence." And the trader James Adair maintained that "the Cherokees are an exception to all civilized or savage nations in having no law against adultery; they have been a considerable while under a petty-coat government, and allow their women full liberty to plant their brows with horns as oft as they please, without fear of punishment."

Women in the Southeast sometimes openly solicited sex from Euro-Americans because sex gave women an opportunity to participate in the emerging market economy. Unlike men, who exchanged deerskins, beaver pelts, and buffalo hides with Europeans for manufactured goods, women often had to rely on "the soft passion" to obtain clothing, kettles, hoes, and trinkets. Among some Native peoples a kind of specialization developed according to John Lawson, who claimed that coastal Carolina peoples designated "trading girls." Sometimes prostitution was more widespread. Louis-Philippe insisted that "all Cherokee women are public women in the full meaning of the phrase: dollars never fail to melt their hearts."

Selling sex was one thing; the apparent gift of women by their husbands and fathers was quite another. To Europeans, sex was a kind of commodity, purchased from prostitutes with money and from respectable women with marriage. An honorable man protected the chastity of his wife and daughters as he would other property. Native men in many societies, however, seemed to condone or even encourage sexual relations between Europeans and women presumably "belonging" to them. Even husbands who might object to "secret infidelities" sometimes offered their wives to visitors.

Europeans also viewed the widespread practice of polygamy, or a man taking more than one wife, as adulterous because they recognized only the first as the "real" wife. Many Native people favored sororal polygamy, the marriage of sisters to the same man, and the groom often took sisters as brides at the same time. Since this meant, in European terms, that a man married his sister-in-law, sororal polygamy was incest as well as adultery. Jedidiah Morse, in his *Universal Geography,* wrote: "When a man loves his wife, it is considered his duty to marry her sister, if she has one. Incest and bestiality is common among them." Morse apparently regarded marriage to sisters as serious violations of European sexual mores as human intercourse with animals; in his mind, both constituted perversions.

Polygynous, adulterous, and incestuous or not, marriage meant little to Indians in the estimation of many Euro-Americans. Lawson, for example, described the ease with which the Native peoples of coastal Carolina altered their marital status: "The marriages of these Indians are no further binding than the man and woman agree together. Either of them has the liberty to leave the other upon any frivolous excuse they can make." The trader Alexander Longe relayed a Cherokee priest's view of his people's lax attitude toward marriage: "They had better be asunder than together if they do not love one another but live for strife and confusion." Europeans would have preferred that they stay together and, despite domestic turmoil, raise their children in an appropriately patriarchal household.

When husband and wife parted, children normally remained with their mothers because Native peoples of the Southeast were matrilineal, that is, they traced kinship solely through women. John Lawson attributed this very odd way of reckoning kin, in his view, to "fear of Imposters; the Savages knowing well, how much Frailty possesses Indian women, betwixt the Garters and the Girdle." While paternity might be questioned, maternity could not be. Despite the logic of such a system, Europeans had both intellectual and practical objections. Matrilineality seemed too close to the relationship between a cow and calf or a bitch and puppies: It was, the Iroquois historian Cadwallader Colden asserted, "according to the natural course of all animals." "Civilized" men presumably had moved beyond this "natural course" and had adopted laws, civil and religious, that bound fathers to children and husbands to wives. Europeans who married Native women of matrilineal societies nevertheless had difficulty exercising any control over their children and often abandoned them to their mothers' kin because men had no proprietary interest in their offspring. Thomas Nairne wrote of the Creeks: "A Girles Father has not the least hand or concern in matching her. Sons never enjoy their fathers place and dignity."

Blatant disregard of marital vows and paternal prerogatives was shocking enough, but many Native peoples exhibited little concern for the chastity of their daughters. Jean-Bernard Bossu reported that among Native peoples on the lower Mississippi, "when an unmarried brave passes through a village, he hires a girl for a night or two, as he pleases, and her parents find nothing wrong with this. They are not at all worried about their daughter and explain that her body is hers to do with as she wishes. Furthermore, according to Lawson, "multiplicity of Gallants never [gave] a stain to a Female's reputation, or even the least Hindrance of her Advancement; the more Whorish, the more Honourable."

THE REALITIES OF NATIVE SEXUALITY

European men who traveled through the Native Southeast thought that they had stepped through the looking glass into a sexual wonderland. Actually, they had encountered only a fractured reflection of their own assumptions about appropriate sexual behavior. Native women were not as uninhibited as most whites thought. Europeans failed to realize that Native peoples did have rules regulating marriage and sexual intercourse, although the rules were sometimes quite different from their own. In the Southeast, unmarried people could engage freely in sex, but many factors other than marital status regulated and limited sexuality. A warrior preparing for or returning from battle (sometimes much of the summer), a ballplayer getting ready for a game, a man on the winter hunt (which could last three to four months), a pregnant woman, or a woman during her menstrual period abstained from sex. In other words, Native southerners had to forego sexual intercourse for a far greater percentage of their lives than Europeans.

Furthermore, there were inappropriate venues for sex. Although a Native couple might engage in sex in a room occupied by others, there were places, such as in an agricultural field, where amorous encounters were forbidden. Violation of this rule could have serious consequences. According to the trader James Adair, the Cherokees blamed a devastating smallpox epidemic in 1738 on "the adulterous intercourses of their young married people, who the past year, had in a most notorious manner, violated their ancient laws on marriage in every thicket, and broke down and polluted many of their honest neighbours bean-plots, by their heinous crimes, which would cost a great deal of trouble to purify again." For many Native southerners, therefore a "toss in the hay" would have been a very serious offence.

Native peoples also had rules against incest, but they did not define incest in the same way Euro-Americans did. Intercourse or marriage with a member of a person's own clan, for example, was prohibited, and the penalty could be death. Clan membership, which included all individuals who could trace their ancestry back to a remote, perhaps mythical figure, often ran into the thousands and included many people whom Europeans would not have regarded as relatives. Consequently, the number of forbidden partners was far greater than the number under the European definition of incest. The Cherokees, for example, had seven clans. No one could marry into his or her own clan, nor was the father's clan an acceptable marriage pool. The result was that, for any given Cherokee, almost one third of all Cherokees were off-limits as sexual partners.

Every Native people had particular rules regarding marriage and incest. Many societies permitted men to have more than one wife and to marry sisters. The effect was not necessarily the devaluation of women, as European observers often claimed. Some cultural anthropologists suggest, in fact, that sororal polygamy correlates positively with high female status. In the Southeast where husbands lived with their wives, the marriage of sisters to the same man reduced the number of men in the household and strengthened the control of the women over domestic life. As Morse suggested, sisters often wanted to share a husband just as they shared a house, fields, labor and children.

Ignorant of Native rules, southern colonials tended to view Native women as wanton woodland nymphs over whose sexuality fathers, brothers, and husbands could exercise little control. Many colonists took full advantage of the situation as they perceived it. Some evidence, however, suggests that southeastern Native women were not as amenable to sexual encounters as Europeans suggested. Louis-Philippe's anecdote reveals a woman, however bold and uninhibited, rejecting a sexual advance. When women did engage in sexual activity, many of them probably succumbed to pressure or force rather than charm.

European culture at this time countenanced considerable violence against women. William Byrd's confidential account of surveying the boundary line between North Carolina and Virginia, for example, describes several episodes of sexual aggression. One young woman, he wrote, "wou'd certainly have been ravish't, if her timely consent had not prevented the violence." This cavalier attitude toward a woman's right to refuse sex characterized much interaction between Native women and Europeans. Race almost certainly exacerbated the situation. The records of the South Carolina Indian trade are replete with Native complaints of sexual abuse at the hands of Europeans. One trader "took a young Indian against her Will for his Wife," another severely beat three women including his pregnant wife whom he killed, and a third provided enough rum to a woman to get her drunk and then "used her ill." Obviously, the women in these incidents were not the ones who were lascivious.

Some Native peoples came to regard sexual misbehavior as the most distinguishing feature of European culture. The Cherokee Booger Dance, in which participants imitated various peoples, portrayed Europeans as sexually aggressive, and the men playing that role chased screaming women around the dance ground. As it turns out, from the Native perspective, the British colonists of the American South may not have been so terribly different from Columbus's men after all.

The people who do stand in stark contrast are Native men. James Adair, a resident of the Chickasaw Nation and a trader throughout the Southeast, perhaps knew the region's Native cultures better than any other European in the eighteenth century. As the husband of a Chickasaw woman and an occasional member of Chickasaw war parties against the Choctaws, he wrote with authority that "the Indians will not cohabit with women while they are at war; they religiously abstain from every kind of intercourse, even with their own wives." While Adair believed, perhaps correctly, that the reason for a period of abstinence was religious, the implications for female captives [were] clear. "The French Indians," he wrote, "are said not to have deflowered any of our young women they captivated, while at war with us." Even the most bloodthirsty Native warrior, according to Adair, "did not attempt the virtue of his female captives," although he did not hesitate to torture and kill them. Even the Choctaws, whom Adair described as "libidinous," had taken "several female prisoners without offering the least violence to their virtue, till the time of purgation was expired." Adair could not, however, resist the temptation to slander the Choctaws, the Chickasaw's traditional enemy: "Then some of them forced their captives, notwithstanding their pressing entreaties and tears."

Captivity narratives suggest Indian men raped very few, if any, women victims of colonial wars—"a very agreeable disappointment" in one woman's words. Rules prohibited intercourse immediately before and after going to war may have contributed to the absence of documented sexual violence, but native views on female sexuality and autonomy may have been equally responsible. Indians apparently did not view sex as property or as one of the spoils of war.

Columbus's men do seem to have equated sex and material plunder. The accounts of the destruction of the Hispaniola settlement link his men's desire for women with a desire for gold. In perhaps a more subtle way, British colonists also considered women to be a form of property and found the Native men's lack of proprietary interest in their wives and daughters incomprehensible. It called into question the Indians' concept of property in general and paved the way for Europeans to challenge Native people's ownership of land. From the second decade of colonization in the South, wealth depended on the cultivation of land, and southerners found the argument that Indians had no notion of absolute ownership particularly compelling.

While Native southerners forcefully maintained their right to inhabit the land of their fathers, they did not, in fact, regard land ownership in quite the same way as the Europeans who challenged their rights to it. They fought for revenge rather than for territory, they held land in common, and they permitted any tribal member to clear and cultivate unused tracts. Land did not represent an investment of capital, and Native southerners did not sell out and move on when other opportunities beckoned. Indeed, the land held such significance for most of them that they suffered severe economic, social, and political disruption rather than part with it. In the 1820s and 1830s, frontiersmen, land speculators, and politicians joined forces to divest Native peoples of their land, and southern state governments and ultimately the federal government took up the aggressors' cause. White southerners made a concerted effort to force their Indian neighbors to surrender their lands and move west of the Mississippi to new territory. What difference did it make, many whites asked, which lands the Indians occupied? With squatters encroaching on them, shysters defrauding them at every turn, and federal and state authorities unwilling to protect them, Native peoples in the South struggled desperately to retain their homelands.

They did so for reasons as incomprehensible to Euro-Americans as the sexual behavior of Native women. People who objectified both land and sex had encountered people who did not.

Questions for Discussion

1. What Native practices regarding marriage, family, and male–female relations most influenced European views of Indian sexuality?
2. According to the author, how was the Europeans' desire for material gain related to their exploitation of Native women? How did Indian and European attitudes toward gender and private property differ?
3. Despite European opinion to the contrary, Indians did have strict moral codes regarding sexual behavior. What were they? In your view, why did Europeans fail to acknowledge them?
4. According to the author, what were the basic attitudes of European men toward women in general? Do you agree?

For Further Reading

Paula Gunn Allen, *The Sacred Hoop: Recovering the Feminine in American Indian Tradition* (1986); James Axtell, *After Columbus: Essays in the Ethnohistory of Colonial North America* (1988), *The Invasion Within: The Contest of Cultures in Colonial North America* (1985); James Brooks, *Captives and Cousins: Slavery, Kinship and Community in the Southwest Borderlands* (2002); Martin Daunton and Rick Halpern, eds., *British*

Encounters with Indigenous Peoples, 1600–1850 (1999); Ramon Gutierrez, *When Jesus Came, the Corn Mothers Went Away: Marriage, Sexuality, and Power in New Mexico, 1500–1846* (1991); Theda Perdue, *Cherokee Women: Gender and Culture Change, 1700–1835* (1998); Virginia Peters, *Women of the Earth Lodges: Tribal Life on the Plains* (1995); Ann Marie Plane, *Colonial Intimacies: Indian Marriage in Early New England* (2000); Nancy Shoemaker, ed., *Negotiators of Change: Historical Perspectives on Native American Women* (1995); Henrietta Stockel, *Chiricahua Apache Women and Children* (2000); Walter Williams, *The Spirit and the Flesh: Sexual Diversity in American Indian Culture* (1986).

Religion, Childhood and Society in the Northern Colonies

Steven Mintz

Tens of thousands of women and men left Great Britain for England's North American colonies in the seventeenth century. They migrated for a variety of reasons. Chaotic economic conditions, especially in the early decades of the century, prompted many to seek a new life in the New World. But religious values also played a crucial role in decisions to leave the British Isles. This was especially true of the Puritans, who settled New England in the middle decades of the seventeenth century, and the Quakers, who dominated immigration to the Middle Colonies later in that century.

The Puritans were convinced that European religious and political institutions were not only morally corrupt but beyond redemption. From their perspective, Europe was no place for devout Christians. So they left, determined to create a sanctified community in the New World. They would model their community on New Testament descriptions of how the early Christians combined strict religious devotion and social cohesion.

Puritan immigrants to New England believed they were sent by God on a divine mission, an "errand into the wilderness" as one of them put it. The ultimate purpose of their journey was nothing less than the redemption of humanity. They hoped their model Christian social order in the New World would be

SCHEME

For the Settlement of a NEW COLONY to the Westward of *Pennsylvania*, for the Enlargement of his Majesty's Dominions in *America*, for the further Promotion of the Christian Religon among the *Indian* Natives, and for the more effectual Securing them in his Majesty's Alliance.

THAT humble Application be made either to his Majesty or the General Assembly of *Connecticut*, or to both, as the Case may require, for a Grant of so much Land as shall be necessary for the Settlement of an ample Colony, to begin at the distance of one Hundred Miles Westward of the Western Boundaries of *Pennsylvania*, and thence to extend one Hundred Miles to the Westward of the River *Mississippi*, and to be divided from *Virginia* and *Carolina* by the Great Chain of Mountains, that runs along the Continent from the North-Eastern to the South-Western Parts of *America*.

THAT humble Application be made to his Majesty for a Charter to erect the said Territory into a seperate Government, with the same Privileges which the Colony of *Connecticut* enjoys, and for such Supplies of Arms and Ammunition as may be necessary for the Safety and Defence of the Settlers, and that his Majesty would also be pleased to take the said New Colony under his immediate Protection.

THAT Application be made to the Assemblies of the several *British* Colonies in *North-America*, to grant such Supplies of Money and Provisions as may enable the Settlers to secure the Friendship of the *Indian* Natives, and support themselves and Families till they are established in said Colony in Peace and Safety, and can support themselves by their own Industry.

THAT at least Twelve Reverend Ministers of the Gospel be engaged to remove to the said New Colony with such Numbers of their respective Congregations as are willing to go along with them.

THAT every Person from the Age of Fourteen Years and upwards (Slaves excepted) professing the Christian Religion, being Protestant Subjects of the Crown of *Great-Britain*, and that will remove to said new New Colony with the First Setlers thereof, shall be intitled to a sufficient Quantity of Land for a good Plantation, without any consideration Money, and at the annual Rent of a Pepper Corn :--------Said Plantation to contain at least Three Hundred Acres two Hundred Acres of which to be such Land as is fit either for Tillage or Meadow.

THAT every Person under the Age of Fourteen Years (Slaves excepted) who removes to said Province with the First Settlers thereof, as well as such Children as shall be lawfully born to said First Settlers in said Province, or in the Way to it, shall be intitled to Three Hundred Acres of Land when they come to the Age of Twenty-one Years, without any Purchase Money, at the Annual Quit-Rent of Two Shillings Sterling for every Hundred Acres ; the Quit-Rent arising from such Lands to be applied to the Support of Government, the Propagation of the Christian Religion among the *Indian* Natives, the Relief of the Poor, the Encouragement of Learning; and in general to such other publick Uses, as shall be judged by the Legislature of the Province to be most conducive to the General Good.

THAT every Person who is intitled to any Land in the Province, shall be at Liberty to take it up when they please ; but when taken up shall be obliged to clear and fence at least Fifteen Acres on every Farm of Three Hundred Acres, within Five Years after the Appropriation of said Land, and also to build a Dwelling-House of at least Fifteen Foot square with a good Chimney on the Premises within the said Term, on Pain of forfeiting said Land.

THAT the said Plantations shall be laid out in Townships, in such Manner as will be most for the Safety and Convenience of the Settlers.

THAT in order to prevent all Jealousies and Disputes about the Choice of said Plantations, they shall be divided by Lot.

THAT as soon as possible after a sufficient Number of Persons are engaged, a proper Charter obtained, and the necessary Preparations are made for the Support and Protection of the Setlers, a Place of general Rendezvous shall be appointed, where they shall all meet, and from whence they shall proceed in a Body to the new Colony ; but that no Place of Rendezvous shall be appointed till at least Two Thousand Persons able to bear Arms are actually engaged to remove exclusive of Women and Children.

THAT It be established as one of the fundamental Laws of the Province, that Protestants of every Denomination who profess the Christian Religion, believe the Divine Authority of the Sacred Scriptures of the Old and New Testament, the Doctrine of the Trinity of Persons in the Unity of the Godhead, and whose Lives and Conversations are free from Immorality and Prophaneness, shall be equally capable of serving in all Posts of Honour, Trust or Profit in the Government, notwithstanding the Diversity of their religious Principles in other Respects : But that none of any Denomination whatsoever, who have been guilty of Prophaning the Name of God, of Lying, Drunkenness, or any other of the groser Immoralites, either in their Words or Actions, shall be capable of holding any Office in or under the Government till at last one Year after their Conviction of such Offence --------The Christianizing the *Indian* Natives, and bringing them to be good Subjects, not only to the Crown of *Great-Britain*, but to the King of all Kings, being one of the essential Designs of the Proposed New Colony, it is a Matter of the utmost Importance that these poor ignorant Heathen should not be prejudiced against the Christian Religion by the bad Lives of those in Authority .

THAT Protestants of every Denomination who profess the Christian Religion, shall have the free and unlimited Exercise of their Religion, and shall be allowed to defend it, both from the Pulpit and the Press, so long as they remain peaceable Members of Civil Society, and do not propagate Principles inconsistent with the Safety of the State.

THAT no Member of the Church of *Rome* shall be able to hold any Lands or Real Estate in the Province, nor be allowed to be Owners of, or have any Arms or Ammunition in their Possession on any Pretence whatsoever, nor shall any Masshouses, or Popish Chapels, be allowed in the Province

THAT no Person shall be obliged to pay any Thing towards the Support of a Minister of whose Congregation he is not a Member, or to a Church to which he does not belong.

THAT the *Indians* shall on all Occasions be treated with the utmost Kindness, and every justifiable Method taken to gain their Friendship ; and that whoever injures, cheats, or makes them drunk, shall be punished with peculiar Severity.

THAT so soon as the Province is able to support Missionaries, and proper Persons can be found to engage in the Affair, a Fund shall be settled for the Purpose, and Missionaries sent among the neighbouring *Indian* Nations ; and that it shall, in all Time coming, be esteem'd as one of the First and Most Essential Duties of the Legislature of the Province, by every proper Method in their Power, to endeavour to spread the Light of the glorious Gospel among the *Indians* in *America*, even to its most Western Bounds.

THAT, as the Conversion of the *Indians* is a Thing much to be desired, from the weightiest Considerations, both of a religious and political Nature, and since the Colony during its Infancy will be unable to provide the necessary Funds for that Purpose, some proper Person or Persons shall be sent to *Europe*, duly authorized from the Government, to ask the Assistance of such as desire to promote that great and good Work,

This 1755 "scheme" for settling western Pennsylvania mentions the hope of converting Native Americans to Christianity. Did British settlers agree about what constituted "true" Christianity?

emulated by people in the Old World, setting the stage for the Christian millennium. "We must consider that we shall be as a Citty upon a Hill," said their leader John Winthrop. "The eyes of all people are upon us." Theirs would be a community constructed upon a solid scriptural foundation, a Protestant theocracy in which civil society was governed by biblical mandates.

As Steven Mintz points out in the next essay, the Puritan desire to create a model Christian community in the New World influenced their attitudes toward children. According to Mintz, the Puritans devoted more time and effort than anyone else in the seventeenth century to thinking about children, their nature, their future, and how to secure their spiritual and physical well-being. With good reason—if their children failed to grow into model Christians as adults, the Puritan holy experiment in America was doomed from the start. Puritans were obsessed with childhood because they were convinced that proper childrearing was the key to their community's future. One way to understand the kind of society the Puritans wanted to create, therefore, is to study how they thought about and treated their children.

Of course, Puritans have the reputation of being cold-hearted disciplinarians determined to keep young people (and anyone else for that matter) from having a good time. And it is true that they believed children came into life burdened by original sin; for them, even newborn infants were innately corrupt beings whose wills had to be broken if they were to attain eternal salvation. They not only insisted that their children obey and respect them, but acted on that belief in ways that most (though by no means all) in today's child-centered American society would find reprehensible. For example, in 1641 Massachusetts passed a law that called for the execution of children over the age of fourteen who cursed or struck their parents. During the seventeenth century, Puritan-dominated Rhode Island, Connecticut, and New Hampshire passed similar laws.

But the Puritans were not as "puritanical" as these attitudes suggest. In fact, no child was ever executed under these laws, and New England legislators passed numerous laws to protect children from abusive parents and to ensure their welfare. And there is ample evidence that Puritan parents doted on and were devoted to their children.

The important issue, however, is not just how kindly or harshly Puritans treated their children. Rather, it is this: What can Puritan religious values and their attitudes toward children tell us about the kind of society they wished to create in the New World?

There are related and equally important questions: How did Puritan attitudes toward children compare with those of non-Puritans in other British colonies? What can such comparisons tell us about the diversity of goals and values of early British settlers?

The second part of Mintz's essay describes childhood and society in England's Middle Colonies, particularly among the thousands of Quakers who pioneered settlements in West Jersey, Pennsylvania, and Delaware during the last quarter of the seventeenth century. Like the Puritans, Quakers fled persecution in England; also like the Puritans, they hoped to create a utopian religious community in America. But this was where the similarities ended.

The God of the Puritans was an Old Testament patriarchal figure. He was equally capable of wrath and love and demanded unquestioning obedience from his human creatures. Puritans were convinced that human beings were incapable of attaining salvation on their own: only God could save them. And, since God already knew who was going to heaven and who was headed in the opposite direction, everyone's fate was predestined.

In contrast, Quakers worshipped a God of love. Their God was more in line with the message of forgiveness and the humble gentleness associated with the Jesus of the New Testament than with the angry and frequently vengeful God of the Old Testament. Quakers believed everyone possessed what they called an "inner light," a capacity for grace and an intuitive understanding of the divine. The inner light linked the individual directly with God. Formally trained clergy, therefore, were unnecessary. Where Puritans were determined patriarchs—men were supposed to be unquestioned rulers within the family; Quakers had a far more equitable approach to gender. "In God there is no sex," was a Quaker saying, and while men held exclusive sway over public life, Quaker women could be missionaries and they controlled their own religious "meeting," including the power to make decisions about church finances and other business matters. (Quaker children spoke of "my father's and mother's house," a phrase not likely to be heard in Puritan New England.) With regard to children, Quakers believed they were born innocent—that is, free of original sin. Also, except as a last resort, children should never be physically punished; rather, they should be reasoned with by carefully explaining to them what they had done wrong. Finally, where Puritans were determined to construct a theocratic social order based on religious conformity, Quakers envisioned a society based on religious tolerance (as long as one was a Christian) and peaceful relations among neighbors.

From the very beginning, then, Britain's North American colonies were marked by a social and cultural diversity that to some degree was based on religious differences and the distinctive ways they organized family life.

Source: Steven Mintz, *Huck's Raft: A History of American Childhood* (Cambridge, MA: Harvard University Press, 2004), pp. 8, 10–23, 27–28, 37–41, 47–52.

CHILDHOOD IN COLONIAL NEW ENGLAND

A Puritan childhood is as alien to twenty-first century Americans as an Indian childhood was to seventeenth-century New Englanders. The Puritans did not sentimentalize childhood; they regarded even newborn infants as potential sinners who contained aggressive and willful impulses that needed to be suppressed. Nor did New Englanders consider childhood a period of relative leisure and playfulness, deserving of indulgence. They considered crawling bestial and play as frivolous and trifling, and self-consciously eliminated the revels and sports that fostered passionate peer relationships in England. In the Puritans' eyes, children were adults in training who needed to be prepared for salvation and inducted into the world of work as early as possible. Nevertheless, it would be a mistake to misrepresent the Puritans as unusually harsh or controlling parents, who lacked an awareness of children's special nature. The Puritans were unique in their preoccupation with childrearing, and wrote a disproportionate share of tracts on the subject. As a struggling minority, their survival depended on insuring that their children retained their values. They were convinced that molding children through proper childrearing and education was the most effective way to shape an orderly and godly society. Their legacy is a fixation on childhood corruption, child nurture, and schooling that remains undiminished in the United States today.

"Why came you unto this land?" Eleazar Mather asked his congregation in 1671; "was it not mainly with respect to the rising Generation? Was it to leave them a rich and wealthy people? Was it to leave them Houses, Lands, Livings? Oh, No; but to leave God in the midst of them." Mather was not alone in claiming that the Puritans had migrated to promote their children's well-being. Mary Angier declared that her reason for venturing across the Atlantic was "thinking that if her children might get good it would be worthy my journey." Similarly, Ann Ervington decided to migrate because she feared that "children would curse [their] parents for not getting them to means." When English Puritans during the 1620s and 1630s contemplated migrating to the New World, their primary motives were to protect their children from moral corruption and to promote their spiritual and economic well-being.

During the 1620s and 1630s, more than 14,000 English villagers and artisans fled their country to travel to the shores of New England, where they hoped to establish a stable and moral society free from the disruptive demographic and economic transformations that were unsettling England's social order. In the late sixteenth and early seventeenth centuries England experienced mounting inflation, rapid population growth, and a sharp increase in the proportion of children in the population. A 50 percent decline in real wages between 1500 and 1620 prompted a growing number of rural sons and daughters to leave their impoverished families and villages at a very young age to seek apprenticeships or to find employment as live-in servants or independent wage earners. . . .

The Puritan preoccupation with childhood was a product of religious beliefs and social circumstances. As members of a reform movement that sought to purify the Church of England and to elevate English morals and manners, the Puritans were convinced that the key to creating a pious society lay in properly rearing, disciplining, and educating a new generation to higher standards of piety. As a small minority group, the Puritans depended on winning the rising generation's minds and souls in order to prevail in the long term. Migration to New England greatly intensified the Puritans' fixation on childhood as a critical stage for saving souls. Deeply concerned about the survival of the Puritan experiment in a howling wilderness, fearful that their offspring might revert to savagery, the Puritans considered it essential that children retain certain fundamental values, including an awareness of sin.

In New England, the ready availability of land and uniquely healthy living conditions, the product of clean water and a cool climate, resulted in families that were larger, more stable, and more hierarchical than those in England. In rural England, a typical farm had fewer than forty acres, an insufficient amount to divide among a family's children. As a result, children customarily left home in their early teens to work as household servants or agricultural laborers in other households. . . . But in New England, distinctive demographic and economic conditions combined with a patriarchal ideology rooted in religion to increase the size of families, intensify paternal controls over the young, and allow parents to keep their children close by. A relatively equal sex ratio and an abundance of land made marriage a virtually universal institution. Because women typically married in their late teens or early twenties, five years earlier than their English counterparts, they bore many more children. On average, women gave birth every two years or so, averaging between seven and nine children, compared with four or five in England. These circumstances allowed the New England Puritans to realize their ideal of a godly family: a patriarchal unit in which a man's authority over his wife, children, and servants was a part of an interlocking chain of authority extending from God to the lowliest creatures.

The patriarchal family was the basic building block of Puritan society, and paternal authority received strong reinforcement from the church and community. Within their households, male household heads exercised unusual authority over family members. They were responsible for leading their household in daily prayers and scripture reading, catechizing their children and servants, and teaching household members to read so that they might study the Bible and learn the "good lawes of the Colony." Childrearing manuals were thus addressed to men, not their wives. They had an obligation to help their sons find a vocation or calling, and a legal right to consent to their children's marriage. Massachusetts Bay Colony and Connecticut underscored the importance of paternal authority by making it a capital offense for youths sixteen or older to curse or strike their father.

The Puritans repudiated many traditional English customs that conflicted with a father's authority, such as godparenthood. The family was a "little commonwealth," the keystone of the social order and a microcosm of the relationships of superiority and subordination that characterized the larger society. Yet even before the first generation of settlers passed away, there was fear that fathers were failing to properly discipline and educate their young. In 1648 the Massachusetts General Court reprimanded fathers for their negligence and ordered that "all masters of families do once a week (at the least) catechize their children and servants in the grounds and principles of Religion." Connecticut, New Haven, and Plymouth colonies followed suit in 1650, 1655, and 1671 with almost identical injunctions to ensure that "such children and Servants may [not] be in danger to grow barbarous, rude and stubborn, through ignorance.". . .

Childbirth in colonial New England was a difficult and sometimes life-threatening experience. During the seventeenth century, between 1 and 1.5 percent of births ended in the mother's death, the result of exhaustion, dehydration, infection, hemorrhage, or convulsions. Since the typical mother gave birth to between seven and nine children, her lifetime chances of dying from childbirth ran as high as one in eight. Understandably, many Puritan women regarded childbirth with foreboding, describing it as "that evel hour I loock forward to with dread." Likewise, the death of infants and children was common. The Puritan minister Cotton Mather said that a dead child was "a sight no more surprising than a broken pitcher," and almost all families experienced the loss of at least two or three children. Of the fourteen children Samuel Slater had with his first wife, only six reached adulthood. In New England's healthiest communities, around 10 percent of children died in their first year, and three of every nine died before reaching their twenty-first birthday. In seaports like Boston or Salem, death rates were two or three times higher. Epidemics of smallpox, measles, mumps, diphtheria, scarlet fever, and whooping cough were special sources of dread. During a 1677 smallpox epidemic, a fifth of Boston's population, mainly children, died. Cotton Mather saw eight of his fifteen children die before reaching the age of two. "We have our children taken from us," he cried out, "the Desire of our Eyes taken away with a stroke."

According to Puritan doctrine, infants who died unconverted were doomed to eternal torment in hell. Although parents were supposed to accept these deaths with resignation, many could barely contain their grief. Over time the Puritans softened the Calvinist emphasis on infant depravity. By the end of the seventeenth century, a growing number accepted the possibility that baptism washed away a child's sins and protected it from damnation. . . .

A Puritan childhood was enveloped in religion. Within two weeks of birth, a father brought his infant to the meetinghouse to be baptized. At this ceremony, a father renewed his covenant with God and promised him his seed. It was the father's duty to baptize the newborn because "the mother at that time by reason of her travail and delivery is weake, and not in case to have her head much troubled with many cares." It was at the baptismal ceremony that the child's name was announced. Although some parents bestowed common English names on their children, many first-generation Puritans, who had joined the movement after breaking with their parents, underscored this new beginning by choosing names with religious and moral significance. Some drew names from scripture (such as Zachariah) or their English equivalents (like "Thankful"); others chose phrase names (such as "If-Christ-had-not-died-for-thee-thou-hadst-been-damned"). Roger Class and his wife named their children Experience, Waitstill, Preserved, Hopestill, Wait,

Thinks, Desire, Unite, and Supply. These names gave tangible expression to the first generation's basic values and religion's importance to their lives. . . .

The Puritans regarded childhood as a time of deficiency, associating an infantile inability to walk or talk with animality, and considered it essential to teach children to stand upright and recite scripture as quickly as possible. To prevent infants from crawling, they dressed young children, regardless of sex, in long robes or petticoats, and placed them in wooden go-carts, similar to modern-day walkers. Neck stays kept infants' heads upright, while young girls wore leather corsets to encourage an erect and mature bearing. Wooden rods were sometimes place along children's spines to promote proper posture.

In Europe infants were wrapped tightly in swaddling bands to ensure that children's bones grew straight and that they did not get into their parents' way. There is no conclusive evidence that the New England Puritans swaddled children. In New England's larger families, older siblings or servants were assigned to watch infants. Still, many young children experienced accidents that indicate a lack of close supervision. Children suffered burns from candles or open hearths, fell into rivers and wells, ingested poisons, broke bones, swallowed pins, and stuffed nutshells up their noses. Unlike parents today, Puritan parents did not "baby-proof" their homes by screening fireplaces, covering wells, or blocking stairways. Stoically accepting accidents as a fact of life, parents instead stressed safety through obedience and assumed that a child's well-being was best served by teaching a child the skills and rules necessary to function in the adult world.

The Puritans were set apart from other religious sects by their emphasis on household religion. Although the meetinghouse was the place for public worship (the term *church* referred to the congregation's members, not to the physical structure), the household was the place for young people's initial religious and moral instruction. In 1650 the Connecticut General Court gave "masters of families" responsibility to "once a week at least catechize their children and servants in the grounds and principles of religion." Bible readings, prayers, self-examination, psalm-singing, and family instruction formed the household curriculum designed to lead children and servants to faith. . . .

The emphasis on early moral instruction led the Puritans to view children's play with ambivalence. Puritan children had swings, rode hobbyhorses, and drew on slates. Girls cut out paper dolls with scissors, recited poetry, and played with dollhouses and cradles. Boys flew kites, sailed toy boats, constructed wigwams and played at being Indians, collected rocks and bird eggs, and made pets of squirrels, dogs, and cats. Seventeenth-century records provide a litany of complaints about children playing ball or flying kites, robbing birds' nests and orchards, and throwing stones and snowballs at passersby. Yet the dominant view was that play was a sinful waste of time, "a snare of the Old Deluder, Satan." Samuel Sewall and Cotton Mather complained about their children's "inordinate love of play" and worried about the energies diverted to it. They especially abhorred game-playing on the Sabbath and any games involving cards and dice. . . .

As early as possible, children were taught to prepare for death. Ministers admonished children to reflect on death, and their sermons contained graphic descriptions of hell and the horrors of eternal damnation. Cotton Mather offered this advice: "Go into Burying-Place, Children; you will there see *Graves* as short as your selves. Yea, you may be at *Play* one Hour; *Dead, Dead* the next." With his own family, he seized on opportunities to reinforce this lesson. In one incident, he explained, "I took my little daughter, Katy, into my study, and there told my child, that I am to die shortly, and she must, when I am dead, remember every thing, that I said unto her." Awareness of death was inculcated by showing young children corpses and hangings. . . . At least some Puritan children picked up the message that they needed to recognize their sinfulness and strive for repentance and salvation. Samuel Sewall's daughter Betty "burst out" after dinner "into an amazing cry . . . Her Mother ask'd the reason; she gave none; at last she said she could goe to Hell, her Sins were not pardon'd. . . ."

During the seventeenth century, a growing perception that parents were failing to properly educate their children led many communities to transfer instructional responsibilities to schools. In 1647 Massachusetts Bay Colony had ordered every town of fifty families to "appoint one within their own towne to teach all such children as shall resort to him to write and read." In 1670 the Massachusetts General Court described a "great & general neglect of instructing & governing the rising generation, both in families & churches." By the end of the century, young New Englanders increasingly went to school to learn to write and cipher. This early rise of public schooling has been seen as a Puritan innovation, but it would be a mistake to exaggerate the Puritans' commitment to formal schooling. The Massachusetts school law was not rigidly enforced, and many towns failed to regularly provide teachers. All eight towns required to maintain a grammar school did so, but only a third of the smaller towns required to establish reading and writing schools obeyed the law, and no statute required children to attend school. While Puritan New Englanders had a much higher rate of literacy than the English, this phenomenon primarily reflected the lack of a large population of illiterate laborers rather than the Puritan belief that access to books distinguished Protestantism from the tyranny of Catholic priests.

Formal school terms were often quite brief, sometimes no more than a few months, and literacy was highly gendered. The Puritans were generally content to teach girls only reading, while encouraging boys to learn both reading and writing. Among the early settlers, about 60 percent of the men and 30 percent of the women could sign their own wills. By the end of the colonial period, 90 percent of the males and 50 percent of the females signed their wills. Grammar schools and Latin schools were reserved almost exclusively for boys. . . .

For much of the seventeenth century, paternal control over property had strengthened a father's authority over his offspring. In England the practice of primogeniture had restricted the prospects of land to the eldest son, but in New England all sons expected to inherit land. Having far more acres than people, the first settlers in New England fell into a pattern of distributing their estates among all their male heirs, with generous portions for their daughters, too. New England fathers used their control over property to influence their children's choice of vocation and decisions about the timing of marriage and the marriage partner. Paternal control over property also ensured that children took care of their parents in their old age. Typically fathers retained legal title to their land until their death, delaying their children's achievement of full adulthood until a relatively late age. Fathers controlled family assets to ensure that their sons labored for them productively and maintained them and their widows in old age. The strength of paternal authority extended to daughters as well. In the seventeenth century, daughters generally married in strict birth order to alleviate the father's fear that if younger daughters married earlier, it would be more difficult for older daughters to find husbands.

By the end of the seventeenth century, however, paternal authority had noticeably weakened. No longer was there sufficient land to sustain its distribution to all heirs. Geographic mobility increased markedly in the last two decades of the seventeenth century, as growing numbers of young people in their mid to late teens or early twenties left home for eastern seaports or commercial towns or newly settled frontier regions to find new opportunities. At the same time, nonagricultural employment expanded, particularly in household manufacturing, shipping, and trade, helping to draw young people off the land. An increase in geographic mobility and occupational opportunities allowed men and women to marry at an earlier age without a father's permission. The patriarchalism so dominant in early New England faded considerably during the early eighteenth century. Rather than wait for their inheritance, sons increasingly bought their portions, and hence their economic independence, from their father or siblings and left to farm on available land on the frontier or to make a new start in other towns. Although parents often aided them in this resettlement process, sons were removed from day-to-day paternal and church supervision, something their seventeenth-century counterparts had rarely managed. As a result, paternal control of marital decisions weakened significantly. . . .

CHILDHOOD IN THE MIDDLE COLONIES

The Middle Colonies, from New York to Delaware, were more pluralistic than any other portion of colonial America. Embracing the principle of religious toleration, this region attracted a diversity of immigrants who spoke a variety of languages. It was here, especially among the Quakers, where patterns of childhood and family life emerged that anticipated those that became common among the middle class during the nineteenth century.

When George Mittelberger, a schoolteacher from the German duchy of Wurttemberg who sailed to Pennsylvania in 1750, departed his ship, he witnessed a shocking scene. To pay for their passage to the New World, many German immigrants sold their children into service [indentured servitude] "like so many head of cattle" so that "the parents can leave the ship free and unrestrained." Children from five to fifteen years in age were bound out to service until they were twenty-one. Frequently, Mittelberger observed, the parents "do not know where and to what people their children are." He wrote that it "often happens that such parents and children, after leaving the ship, do not see each other again for many years, perhaps no more in all their lives."

Alongside the indentured children that Mittelberger described, another pattern of childhood arose in the Middle Colonies, decisively different from . . . New England. Especially pronounced among the Quakers, this family pattern was characterized by unusually intense emotional bonding between parents and children, indulgent childrearing, and an acceptance by parents of early youthful independence. In the Middle Colonies, most families lived in small nuclear households isolated from extended kin and free from the community controls found in New England. It was within these private, inward-turning households that new patterns of childhood were pioneered. Today we customarily distinguish between two-parent families, single-parent families, and extended families in which two-parent or single-parent families are augmented by other kin. Three centuries ago, very different conceptions of families prevailed. The gentry family—a unit based on lineage and ownership of a landed estate, passed down from generation to generation through the eldest son—proved difficult to sustain in the American colonies. Even the great landed families of New York and the southern colonies abandoned primogeniture and provided large inheritances to every one of their children. A second kind of family—the farm or artisanal household—was a unit of production that included not only a husband, wife, and their children but also the servants, apprentices, laborers, and other dependents. Common in New England, this was a patriarchal unit in which proprietors and masters exercised direct command over their dependents' labor. A third familial model—the clan—consisted of a group of interrelated families that lived in separate households but interacted socially and economically. Especially in seventeenth-century New England, it was not uncommon for the sons and daughters of one family to marry the children of another. Indeed, whole communities in early New England often consisted of a small number of interrelated families.

It was during the eighteenth century in the Middle Colonies that a fourth kind of family emerged: the private family, consisting of a father, mother, and children bound together by ties of affection. Not simply a unit of production or a vehicle for transmitting property or craft skills, the private family was an emotional entity and an instrument for shaping children's character. Within the private family, space was restructured; particular areas were set aside for cooking, eating, sitting at ease, and sleeping. The shift toward a privatized family was also apparent in burial practices; rarely did inhabitants of the Middle Colonies bury their dead alongside extended family members. Language, too, reflected the emphasis on the private family. Settlers in the Middle Colonies rejected the custom of referring to distant relatives as aunts, uncles, and cousins. Indeed, the very spelling of the family's surname varied from one household to another.

Favorable circumstances, such as the sheer abundance of arable land, encouraged the development of private families in the Middle Colonies, as did religion. Much more than Puritans, the Quakers and other religious sectarians in the Middle Colonies sought to keep children isolated from the corruptions of the outside world. The Quakers, in particular, were convinced that the best way to promote children's religious salvation was to maintain "holy conversation" with their parents, who had already learned religious truth. More than any earlier group of English immigrants, the Quakers extolled a family life centered on the affection and companionship between a husband and wife and the love, care, and emotional support of their children. Unlike the Puritans, the Quakers emphasized equality over hierarchy, gentle guidance over strict discipline, and early autonomy for children. Precisely because the Quaker Meeting exercised strong communal control over marriage, parents could afford to be more indulgent. Nor did Quaker fathers govern children through the inheritance system. They generally gave their sons outright gifts of land at the time of marriage without any restrictions or stipulations. Sons of the first settlers received an average of over 200 acres of land, and daughters received the equivalent in cash and goods.

The steady influx of new immigrant families into the Middle Colonies, which slowed the development of dense extended family networks, also encouraged the growth of private families. Unlike New England, where immigration declined after 1640, or the Chesapeake, where most new arrivals came as forced laborers, either as indentured servants or as slaves, the Middle Colonies attracted many non-English immigrants, particularly Germans and Scots-Irish. Many of the first immigrants arrived as single young men or teenagers and usually lived with a master's family. Beginning in the 1730s, however, poor economic conditions in Germany, Scotland, and Ireland led to the migration of entire families, usually consisting of a young married couple with one or two children or an older couple and their teenaged children. Even poor tenant farmers maintained separate households. Private families were especially common in the growing towns and seaports, like Philadelphia, where few journeymen resided in the homes of their masters and few laboring families took extended kin or non-kin into their homes.

In contrast to New England, where paternal control of land allowed fathers to exert a powerful influence on the sons' lives well into their twenties or even thirties, in the Middle Colonies a large proportion of sons moved away from their parents in their teenage years. Even Quaker parents found it difficult to ensure that their children married within the faith and stayed close by. . . .

During the second half of the eighteenth century, regional variations in childhood narrowed as increasing geographic mobility, new employment opportunities, evangelical religious revivals, and military conflict contributed to greater youthful autonomy. Dwindling land supplies in New England and soil exhaustion of the tobacco lands of the Tidewater and

Piedmont encouraged many sons to leave family farms for western lands or fresh starts in towns and cities. As a result, boys got their start in life considerably earlier than before and had more occupational choices. Meanwhile the emotional evangelical religious revivals sweeping through the colonies challenged older forms of authority and allowed youths to assert an independent religious identity much earlier. The Great Awakening of the 1730s and 1740s had pronounced effects on the young, encouraging new childrearing practices, reducing the age of conversion, and promoting a new code of values among many. Evangelical families placed a heavy emphasis on suppressing children's willfulness, shaping their conscience, and disciplining their passions to prepare them for the experience of religious rebirth. The age of religious conversion fell sharply, often into the teen years, and young people in increasing numbers decided independently which churches to join. . . .

Young men's participation in military combat dramatically altered the experience of adolescent white males. Warfare was common during the mid-eighteenth century. Roughly 30 to 40 percent of adolescent males saw action in warfare in the period from 1740 to 1781, against either the Indians, the French, or the British. Wars drew youth away from their parents' homes and accelerated the process by which young people attained independence and adult status.

Even before the Revolution, a new ideology highly critical of patriarchal authority had begun to circulate throughout the colonies. Much more widely read than political discourses such as John Locke's *Second Treatise on Liberty* were childrearing tracts, such as his *Essay Concerning Human Understanding* and Jean-Jacque Rousseau's *Emile.* In widely read works of fiction by Daniel Defoe, Henry Fielding, Samuel Richardson, Laurence Sterne, and numerous lesser-known writers, the patriarchal family came under attack as unduly repressive and incompatible with the spirit of the times. Readers learned that parental example was more effective than coercion governing children; that the ideal parent sought to cultivate children's natural talents and abilities through love; and that young people had a right to choose an occupation and a spouse free from parental intrusion.

The growing emphasis on youthful independence represented a striking reversal in public attitudes. During the seventeenth century most young colonists, regardless of region and social class, had lived in a state of dependency upon their parents or upon a master and a mistress. Through their control over dowries, inheritance, landed property, and access to training and apprenticeships, fathers and masters determined when young people were able to leave home, marry, and achieve the independence of full adulthood. It is not an accident that the very terms used to describe young people—*boy* and *girl*—were words also applied to servants, regardless of age, since subordination and dependency characterized both the condition of service and the condition of childhood and youth. Nothing symbolized this emphasis on domestic hierarchy better than the practice among young people of uncovering their heads and bowing in their presence of their parents. By the mid-eighteenth century, however, adult control over young people's access to economic independence had diminished, and young people were exercising greater autonomy over their leisure activities and courtship practices. A flood of advice books, philosophical treatises, novels, plays, and poems condemned prolonged submission to paternal rule and defended youthful freedom as a natural right. This antipatriarchal, antiauthoritarian ideology helped to sensitize the colonists to arbitrary British colonial authority. In defending the colonists' struggle for independence from British colonial rule, the radical pamphleteer Thomas Paine drew a pointed analogy to the importance of granting children early autonomy. "Nothing hurts the affections both of parents and children so much," he wrote in *The Crisis* in 1878, "as living too closely connected, and keeping up the distinction too long."

Questions for Discussion

1. How did Puritan and Quaker views of children differ? In your opinion, what are the respective legacies of Puritan and Quaker attitudes toward children in today's society?
2. What impact did the New England climate have on the health and economic prospects of Puritan families?
3. How did religion influence the social and political development of New England and the Middle Colonies? Specifically, what role did it play regarding immigration, ethnic and religious diversity, and land ownership?
4. What was patriarchy? How did Quakers and Puritans differ in their views of patriarchy?
5. The author described four distinct family types in the seventeenth-century colonies. What were they? Which most closely resembles the "typical" American family today?

For Further Reading

James Axtell, *The School upon a Hill: Education and Society in Colonial New England* (1974); Cornelia Hughes Dayton, *Women Before the Bar: Gender, Law, and Society in Connecticut, 1639–1789* (1995); John Demos, *A Little Commonwealth: Family Life in Plymouth Colony* (1970); Richard S. Dunn and Mary Maples Dunn, eds., *The World of William Penn* (1986); David Hackett Fischer, *Albion's Seed: Four British Folkways in America* (1989); J. William Frost, *The Quaker Family in Colonial America* (1973); Philip Greven, *The Protestant Temperament: Patterns of Child-Rearing, Religious Experience, and the Self in Early America* (1977); Joseph Illick, *Colonial Pennsylvania* (1976); Barry Levy, *Quakers and the American Family: British Settlement in the Delaware Valley, 1650–1765* (1988); Anne S. Lombard, *Making Manhood: Growing Up Male in Colonial New England* (2003); James Marten, ed., *Children in Colonial America* (2007); Steven Mintz and Susan Kellogg, *Domestic Revolutions: A Social History of American Family Life* (1988); Gerald F. Moran and Maris A. Vinovskis, *Religion, Family, and the Life Course: Explorations in the Social History of Early America* (1992); Edmund Morgan, *The Puritan Family* (1966);

Gary Nash, *Quakers and Politics: Pennsylvania, 1681–1726* (1968); Peter Gregg Slater, *Children in the New England Mind* (1977); C. John Sommerville, *The Discovery of Childhood in Puritan England* (1992); Laurel T. Ulrich, *Good Wives: Image and Reality in the Lives of Women in Northern New England, 1650–1750* (1982); Helena Wall, *Fierce Communion: Family and Community in Early America* (1990); Robert Wells, *The Population of the British Colonies in America before 1776* (1975); Bernard Wishy, *The Child and the Republic: The Dawn of Modern American Child Nurture* (1968); Michael Zuckerman, *Friends and Neighbors: Group Life in America's First Plural Society* (1982).

4

Settling South Carolina
Family Ties and the Quest for Wealth in the New World

Lorri Glover

As we saw in the preceding chapter, from the beginning of British settlement in North America, distinctive regional cultures evolved in New England and the Middle Colonies. This was also the case between the northern and southern colonies. Climate and geography had a lot to do with it. The northern British colonies had a temperate climate and a relatively disease-free environment (at least through the seventeenth century). Both of these factors helped promote stable communities. Environmental circumstances in the southern colonies during the seventeenth century were starkly different. A combination of crop failures, torrid temperatures, and contaminated drinking water produced malnutrition, along with epidemics of malaria, typhus, and other deadly diseases.

In seventeenth-century New England, a man who reached the age of twenty could expect to live to about seventy; his counterpart in Virginia (South Carolina is discussed in the following essay) lived to about forty-three. One-half of the women in Virginia did not live past twenty. The experiences of children in this region differed profoundly from those in the northern colonies. Infant mortality rates in the southern colonies were two to three times higher than in New England. Early death had a devastating impact on social and family stability in this region. High death rates shortened marriages. For instance, the average Virginia marriage in the seventeenth century lasted just seven years. Two-thirds of all children in that colony lost at least one parent by the time they turned eighteen. This

Ships bringing settlers to colonial South Carolina. By contrast with the family-oriented, community-based settlements in New England, emigrants to the south have often been portrayed as individual entrepreneurs hunting for wealth and adventure. Does the following article reinforce or undermine this view?

meant that relationships between parents and children were often cut short. Orphans were common, and many children were raised by step-parents or relatives such as aunts and uncles. When death or poverty broke up families entirely, orphans might be placed in apprenticeships or sold into indentured servitude, where they lived under the authority of unrelated adults.

Patterns of settlement in the South added to family and social instability. By contrast with the largely family-oriented migrations to New England, the vast majority of settlers in seventeenth-century Virginia and Maryland were men. They outnumbered women by six to one. In addition, many of the women and men who migrated there were indentured servants who were not allowed to marry until their term of service was over (four of five emigrants to the Chesapeake Bay area in the seventeenth century were indentures). Southern colonists married late, had low rates of fertility (two to three children per family), and died young—all of which promoted premarital sexuality and illegitimate children. In seventeenth-century New England, less than 10 percent of brides were pregnant on their wedding day, compared with about 33 percent in Maryland and Virginia.

It is important to note that by the mid-eighteenth century, the demographic circumstances in the southern colonies had largely stabilized and had become more consistent with patterns in Britain's northern possessions.

Besides their distinctive environment and climate, seventeenth-century British colonies in the South differed from those in New England in another way: the reason they were settled. By contrast to the central role played by religion in the decisions of Quakers and Puritans to leave England, those who came to the southern colonies desired the material things of this world. Most migrants to Virginia, Maryland, and the Carolinas craved land and profits above all else. The same sultry southern climate that spawned disease also created a soil of remarkable richness. Southern soil was among the most fertile in the world. The cultivation of tobacco, rice, and indigo in the seventeenth century, and cotton by the late eighteenth century, would make this region fabulously wealthy. It would also make it a slave society.

In the following article Lorri Glover describes the origins of South Carolina. Glover shows that those who settled in what she calls South Carolina's *"lowcountry"*—the narrow, fertile coastal region on the colony's eastern seaboard—had three goals. They wanted to acquire land, engage in transatlantic trade, and make money. And it was a business venture in which success and profits often depended on transatlantic family ties that connected relatives in England and the West Indies to those in South Carolina. According to Glover, family connections—or their absence—often determined the success—or failure—of those who migrated to South Carolina in the seventeenth century.

Source: Glover, Lorri. *All Our Relations: Blood Ties and Emotional Bonds among the Early South Carolina Gentry.* Excerpts pp. 1–3, 5–11, 15–16, 21–22. © 2000 The Johns Hopkins University Press. Reprinted with permission of The Johns Hopkins University Press.

In the spring of 1670, the first group of permanent English settlers arrived on the shores of what is today Charleston, South Carolina. Stephen Bull, a member of an established, wealthy English family, sailed with those first ninety-odd immigrants. As the *Carolina* approached the bay, he saw stretched before him potentially limitless opportunities. Carolina offered a relatively temperate climate, a long growing season, good rivers, rich soil, and free land. When Bull arrived on the shores of Carolina he brought with him nine servants and the Bull family name. For the former he received 1,050 acres of rich land along the Ashley River, but the latter proved far more lucrative. Bull's relatives financed his settlement in Carolina and eagerly anticipated his success there. All the Bull family resources stood ready to ensure that this came to pass. Further, his familial connections earned him the favor of the lord proprietors and an appointment as proprietary deputy on the Grand Council. Bull and his descendants numbered among South Carolina's wealthiest and most politically influential families from the late seventeenth century until the American Revolution. . . .

Edward Hyrne, conversely, spent his years in the lowcountry barely eking out an existence. In early 1700 Edward and his wife, Elizabeth, fled England, Edward's creditors, and the disapproval of their families and determined to start again in Carolina. Ill-prepared to deal with the lowcountry environment, alone in a new place, and impoverished, the Hyrnes found "our necessities are very great and pressing." Lacking both the financial and familial connections necessary to succeed, Edward and Elizabeth watched again and again as their dreams of prospering in Carolina died. Around 1706 Edward reluctantly traveled to England and issued a desperate appeal to Elizabeth's brother for financial support. While Edward's brother-in-law begrudgingly agreed to provide some money for his sister and nephews, he assured Edward that only a court order could make him acquiesce to all the Hyrnes' financial appeals. The trip a failure, Edward attempted to return to Charleston. But before he could board the next ship, he was arrested and thrown into debtor's prison.

Bull and Hyrne, like most other early Carolinians, did not rise or fall solely—or even primarily—on their own merit. Ambition, wealth, and chance all contributed to a successful Carolina venture, but the single most important determinant in the fate of the earliest colonists was familial connections. Bull went to Carolina not as an individual entrepreneur, but rather as an emissary of the Bull clan. Edward Hyrne, on the other hand, fled to Carolina to escape his creditors and the disdain of his wife's family. While Bull enjoyed the support of his kin abroad and parlayed his family name into political appointments, social status, and economic gain, the Hyrnes remained alone, estranged from their relatives, bereft of a kinship network either in England or in the colony. Bull prospered beyond his own grand dreams. Halfway through the winter of 1700–1701, Edward Hyrne reported that only the kindness of strangers kept him and his family from starving to death.

When one understands the nature of Carolina settlement, it is not at all surprising that Bull spent his last days on South Carolina's Grand Council and Hyrne spent his in debtor's prison.

Settling South Carolina was, from the beginning, a family affair. The free white men and women who first came to colonial South Carolina did so primarily with the endorsement and encouragement, and in some cases at the behest, of their families. Indeed, many migrated as emissaries for relatives in Europe or the West Indies with the intention of expanding established family empires along the Carolina coastline.

Lowcountry immigrants were hardly alone in this initial reliance on kin. Indeed, family and kin were essential to European colonization throughout early America. From the "little commonwealths" of Puritan New England to the ethnic enclaves of New York and Philadelphia to the Calvert dynasty in Maryland, family—in all its myriad forms—lay at the heart of most colonization efforts. Even early Virginia, long accused of only "looking out for number one," apparently joined together in elaborate familial and neighborhood networks.

Although most early British-Americans depended on family during initial migration, their commitment to transatlantic kin often waned over time. Subsistence farmers and planters could afford to sever Old World connections and seek personal and familial independence because they saw little long-term need for extended family ties. They sold goods in local markets or bartered with neighbors for the things they could not produce themselves. For many, extended family could seem more like a burden than a blessing. In fact, the quest for autonomy sometimes drove private households away from extensive kinship networks.

South Carolina elites, on the other hand, carried their reliance on kin far beyond the initial period of settlement. From the beginning, Charleston was planned as a center for transatlantic businesses. Because they migrated expressly to build international family empires, Charleston's businessmen needed their relatives abroad to provide financial assistance and serve as liaisons in their trading ventures far longer than other British-Americans. That, after all, was what drove seventeenth- and eighteenth-century businesses. Furthermore, throughout the colonial era, lowcountry elites remained both more interrelated and more homogeneous than the gentry in any other city in British North America. Philadelphia, Boston, and New York developed over time into larger, more heterogeneous urban centers. They remained far less intimately connected to slaveholding than Charleston and maintained far more diverse populations. Charleston, conversely, fell under the control of a uniquely homogeneous, insular, cooperative, interrelated ruling class, much like their neighbors in Barbados.

These well-laid plans for expanding family empires ran afoul of the harsh lowcountry environment, and siblings and kin took on even greater weight when colonists realized their "earthly paradise" was a death trap. Among the first generation of colonists, demographic and social instability in Carolina extended their initial reliance on relatives abroad. At the same time, short life expectancy coupled with the preponderance of disease and frequent emigration necessitated an even deeper dependence on intergenerational kin within the colony.

It took only a few years after the founding of Charleston for the word to spread from Europe to the West Indies to the northern and mid-Atlantic colonies: "Those who wish to die quickly, go to Carolina." Dysentery, malaria, smallpox, "bloody flux," and a host of other debilitating diseases plagued early lowcountry settlers. Epidemics of yellow fever, mumps, measles, and whooping cough swept the colony in wave after wave. In the summertime, residents often complained that the smells of death filled the streets. The subtropical climate and disease-carrying mosquitoes would have brought trouble enough on their own. But Carolinians drank dangerously contaminated water and fought year after year with Native Americans, which heightened the general precariousness of life in the lowcountry.

Colonial South Carolinians died at alarming rates and at unusually early ages. Between 1680 and 1720 almost half the men residing in St. John's parish who survived childhood died before they reached their fiftieth birthday. Another 37 percent died in their fifties. During that same period in neighboring Christ Church parish, 73 percent of men who lived to age twenty died before age fifty. Between 1721 and 1760 that figure rose to 85 percent. Women fared no better. In St. John's between 1680 and 1720, 55 percent of women reaching adulthood never saw their fiftieth birthday. Both women and men considered themselves old—and lucky—if they survived more than fifty years. Mortality rates did not stabilize until the last third of the eighteenth century, and even then South Carolina remained a hotbed of diseases. When he arrived in Charleston in 1757, James Glen informed his brother-in-law that he and his companions had "been seized by Fluxes, Vomiting, and all the Symptoms which attend intermitting Fevers and Am told that this Disorder is a Tribute paid by most Strangers upon their arrival here."

Young Carolinians grew up in a society pervaded by parental sickness and death. Most children of the first generation of colonists could expect to lose one or both of their biological parents. Ann Clark and her sister lived with their late mother's former husband and his new wife because both biological parents had died when the sisters were young girls. Mary Smith raised Ann Smith Waring, the orphaned daughter of Mary's stepdaughter and stepson-in-law. Sarah Amory went to live with her mother's friend, Sarah Rhett, after Amory's father, mother, sister, and brother all died in the yellow fever epidemic of 1699–1700. Orphaned children like these often found themselves turning to siblings and kin to fill the emotional and practical roles of dead parents. . . .

Somewhat surprisingly, this turbulent social and familial environment did not derail colonization efforts. Despite the harsh climate and the tremendous potential for failure, each passing year more and more immigrants traveled to the lowcountry. In 1672 fewer than 400 whites lived in South Carolina. By the middle of the eighteenth century, 25,000 whites called the colony home. They lived alongside nearly 40,000 blacks who had been stolen from their homes in West Africa and were forced to toil in the shipyards and rice fields that formed the foundation of South Carolina wealth.

Given Carolina's well-earned deadly reputation, it is hard to imagine why so many free immigrants took so great a gamble. Some, no doubt, were ignorant of the realities, while others were misled by propaganda. For many, religious toleration offered the greatest incentive. In 1680 the proprietors began a vigorous campaign to recruit French Huguenots and English dissenters. By the beginning of the eighteenth century, more than 500 Huguenots had answered the call. Families of English dissenters soon followed. Even after the establishment of the Church of England in 1706, the lowcountry remained religiously diverse and tolerant. For other settlers, adventure, not religion, provided the allure. When asked about his daughter's move to Carolina in the 1720s, one father explained that she "has a rambling Head and a Mind to see strange places." And some, like Edward Hyrne, fled to Carolina hoping to escape the disapproval of their families.

More than anything else, however, land and the potential wealth and power that accompanied landownership drew people to the Carolina lowcountry. For women and men living in England and the overpopulated islands of the West Indies, the lure of land seemed too compelling to ignore.

Affra Harleston and John Coming rolled the dice in the late seventeenth century. Shortly after marrying, they moved to Carolina intent on starting a family dynasty. But they remained childless, and their hopes floundered. John and Affra decided to ask his nephew Elias Ball and her nephew John Harleston to come live with them and eventually inherit the Coming lands. Both nephews balked at the offer, and a disappointed John Coming changed his will and left everything to Affra. She did not long survive as an isolated widow, and upon her death left all her worldly goods to the two nephews. Eventually the two young men, along with John Harleston's sister, decided to try the family luck again. With the bequest from their aunt and their mutual cooperation, they succeeded where Affra had failed. In fact they founded one of Carolina's oldest, most powerful families—the Balls. Their experience illustrates that although land lured people to Carolina, family connections allowed them to thrive.

Most migrants left England and the Caribbean for the turbulent but alluring Carolina lowcountry imagining that they would conserve British familial and cultural practices. Transplanted Carolinians, whether they originated in England or the West Indies, envisioned themselves primarily as Britons, so British values were the ones they sought to emulate. But, in reality, their drive to acquire wealth sometimes overrode their desire to replicate traditions. In some cases, Carolinians adopted kin strategies that diverged from English standards because these tactics advanced their economic standing in the colony. Demographic factors disrupted relationships within the patriarchal family and forced Carolinians to abandon other English traditions and deepen their reliance on siblings and kin. Finally, the widespread availability of rich land contributed to Carolinians' reassessment of family relationships. Demographic instability, land acquisition, and business agendas collectively produced a system of family relationships and functions that differed significantly from early modern English traditions. Some changes grew out of conscious kin-strategies; others resulted from unavoidable differences in climate and geography. But in both cases, the changes that Carolina society underwent encouraged colonists' identification with extended kin and put them on a path that increasingly diverged from the world they had left behind.

For example, in the late seventeenth and early eighteenth centuries, while English men and women increasingly entered into marriages based on mutual affection, South Carolina elites revivified the traditional connections between marriage and money. Marriage remained far more financially focused for a longer time in Carolina than it did in other parts of the British Empire. Visitors to the lowcountry from England as well as from other colonies regularly criticized Carolinians for pursuing economically advantageous marriages and talking openly about their choices.

Carolinians cast off other English practices as well. Remarriage, for instance, became far more acceptable and commonplace among Carolinians. English communities frowned on remarriage after the death of a spouse. . . . South Carolinians, inhabiting a demographically unstable region and greedy for wealth and power, formed a different opinion on the subject of remarriage. Economic agendas and high death rates pushed early settlers toward remarrying more often than their British contemporaries. Aware of the fiscal and physical necessity of kin ties, Carolinians eagerly and quickly remarried after the death of a spouse. Charles Pinckney's first wife died in January 1744, and by May his second wife was drafting thank you notes for wedding gifts. Like Charles Pinckney, Thomas Dale remarried less than six months after his wife died. He then begged his friends in England to "pray keep the Secret for some time because it does not look very decent with you tho' we do not mind it here. . . ."

As Carolinians remarried more often and more quickly than their English kinsmen, they also narrowed the definition of incest and chose close kin as spouses. Cousin and exchange marriages (between sets of siblings from two different families) pervaded the family trees of South Carolinians throughout the colonial era. The first generations of colonists employed these practices, hoping to extend and intensify kin ties and to protect family estates from fragmentation. In subsequent generations, elites used these kin-based unions as a critical component in the construction of their powerful interrelated class. The determination to enter into such marriages, however, diverged from the standards set by English elites. Indeed, while Carolinians looked first to cousin and exchange marriages as a potential solution to the emotional and financial fragmentation of their families and later as the building blocks for class identity, English gentry repudiated such unions. One study that sampled families from the eighteenth-century House of Lords found that these elites married their cousins and in-laws very rarely. Between 1720 and 1780 cousin marriage took place in less than 1 percent of cases. Exchange marriages happened even more infrequently.

Carolinians' choice to take kinfolk as mates, despite British aversion to the practice, grew out of their redefinition of incest. . . . As with remarriage customs, both the precariousness of life and the acquisitiveness of colonists contributed to this divergence in incest taboos. Survival and economic advancement mattered more to the first generations of colonists than honoring religious dictates. Kin-based unions enhanced emotional ties within the family and simultaneously diminished the dilution of family holdings. Once Carolinians got around the moral dilemmas posed by marrying certain relatives—an easily accomplished task given the essentially irreligious nature of the colonial population—narrowing the incest taboo appeared practical and profitable and thus justifiable.

Just as Carolinians' circumscription of marriage prohibitions distinguished them from their mother country, so too did their abandonment of primogeniture. English families engaged in primogeniture throughout the early modern era because they needed to protect family resources, particularly land, across the generations. The limited availability of land and the necessity of land holding for financial stability led English fathers to bequeath the family patrimony to the eldest son. But in South Carolina the perceived widespread availability of land (actually the property of local Yamassee and other Indian nations) and the diminished intergenerational concerns of colonists made primogeniture unnecessary. In its place, colonists adopted a system of partible inheritance. . . .

By limiting inheritance to first-born sons, primogeniture imposed a rigid age and gender ranking among siblings. This ranking tended to exacerbate sibling tensions and rivalry since it led siblings to see one another more as competitors than as allies. The success of one sibling at the expense of the others could also provoke resentment within the sibling group. And the privilege of age and gender over ability imperiled family holdings and caused tensions. . . . Conversely, partible inheritance encouraged cooperation and egalitarianism within generations but complicated estate planning across generations. The abandonment of primogeniture democratized economic relationships among sons (and to a lesser degree, daughters) who all shared in family holdings. It thus had the unintended effect of alleviating some of the sibling resentment that often accompanied the system of primogeniture. Age and gender no longer rigidly dictated place in the family. The eradication of the economic need to rank children diminished conflicts between siblings, who learned that they should share and expand family holdings rather than compete over them. . . .

Siblings and kin groups not only contributed to the success and persistence of particular colonists but also dramatically shaped economic and political life in South Carolina. Kin support proved essential to the development of early merchant firms, businesses, and plantations in and around Charleston. Not surprisingly, the colony's counting houses and plantations operated as family businesses—partnerships between brothers, cousins, uncles, and nephews. With the aid of their kin, early lowcountry elites laid the foundation for future family interests. In the late seventeenth century, Stephen Bull and his brother John, a London merchant, helped establish the lucrative deerskin trade in Carolina. Another London merchant, William Wragg, financed his nephews' move to South Carolina. With the aid of their wealthy and well-connected uncle, William and Joseph Wragg built the largest slave-trading business in early-eighteenth-century South Carolina. In many cases, family connections made all the difference in colonial business ventures. As one early Carolinian explained, "The connexions, capital, & application to Business, those Younger Gentlemen together with the aid of their Fathers & other able friends will give them an Ascendant over other Houses."

Although relatives abroad expected a return on their investment in Carolina, their willingness to aid kin in Charleston was not strictly contingent upon financial restitution. Families and kin recognized the great risk associated with loaning money to Carolinians and anticipated the inability of their kin to repay their debts. Elias Ball assured his nephew and namesake in Charleston that he trusted the younger Elias would *want* to honor his debts, but feared he would never be able to repay a loan. Still, the elder Elias loaned his nephew money—not only for the initial venture, but also for many years after.

Relatives did demand family allegiance in return for their financial backing. Since for both Britons and Carolinians family was as much an economic as an emotional institution, restitution and respect became interwoven. When the two Elias Balls did disagree, the conflict arose not over the younger Elias's ability to repay debts to his English kinsman, but over a perceived lack of respect for the sacrifices the elder Elias had made. In the end, the two men reconciled their differences and made promises of lifelong friendship because they believed that cooperating together was the lucrative and the right thing to do.

Elias Ball and others like him appeared to be motivated by a sense of cooperation that superseded individual interests. A desire for extensive family prosperity, not simply personal gain, governed their behavior. Siblings and close kin frequently collaborated to advance their collective status. Brothers coordinated the migration of younger siblings or moved to Charleston together. They also worked hard to maintain connections to relatives abroad, which brought access to markets and credit while simultaneously diminishing the risk of individual failure. Carolina remained, in the truest sense of the phrase, a family affair. Lowcountry elites' focus lay more in the extension of family influence abroad and within the colony than on individual aggrandizement.

The commitment to aid kin and the quest for family power influenced politics as well as business. Early Charlestonians frequently called on their siblings and kinsmen for the political connections needed for financial and social success. While Peter Colleton lived in South Carolina in the late seventeenth century, he asked his London nephew John More to use his power as a magistrate to advance Colleton's agenda. When Colleton and other early immigrants experienced a growing problem with privateers, he encouraged his nephew to lobby for the passage of a parliamentary act against such activities. Colleton further lobbied More to "doe you your selfe put the law in Execution as far as you have power as you are a Magistrate by Imprisoning any that are going into the Service of forraigne princes or that you Suspect are of themselves going upon any pyraticall Designe & by seizing any prize brought in that land." Although himself a financial failure, Charles Lowndes left his two youngest sons, Rawlins and Charles, something more valuable than money: a legacy of important friendships and familial connections in England, the Islands, and South Carolina. The Lowndes brothers successfully parlayed those connections into respected careers in public office. . . .

Those who failed to secure the aid of family members in the Carolina venture ran a high risk of personal unhappiness and financial failure. John Jenny went back to his native Barbados in 1680 after experiencing one failure upon another in Charleston. His brother, who had remained in Barbados, explained that John returned "in such a weak condition and so discouraged, that he thinks he shall never see that place again. . . .

Elizabeth Massingberd and Edward Hyrne faced the same problems when they moved to Carolina without the help of their kindred. In addition to marrying against the wishes of the Massingberd family, Edward was at least twenty-five years older than his seventeen-year-old bride. The Massingberds hated Edward because, among other things, as port collector he "misapplied" almost 1,400 pounds. When he married Elizabeth, Edward was deeply in debt and facing criminal charges, so he wisely decided it best "to remove himself from the proximity of his creditors." Much to her family's dismay, Elizabeth followed her new husband to Carolina. Alone, forced to work hard, often sick, and poor, she begged her family to send her supplies and money. The Hyrnes did everything they could to curry favor with Elizabeth's family in England. They alternatively pleaded and insisted that her brother Burrell Massingberd, the executor of Elizabeth's father's estate, relinquish Elizabeth's inheritance. The Hyrnes even named their first child after Burrell, hoping he might feel a special affinity for his nephew and namesake, Burrell Hyrne, and send money for his education.

The Hyrnes, however, found themselves continually disappointed. Neither their pleas for money nor their covert attempts to forge a relationship between their children and Elizabeth's family (and their purses) met with much success. Elizabeth wrote at length of the travails that they encountered. Their first few years in South Carolina were filled with heartache. Two of their children died, and their house burned. In the fire they lost most of their food and household possessions. This setback intensified their appeals to the Massingberds, who remained resolute. The Massingberds' refusal to support the Hyrnes condemned them to failure. . . .

The colonization of early Carolina, not unlike that of much of British North America, rested on family ties. While hardly unique in the Atlantic world in this regard, Carolinians did encounter a number of factors that intensified their sibling and kin connections. The heavy reliance on kin abroad during initial colonization and early migrants' commitment to transatlantic trading meant that kinship played an especially important role in the colony. The demographic realities in the lowcountry accentuated this reliance on kin at the same time that it altered the shape of families. Succeeding, even surviving, in the lowcountry required both the protection of family relations abroad and the expansion of family networks in Carolina. The physical and fiscal reality of life in the lowcountry thus deepened Carolinians' attachment to and their identification with siblings and intergenerational kin.

Questions for Discussion

1. According to the author, family connections were central to the colonization of all Britain's North American colonies, but they were especially vital in the settlement and development of South Carolina. What evidence does she present to support this claim?
2. What was the impact of the "lowcountry" environment on settlers? Despite the colony's forbidding climate, the free and slave populations continued to grow. Why?

3. Over time, as each American colony developed, many British traditions were gradually discarded. How did this happen in South Carolina? Why? With what impact on family life?

4. American ideas about success and opportunity imply that the *individual* succeeds or fails on his or her own merits. How does this square with the experiences of South Carolina's early settlers?

For Further Reading

Cara Anzilotti, *In the Affairs of the World: Women, Power, and Patriarchy in Colonial South Carolina* (2002); T. H. Breen, *Tobacco Culture: The Mentality of the Great Tidewater Planters on the Eve of Revolution* (1985), *Puritans and Adventurers: Change and Persistence in Early America* (1980); Kathleen M. Brown, *Good Wives, Nasty Wenches, and Anxious Patriarchs: Gender, Race, and Power in Colonial Virginia* (1996); Peter Coclanis, *The Atlantic Economy During the Seventeenth and Eighteenth Centuries* (2005); S. Max Edelson, *Plantation Enterprises in Colonial South Carolina* (2006); Stephen Innes, ed., *Work and Labor in Early America* (1988); Rhys Isaac, *The Transformation of Virginia, 1740–1790* (1982); Allan Kulikoff, *Tobacco and Slaves: The Development of Southern Cultures in the Chesapeake, 1680–1800* (1986); Karen Ordahl Kupperman, ed., *America in European Consciousness* (1995); Daniel Littlefield, *Rice and Slaves: Ethnicity and the Slave Trade in Colonial South Carolina* (1981); Gloria Main, *Tobacco Colony: Life in Early Maryland, 1650–1720* (1982); Steven Otis, *A Colonial Complex: South Carolina's Frontier in the Era of the Yamasee War, 1680–1730* (2004); Darrett B. and Anita H. Rutman, *A Place in Time: Middlesex County, Virginia, 1650–1750* (1984); Daniel Blake Smith, *Inside the Great House: Planter Family Life in Eighteenth-Century Chesapeake Society* (1980); Thad Tate, *Colonial Virginia: A History* (1986); Robert M. Weir, *Colonial South Carolina: A History* (1997).

CHAPTER

5

From Africans to African Americans

Slavery, Women, and the Family

Carol Berkin

From the sixteenth to the mid-nineteenth century, between 10 and 12 million Africans were forcibly taken from their homelands and sold into slavery in the Western Hemisphere. It was the largest and deadliest forced migration in history. Although more than 90 percent of enslaved Africans were taken to South America and the Caribbean, slavery existed in all of Britain's North American colonies. At first there were relatively few slaves in the colonies. In 1649, about 300 slaves of African descent lived in Virginia, only 2 percent of the colony's population. As late as 1675, the total slave population in all of England's North American colonies did not exceed 4,000. During the 1660s, Virginia passed the first laws legalizing hereditary enslavement for people of African descent. Even so, as late as 1688 there were five white indentured servants for every black slave in that colony.

That would change with the development of the plantation system of cash-crop production in the South. During the second half of the seventeenth century, tobacco cultivation in the Chesapeake Bay region of Maryland and Virginia became an enormously profitable enterprise. As a result, the number of Africans imported as slaves to work on tobacco plantations surged. During the decade of the 1680s, a total of 2,000 African slaves were brought to Virginia. In the 1720s, with tobacco cultivation booming, 2,000 slaves were imported *each year*. With the development of rice cultivation in the 1720s, a similar increase in the slave population occurred in South Carolina. Although

Negroes for Sale.

A Cargo of very fine stout Men and Women, in good order and fit for immediate service, just imported from the Windward Coast of Africa, in the Ship Two Brothers.— Conditions are one half Cash or Produce, the other half payable the first of January next, giving Bond and Security if required.

The Sale to be opened at 10 o'Clock each Day, in Mr. Bourdeaux's Yard, at No. 48, on the Bay. May 19, 1784.   JOHN MITCHELL.

Thirty Seasoned Negroes

To be Sold for Credit, at Private Sale.

AMONGST which is a Carpenter, none of whom are known to be dishonest.

Also, to be sold for Cash, a regular bred young Negroe Man-Cook, born in this Country, who served several Years under an exceeding good French Cook abroad, and his Wife a middle aged Washer-Woman, (both very honest) and their two Children. Likewise. a young Man a Carpenter.

For Terms apply to the Printer.

This late-eighteenth-century advertisement offered for sale men and women who came from the Windward Coast of Africa. What was the connection between the captives' geographical origins in Africa and the nature of South Carolina agriculture at that time?

slavery existed in every colony, the institution sunk its deepest roots in the South because of the fabulous profits from large-scale production of rice, tobacco, indigo, and, later on, cotton.

Like Mary and Anthony Johnson, the married couple described by Carol Berkin in the next essay, the first Africans brought to Virginia in 1619 were indentured servants rather than slaves. Some may have served for life, others for a specific number of years, but until the 1660s they and their children were not doomed to hereditary slavery.

This does not mean Africans were perceived as equal to the white indentured servants who made up the vast majority of the Chesapeake's population. The English had a long-standing aversion to blackness, which they associated with death, disease, anarchy, immorality, and a host of other conditions they found fearful or repulsive. Their interactions with blacks through the slave trade and plantation slavery deepened that aversion. From the moment they arrived in the Chesapeake, and even before they were consigned to lifetime servitude, Africans were treated differently because of the color of their skin.

Racism and slavery were not the only horrors Africans were forced to contend with. For them, America was more than a New World; it was an alien universe as well. Not only were they torn from everything they knew in their African homelands, but the languages and customs of white people were significantly different from anything they had known. That lack of understanding could prove fatal. To make matters worse, many of their fellow enslaved Africans were nearly as alien. Even though most slaves hailed from West Africa, they frequently could not communicate with one another because of language differences. The cultural diversity of West Africa also created barriers between slaves. Some West Africans lived in clans, others did not; some traced their ancestry through male lines, others through the female. The roles of women, men, kin, and children could differ profoundly from one tribe or clan to the next—as could marriage rituals, household structure, and the number of wives a man could have.

These circumstances made it extremely difficult for Africans to create and sustain stable families during the seventeenth century. An unbalanced sex ratio—in the Chesapeake region, African men outnumbered African women by two to one into the early eighteenth century—made family development even more difficult. And the isolation of farms and plantations in the South added to these difficulties.

As the following essay shows, however, over time and with remarkable patience and courage, Africans managed to create viable family structures and vibrant communities in colonial America. In the process, they laid the foundation for an African American culture that continues to exert a worldwide influence.

Source: Carol Berkin, *First Generations: Women in Colonial America* (New York: Hill and Wang, 1996), Chapter 5, pp. 103–128.

Mary came to Virginia aboard the *Margrett and John* in the spring of 1622 soon after the Powhatan Indians launched an attack on the English tidewater settlers. She entered a community still reeling from the violent death of 350 colonists killed in a single morning. That the slaughter took place on

Good Friday carried no special meaning for Mary. She was, after all, neither English nor Christian. She was one of a handful of Africans brought against her will to this struggling Chesapeake colony.

We can say very little about Mary; her age when she arrived in Virginia, her physical appearance, her temperament, her abilities are all unknown. Yet her experiences before arriving in Virginia could not have differed greatly from those of other Africans wrenched from their homeland and carried to America. The accounts we have of the brutality of the slave traders, from both black and white witnesses, of the painful forced march to the Atlantic coast of Africa in which women and men were chained together, of the humiliation of branding, and of the horrors of the "middle passage" allow us to envision her distress even if we lack her personal testimony on such matters. The knowledge we have of her adjustment to America—mastering a foreign tongue, adapting to a new climate, to strange clothing and food, a new physical environment, and a culture whose customs and values were alien—make the loneliness and isolation of her situation certain even if it is undocumented. Her circumstances, then, are more vivid than her personality.

Mary was taken to Richard Bennett's large tobacco plantation on the south side of the James River. Here she witnessed the full consequences of hostile relations between the English and the Indians, for only five of the fifty-seven servants who worked Bennett's Warresquioake plantation had survived the Good Friday assault. Although her English master needed every able-bodied worker he could muster, Bennett may not have set Mary to work in the tobacco fields. His culture identified agriculture with masculinity, and in these earliest decades of Chesapeake society, some masters may have been unwilling to overturn the gendered division of labor they held to be natural. Mary surely demurred from such notions, for in most West African societies women dominated agriculture. These very different traditions produced a surprising harmony in the matter of slave importation. Faced with demands for captives, African villages preferred to surrender up their males and protect their female agriculturalists; faced with a need for fieldworkers, Europeans preferred to purchase men.

What we do know of Mary's life in the colonies is that she had good fortune. Despite the scarcity of Africans of either sex in the Chesapeake, one of Warresquioake's five lucky survivors of the Good Friday attack was a black man named Antonio. Mary took him as her husband in fact, if not in English law. In a society where early deaths routinely interrupted marriages, Mary and Antonio enjoyed a forty-year relationship. Together they made the transition from bound service to freedom, although how and where is unclear, and together they raised four children, whom they baptized in the Christian faith.

Like most freed servants, Mary and her husband—known in their freedom as Mary and Anthony Johnson—migrated from Bennett's plantation, seeking arable land of their own. The Johnsons settled on the Pungoteague River, in a small farming community that included black and white families. By mid-century, they had accumulated an estate of over 250 acres on which they raised cattle and pigs. In 1653, their good luck was threatened by a fire, which ravaged their plantation and brought the Johnson family close to ruin. Mary's neighbors responded with sympathy, and local authorities helped by granting the Johnsons' petition that Mary and her two daughters be exempt from local taxes for their lifetimes. . . .

Whatever else race meant to Mary or her neighbors, it was not yet the basis, or the product, of a broad official policy of exclusion and hierarchy. Africans were clearly a minority, for no more than 300 black Virginians lived among the 15,000 white ones in the year the court granted the Johnsons' appeal. The identity created by that minority could still draw on experiences shared by the English majority. Black men like Anthony Johnson made their appearances in court just as white ones did; white and black intermarried, and bound servants of both races found their way to freedom as Mary and Anthony had done. White masters left property to black servants, black masters hired white laborers, and black planters participated in the scramble for labor by purchasing the labor of newly imported Africans "for life."

In the 1660s, the Johnsons, like other eastern shore colonists, pulled up stakes and moved to Maryland in search of fresh land. . . . Anthony was a tenant, leasing a 300-acre farm in Somerset County, Maryland, which he named Tonies Vineyard. Anthony and Mary's now grown sons and daughters soon joined them in Maryland, establishing farms nearby. Thus when Anthony died shortly after the move, Mary Johnson was surrounded by her family.

In 1672, when Mary sat down to write her will, a new generation of Johnsons was making its mark in this farming community. But a new generation of English colonists was making their task harder. Bad signs were everywhere: in a new colonial policy that forbade free blacks to employ white indentured servants, and in the Virginia and Maryland laws that lengthened terms for servants without indenture, a category to which almost every new African immigrant belonged. Mary's grandchildren, to whom she lovingly willed her cows and their calves, would grow to adulthood in a strikingly biracial society, for the number of African immigrants was rapidly growing. But few of these Africans would enter the world of free men and women as Mary and Anthony had done. The society that had once found room for "Mary a Negro," to become the matriarch of a comfortable family, could spare no such space for Mary's descendants. If it was accidental, it is apt when Mary's grandson John died in 1706, the Johnson family disappeared from the historical record. . . .

In 1623 Mary Johnson was one of only twenty-three Africans in Virginia. By 1650, she was one of perhaps three hundred. Together, free blacks like the Johnson family and servants "for life" like their fieldworker John Casor made up only 3 percent of the colony's growing population. Most had made the transatlantic voyage from Africa to the West Indies and only later arrived on the North American mainland. In the decade of Mary Johnson's death, the African population in the Chesapeake began to rise sharply, reaching 3,000 in Virginia by 1680 and continuing to grow until, by 1700, the colony had almost 6,000 black settlers. African population growth in Maryland was no less dramatic: in 1658 there were only 100 blacks in four Maryland counties, but by 1710 the number had risen to over 3,500, or almost one-quarter of the local population. Nearly 8,000 of Maryland's 43,000 colonists that year were black. Yet the mass involuntary migration of Africans had only begun. Between 1700 and 1740, 54,000 blacks reached the Chesapeake, the overwhelming majority imported directly to these colonies from Biafra and Angola rather than coming by way of the West Indies. Immigrants from the west, or "windward," coast of Africa poured into South Carolina as well. By the time of the American Revolution, over 100,000 Africans had been brought to the mainland colonies. For the overwhelming majority, their destination was the plantation fields of the upper and lower South.

The relentless demand for cheap agricultural labor spurred this great forced migration. As the English economy improved in the 1680s and 1690s, the steady supply of desperate young men and women willing to enter indentured servitude in the colonies dwindled. The advantage of African servants over these English workers was already evident, for by this time, white servants had effectively exerted their "customary right" as English citizens to control working conditions. Planters were forced to abide by customs that prevented labor after sunset, allotted five hours' rest in the heat of the day during the summer months, and forbade work on Saturday, Sunday, and many religious holidays. On the other hand, local courts would not acknowledge or uphold any claims to such "customary rights" by African servants. And as life expectancy increased for black as well as white colonists of the Chesapeake, the initially larger investment in an African laborer began to make good economic sense. Yet the supply of "black gold"—as Chesapeake planters called these slaves— was limited until the monopoly of England's Royal African Trading Society was broken by slaving entrepreneurs. By the turn of the century, the English African slave trade offered a steady, seemingly endless supply of reasonably priced, highly exploitable labor—and mainland colonists leaped to take advantage of it.

Slavery—as a permanent and inheritable condition—developed unevenly across the colonies and within individual colonies. In the Chesapeake, the laws that sharply distinguished black bound labor from white were accompanied by laws that limited the economic and social opportunity of free blacks. Together, these laws established race as a primary social boundary. The process began before the greatest influx of Africans to the region. The 1672 law forbidding free black planters to purchase the labor of white servants squeezed those planters out of the competitive tobacco market. This disarming of African Americans in the economic sphere was echoed in Chesapeake laws that forbade blacks to carry or possess firearms or other weapons. In 1691, Chesapeake colonial assemblies passed a series of laws regulating basic social interaction and preventing the transition from servitude, or slavery, to freedom. Marriage between a white woman and a free black man was declared a criminal offense, and the illegitimate offspring of inter-racial unions were forced into bound service until they were thirty years old. A master could still choose to manumit a slave, but after 1691 he was required to bear the cost of removing the freed woman or man from the colony. Such laws discourage intimacy across racial lines and etched into social consciousness the notion that African origins were synonymous with the enslaved condition. By 1705, political and legal discrimination further degraded African immigrants and their descendants, excluding them from office holding, making it a criminal offense to strike a white colonist under any circumstances, and denying them the right to testify in courts of law. While Mary Johnson had never enjoyed the rights of citizenship available to her husband, Anthony, eighteenth-century African-American men of the Chesapeake lost their legal and political identity as well. Thus, the history of most African Americans in the Chesapeake region, as in the lower South, is the history of women and men defined by slavery, even in their freedom.

Much of a newly arrived slave woman's energy was devoted to learning the language of her masters, acquiring the skills of an agriculture foreign to her, and adjusting to the climate and environment of the Chesapeake. Weakened by the transatlantic voyage, often sick, disoriented, and coping with the impact of capture and enslavement to an alien culture, many women as well as men died before they could adjust to America. Until well into the eighteenth century, a woman who survived this adjustment faced the possibility of a lifetime as the solitary African on a farm, or as the solitary woman among the planter's African slaves. Even when there were other Africans on the plantation, the sense of isolation might persist, for "saltwater," or newly arrived, slaves had no common language, nor did they share the same religious practices, the same kinship systems and cultural traditions. Creole, or native-born slaves, were no less strange to a "saltwater" survivor.

Under such circumstances, African women found it difficult to re-create the family and kinship relations that played as central a part in African identity as they did in Native American identity. In fact, the skewed sex ratio—roughly two [males] to one [female] into the early eighteenth century—and the wide scattering of the slave population, as much as the heterogeneity of African cultures and languages, often prevented any satisfactory form of stable family. Until the 1740s, those women and men who did become parents rarely belonged to the same master and could not rear their children together. The burden of these problems led many African-born women to delay childbearing until several years after their arrival in America. Most bore only three children, and of these, only two were likely to survive. With twice as many male slaves as female, delayed childbearing, and high mortality among both adults and infants, there was no natural increase among the Chesapeake slaves in the late seventeenth or early eighteenth century.

There was little any Chesapeake slave woman could do to rectify the circumstances of her personal life. While women of any race in colonial society lacked broad control over their person or their actions, the restraints of slavery were especially powerful. A woman deprived of physical mobility and unable to allocate the use of her time could take few effective steps to establish her own social world.

Although Mary Johnson may never have worked the fields at Warresquoiake plantation, the slave women who came to the Chesapeake after 1650 were regularly assigned to field labor. Organized into mixed-sex work gangs of anywhere from two to a rare dozen laborers, slave women and men worked six days a week and often into the night. Daylight work included planting, tending, and harvesting tobacco and corn by hand, without the use of draft animals. In the evening, male and female slaves stripped the harvested tobacco leaves from stems or shucked and shelled corn. The crops were foreign to most African-born slave women, but the collective organization of workers was not. Indeed, slaves resisted any effort to deny them this familiar, cooperative form of labor.

By the middle of the eighteenth century, slave women on the largest Chesapeake plantations would wake to a day of labor that segregated them from men. As the great planters shifted from cultivation by the hoe to the plow, and as they branched out into wheat and rye production, lumbering, milling, and fishing, they reinstituted a gendered division of labor. Male slaves were assigned to the new skilled and semi-skilled tasks. While men plowed and mastered crafts, women remained in the fields, left to hoe by hand what the plows could not reach, to weed and worm the tobacco, and to carry the harvested grain to the barns on their heads or backs. When new tasks were added to women's work repertoire, they proved to be the least desirable: building fences, grubbing swamps in the winter, cleaning seed out of winnowed grain, breaking new ground too rough for the plow, cleaning stables, and spreading manure.

If many males were drawn out of the fields and into the workshops or iron mills, few black women in their prime were assigned to domestic duty in the planter's house or taught housewifery skills. Instead throughout the eighteenth century, young girls not strong enough for field labor and elderly women past their productive years in the hoeing gang were assigned to cleaning, child care, and other domestic tasks in the planter's home. Thus, much of the work done by Chesapeake slave women in 1750 differed little from the work done by slave women a half century earlier.

Slave women's work may have remained constant, but other aspects of their lives did not. By 1750, some of these women had the opportunity to create stable families and to participate in a cohesive slave community. These opportunities were linked to changes in the size of plantations and in the composition of their labor forces. Throughout the eighteenth century, great plantations developed, and the number of slaves on these plantations grew, too, ending the isolation the earliest generations had experienced. Many of these slaves were native-born rather than "saltwater," and their energies were not drained by the efforts of adjustment and acculturation. As English-speakers, they shared a common language, and in Christianity, many shared a common religion as well. Both were factors in helping creole slaves begin to create a distinctive community. The gradual equalization of the sex ratio among creoles also helped, and, so did the lower mortality rate. Finally, the evolution of this slave community and slave culture in the Chesapeake was aided by a growing opportunity for slaves to live away from the intrusive eyes of their white masters. The retreat from contact was mutual: many white colonists sought relief from the alien impact of Africanisms by creating separate slave quarters. In these slave quarters blacks acquired a social as well as a physical space in which to organize everyday domestic activities, establish rituals, and develop shared values and norms. Most important, they were able to establish families through which to sustain and uphold this shared culture.

Newly arrived Africans found it difficult to participate in this developing community. On Robert Carter's plantation in 1733, for example, creole slaves lived in families of wives, husbands, and children, while saltwater slaves were housed in sex-segregated barracks. Although the plantation master established these barracks and viewed them as the most efficient way to deal with new arrivals, the isolation of African-born males was not entirely the master's decision. The truth was that few creole women were willing to establish households or families with an African male, preferring to take their husbands from among the creole population. From their point of view, the steady influx of African males may have been a disruptive force in their community. By mid-century, however, this was growing moot, for importation slowed dramatically and what one historian called a "black life cycle" came to define the social world of many creole slaves.

This black life cycle did not develop evenly or uniformly across the Chesapeake, although it was evident in the pre-Revolutionary decades. And while gender ties rarely diminished racial distances, black and white women of the Chesapeake did have life-cycle experiences in common. The earliest creole generations of both races married younger and bore more children than their immigrant mothers' generation. And like white women, creole black women were frequently impelled by an imbalanced sex ratio to marry men considerably older than themselves. Black women delivered their children in the company of other women, just as English colonists continued to do throughout most of the eighteenth century, and midwives saw the mother through these births. The differences are perhaps more telling than the similarities, however. African nursing customs, retained by many slave women, produced wider intervals between children than English weaning patterns. Slave women bore an average of nine children, giving birth every twenty-seven to twenty-nine months. The power of masters to separate wives and husbands—through hiring-out practices or sales—led to wide gaps in many slave women's childbearing histories. Conception and birth cycles in King William Parish, Virginia, reveal other ways in which race interposed upon gender. Two-thirds of the black births in King William Parish occurred between February and July, while white women bore their children in the fall and early winter months. For black women, this meant that the most disabling months of pregnancy fell in the midst of heavy spring planting chores. Perhaps this accounts for the greater risk of childbirth for slave mothers and the higher infant mortality rate among slave children.

Family organization depended on the size of the plantation. On the larger plantations, children under ten could expect to live with both their father and their mother, often in two-family slave cabins. When the parents came from different small plantations, the children lived with their mother, sometimes in cabins that housed all the slaves, whether related or not. The large plantations offered other advantages besides the opportunities for families to live as a unit. Here, mothers could rely on a growing kin network or on friends to help in the complex tasks of childrearing. When husband and wife lived on separate plantations, the couple's main concern was maintaining contact. Where their master's regulation permitted and where there were roads linking plantations, many husbands and fathers undertook nightly and Sunday journeys to visit their families.

Thus, after 1750, a Chesapeake slave woman might be able to live out her life in the company of her family, as Mary Johnson had done. Yet she knew that powerful obstacles stood in her way. Husbands often lived on other plantations. Children between the ages of ten and fourteen, especially sons, were commonly sold. Sisters and brothers were moved to different slave quarters. And on a master's death, slaves were often dispensed along with other property to his heirs. A master who might never separate a family during his lifetime thought it his obligation to his survivors to divide them at his death. Hard times could prompt a master to sell a slave woman's family members in order to provide for his own. A planter's widow might keep her family intact by hiring out her slave's sons or daughters. Even the wedding celebration of a planter's daughter might mean the tragic separation of a slave woman and her own young daughter, sent to serve in the bride's new home. In the 1770s, the westward expansion of agriculture into the Piedmont and beyond led to mass dispersal of slave families among the new farms and plantations. Slave women, and their men, could succeed in creating effective family structures despite the many demands of slavery, but they could not ensure their permanence. . . .

Perhaps it is most useful to say that while legal codes created a uniform definition of enslavement in the Chesapeake, there was no uniform set of conditions under which slaves lived. Nor could there be as long as uniform living conditions for their masters and mistresses failed to exist. The circumstances and the choices made by great planters and struggling ones, by tobacco growers and wheat farmers, by residents of the Piedmont and those of the tidewater, by cruel men and kind ones set the parameters of life for the enslaved. However, if the black life cycle and the slave culture that emerged on larger plantations do not account for all eighteenth-century slave women and men, or even for the majority, they are still significant. Their reconstruction reveals basic social choices that slaves made when conditions permitted. The culture that emerged shaped the expectations and channeled the energies of slaves throughout the Chesapeake.

The slave quarters were the heart of the slave community; the houses and yards surrounding them were the focal points of daily life. Inside each cabin were straw beds, seats made of barrels, pots, pans, and a grindstone for beating corn into meal. The older women looked after the children, the men hunted to provide extra food, and the women defined themselves, in part, by taking up domestic chores and housewifery. The culture that developed within these communities suggests a flexible adaptation of both African and European customs and beliefs. In this Chesapeake slave community dominated by creoles, African traditions were more muted than they would be in the Lower South [where Africans continued to be imported in large numbers]. But on Virginia and Maryland plantations, slaves preserved African folk traditions of magic and magic charms, much, of course, as English colonists preserved their own magic traditions. In music and the instruments used to make it, and in the rhythms and patterns of dance, the slave community drew distinct lines that separated them from the dominant white culture and linked them to their African roots. Christianity, however, became the dominant religion within the quarter, and sometimes this produced tensions between African values and European ones. In the Piedmont, in particular, where many slaves embraced the teachings of the Baptists, evangelical codes of morality condemning adultery and fornication conflicted with an African-based tolerance for premarital intercourse and older sexual mores arising from traditions such as polygyny.

Many slave quarters were bordered by plots of corn and tobacco and by gardens, all cultivated in the residents' limited free time. Using Sundays and the rare holidays they were granted (including, after 1776, Independence Day), Chesapeake slaves made this small-scale agriculture an integral part of community life. In the Piedmont area, historians have traced the rise of an internal economy, built upon the raising and trading of surplus food and livestock from the quarters, upon hunting and foraging, and upon materials stolen, or liberated, from the master's stock of supplies. Slaves on a plantation traded with each other, but they also traded with peddlers traveling through the Chesapeake region, with neighboring plantation workers, and with white masters or mistresses who found it easier to purchase pies or chickens from their slaves than to compete with them in these areas. Slave women played active parts in expanding and sustaining this internal economy, raising and selling poultry and eggs, baked goods, garden products, and handmade baskets. Thus, although few slave women in the pre-Revolutionary Chesapeake were employed in housewifery by their mistresses, they developed a repertoire of household production skills within their own community economy. The records of one general store in Orange County, Virginia, show that by the 1780s, slave women were able to purchase kerchiefs and scarves, calico cloth, ribbons, thread, and even tableware with money made from production and trade.

Whatever initial reaction Piedmont masters may have had to the rise of this internal economy, they soon realized its benefits. The crops produced in the quarter allowed a master to reduce rations for his labor force, and in many cases the yield from slave gardens and fields helped reduce the pilferage of storerooms and the theft of livestock. Masters could demand that older slaves, no longer valuable in the fields, provide for themselves by gardening, farming, or keeping chickens. These masters saw the internal economy as a means to shift the burden of subsistence onto the slaves. For slave women and men, however, it was a means to carve out more autonomous space in their constricted world. This secondary, or internal, economy, in which women played active roles, had the potential to strengthen the slave community, as much because slaves established its protocols and regulated its operation as because of the material benefits it provided. Working collectively and cooperatively, slaves were able to carve out other autonomous realms. Slave midwives and slave doctors shaped the medical care of the quarter, and slave communities established their own burial societies and burial rituals. Slave women and their husbands also took the initiative in naming their children, using naming patterns to reinforce the kinship structures their community had developed. Mothers named their sons and daughters for their own brothers and sisters, and for their husband's siblings. By naming sons for their fathers, slave mothers attempted to reinforce the most often violated and thus most fragile link in the slave family chain: the paternal line.

Physical and psychological distance from the master and from his white culture surely aided the development of a slave culture. Indeed, historians have found that urban slaves and household slaves who lacked this cultural space were more acculturated [to white culture] than the slaves of the quarters. Yet if proximity to slave masters had its costs, distance could extract a price of its own. In the Piedmont, for example, absentee owners often relied on overseers who proved to be both crueler and more intrusive into the personal lives of the slaves than masters. These overseers allowed the men and women of the quarters fewer opportunities to develop distinctive communal patterns in leisure time, in sexual practices, or in family organization. When Piedmont slaves murdered a white man, their most common victim was not a master but an overseer.

When and where it was well established, the slave community influenced the decisions of the more powerful white community around it. For example, in 1693 a Petersburg, Virginia, slave sentenced to die for robbery won support from white residents of the town. These colonists opposed the slave's execution on practical rather than moral grounds: his death would have too unsettling an effect on his large family and thus too unsettling an effect on their lives as well. And in 1774 the master of a twenty-five-year-old mulatto [runaway] woman named Sall took into account the reality of a dense social network based on kinship when he tried to track her down. She came, he noted in his newspaper advertisement for her return, "of a numerous Family of Mulattoes, formerly belonging to a Gentleman of the Name of Howard in York County . . . and where probably she may attempt to go again, or perhaps into Cumberland, or Amelia, where . . . many of her kindred live."

Questions for Discussion

1. The first Africans taken to the Chesapeake region, like Mary and Anthony Johnson, were not subjected to hereditary slavery. Describe the experiences of the Johnsons after their terms of indentured servitude ended.
2. Over time, the freedom of African Americans like the Johnson family was limited by law. Describe those laws. How were these legal restrictions connected to the expansion of slavery in the Chesapeake?
3. From the point of view of planters, what advantages did African slave labor have over the labor of white indentured servants?
4. What was the daily work routine on plantations? How did it differ for female and male slaves?
5. Describe the evolution of the African American family. In what specific ways did it differ from the family life of free persons? What were the relationships between "creole" and "saltwater" Africans?
6. According to the author, by the early eighteenth century, the slave quarter became a seedbed for the development of an autonomous African American culture. How?

For Further Reading

Ira Berlin, *Many Thousands Gone: The First Two Centuries of Slavery in North America* (1998); Ira Berlin and Ronald Hoffman, *Slavery and Freedom in the Age of the American Revolution* (1983); Ira Berlin and Philip D. Morgan, eds., *The Slaves' Economy: Independent Production by Slaves in the Americas* (1991); John Blassingame, *The Slave Community: Plantation Life in the Antebellum South* (1972); T. H. Breen and Stephen Innes, *"Myne Own Ground": Race and Freedom on Virginia's Eastern Shore, 1640–1720* (1980); Sylvaire Diouf, *Servants of Allah: African Muslims Enslaved in America* (1998); Wilma Dunaway, *The African American Family in Slavery and Emancipation* (2003); Stanley Elkins, *Slavery*, 3rd ed. (1976); Eugene Genovese, *Roll, Jordan, Roll: The World the Slaves Made* (1976); Herbert Gutman, *The Black Family in Slavery and Freedom, 1750–1925* (1976); Gwendolyn Midlo Hall, *Africans in Colonial Louisiana: The Development of Afro-Creole Culture in the Eighteenth Century* (1992); Walter Johnson, ed., *The Chattel Principle: International Slave Traders in the Americas* (2004); Winthrop Jordan, *White Over Black: American Attitudes Toward the Negro, 1550–1812* (1968); Peter Kolchin, *American Slavery, 1619–1877* (1993); Allan Kulikoff, *Tobacco and Slaves: The Development of Southern Cultures in the Chesapeake, 1680–1800* (1986); Beverly C. McMillan, ed., *The Transatlantic Slave Trade and the Making of the Americas* (2002); Edmund Morgan, *American Slavery American Freedom: The Ordeal of Colonial Virginia* (1975); Phillip D. Morgan, *Slave Counterpoint* (1998); Gerald Mullin, *Flight and Rebellion: Slave Resistance in Eighteenth Century Virginia* (1974); Colin A. Palmer, *The First Passage: Blacks in the Americas, 1502–1617* (1995); Brenda Stevenson, *Life in Black and White: Family and Community in the Slave South* (1996); Hugh Thomas, *The Slave Trade: The Story of the Atlantic Slave Trade, 1440–1870* (1997); Lorena Walsh, *From Calabar to Carter's Grove: A History of a Virginia Slave Community* (1997); Deborah Gray White, *Ar'n't I A Woman? Female Slaves in the Plantation South* (1999); Peter Wood, *Strange New Land: African Americans, 1617–1776* (1995).

Patriot Father, Loyalist Son

Benjamin and William Franklin

Sheila L. Skemp

The American Revolution was a civil war as well as a struggle for independence from Great Britain. John Adams, the staunch Massachusetts patriot and second president of the United States, famously estimated that one-third of Americans were "loyalists" (that is, remained loyal to England), one-third were "rebels" (or patriots), and another third were neutral. Historians continue to debate the issue. But it is clear that during the War for Independence, a sizable portion of the white population either opposed independence or declared a "plague on both your houses" by choosing neither side during the conflict.

For example, regional affiliation mattered: perhaps 90 percent of New England adhered to the patriot cause; it is possible, however, that a majority of Americans who lived in the recently settled, more thinly populated western regions of the colonies were either loyalist or neutral. Religion could be an issue. In Pennsylvania and Delaware, most Presbyterians supported rebellion against England, but the majority of Quakers in those colonies—whose religious values prohibited participation in war—were "passive loyalists," in the words of one historian. Loyalists could come from any social or economic group. For instance, when Massachusetts banished 300 loyalists in 1778, only one-third of them could be described as well-off, well-educated "gentlemen." Two-thirds of the banished Massachusetts loyalists were middling farmers, unskilled laborers, artisans, and owners of small shops. Rebels and loyalists, then, could hail from almost every region, social status, or ethnic group.

The TORY'S Day of JUDGMENT.

Loyalists being tarred and feathered by New England patriots. Despite persecution, significant numbers of Americans opposed independence from Great Britain. Why?

The attitudes of nonwhite Americans toward independence were important as well. At the start of the conflict, most Native American tribes declared their intention to remain neutral. In the end, however, many Indians realized that land-hungry Americans were a greater threat to their future well-being than the continued dominion of Great Britain. The vast majority of Indians who fought during the war, therefore, sided with the British. This was true of African Americans as well, who hoped that a British victory would spell the end of slavery. But many more enslaved black Americans took advantage of the chaos created by the war to flee their owners than fought for either side. Thomas Jefferson estimated that in one year alone—1778—more than 30,000 Virginia slaves ran to freedom.

The War for Independence sometimes divided families as well. The most famous example was Benjamin Franklin and his son William, described by Sheila L. Skemp in the next essay. Benjamin Franklin was the most renowned and perhaps most revered American of his time—his "rags to riches" American journey continues to fascinate numerous biographers and millions of Americans. Franklin's son William was illegitimate—born of an illicit affair between Benjamin Franklin and an unknown woman. The elder Franklin was not particularly attentive to family matters. His affair with William's unknown mother may have occurred the same year he married his wife, Deborah, in 1730. But it appears that he and William were very close. Young William helped Benjamin conduct his famous experiments on electricity. His father sponsored William Franklin's training as a lawyer, and in 1763 the elder Franklin's political connections helped secure William's appointment as Royal Governor of New Jersey.

Benjamin Franklin had a deep affection for the British Empire and, like many colonists, was slow to embrace the idea of American independence. Once committed to rebellion, however, Franklin pursued it passionately and played a crucial role in its ultimate success. But William Franklin, like most other Royal appointees in the colonies, never veered from his loyalty to the Crown. The result was a gradual and ultimately bitter split between father and son.

There is an additional aspect of the Revolution that relates to private issues such as fathers, sons, and family that has an interesting twist in the case of the Franklins. A number of historians, including Skemp, have suggested that the American Revolution was not only a political rebellion against a king who was viewed by rebels as a tyrant. It was also a symbolic revolt against the king as a father figure by rebellious sons intent upon living their own lives in their own way. In other words, the Revolution was a revolt against patriarchy. It was a declaration of independence by American sons who longed for a degree of personal autonomy that was incompatible with traditional notions of obedience and deference toward paternal authority. And it didn't matter whether that authority sat on a throne in a palace or in a rocking chair at home.

How does this play out in the case of Benjamin and William Franklin? William certainly rebelled against his biological father, but not against the king-as-father-figure, to whom he remained deeply loyal. Could William's status as an illegitimate child who did not know his mother help account for his decision to remain loyal to England? Perhaps his loyalty to England—known as the "*Mother* Country" to the colonists—mattered as much or more to William as his connection to his biological father. For William, loyalty to king and mother country may have enabled him to retain a father figure, while giving him the "mother" he never knew.

Whatever the metaphorical meaning of the Revolution in terms of fathers and sons, the rebellion itself was a very complex matter. It cannot be explained simply by looking at the disagreement between a father and his son in one elite American family such as the Franklins. But what Skemp does show is that major issues of the Revolutionary era, such as the Stamp Act crisis and the Boston Tea Party, were more than important political events. They also affected people in the most intimate areas of their lives. Her essay demonstrates how public issues affect private lives.

Source: From *Benjamin and William Franklin* by Sheila L. Skemp. © 1994 by Bedford/St. Martin's. Reproduced by permission of Bedford/St. Martin's.

The Boston Tea Party set the stage for a series of events that ultimately separated America from England. Those same events led Benjamin and William Franklin to choose opposite sides in a war that both men would have preferred to avoid. By the middle of 1774 the two men simply quit discussing political issues, and by the end of 1775 they no longer communicated at all.

After Parliament passed the legislation that became known as the Coercive Acts in 1774, both Franklins attempted to find some way to resolve the issues that were tearing the empire apart. This time they operated from very different perspectives. Benjamin urged the colonists to cut off all commercial intercourse with England, arguing that if the mother country had backed down before in the face of colonial unity, it would surely do so again. William was convinced that England would not retreat. He insisted that the colonists had to exhibit a willingness to compromise if they seriously wanted a rapprochement. Ironically, he relied on his own father to work out the detail of such a compromise.

While the two men surely realized that their political views were diverging in the early 1770s, they continued to try to nurture the personal side of their relationship. Benjamin purchased English goods for the governor and his wife, taking care that every tea urn, every mahogany chair that he sent to America met his son's exacting standards. Whenever he could, he called William's achievements to the attention of the ministry. . . . For his part, William continued to support his father, even as he grew uneasy about his politics. He worried about Benjamin's health, urging him to come home before old age caught up with him. He refused to criticize his father, no matter how great the temptation might have been. When William Strahan wrote to warn him that Benjamin was out of touch "with the [British] Ministry in general," telling him that some people assumed he held "the same political opinions with [his] father," William's reply was circumspect, although he did put some distance between himself and the elder Franklin. There was, he insisted, "no reason (other than the natural connexion between us) to imagine that I entertain the same political opinions with my father. My sentiments are really in many respects different from those which have been published on either side of the question." He knew that he often suffered from his "natural connexion" with Benjamin, but he refused to repudiate a man whose affection he cherished.

Yet despite their best intentions, an aura of animosity increasingly pervaded the letters between father and son in the years before the Revolution.

That this should have been the case is hardly surprising. Both men were deeply embroiled in the controversies of the day, and while they both tried to avoid an argument, neither could resist the temptation to lash out from time to time.

As Benjamin grew disenchanted with the ministry, he tried to convey his mood to his son. Generally, he engaged in reasoned discourse, but on occasion he abandoned his pose of disinterested equanimity altogether. . . . Apparently forgetting that he had once helped launch William's career as a Crown servant and that he had also sought royal preferment for himself, he now insisted that he "rather wish[ed] to see all I am connected with in an Independent Station, supported by their own Industry." Whenever Benjamin discussed [grandson] Temple's prospects with William, he implied that he hoped the boy would not follow in his father's footsteps. Independence, not royal patronage, should be the key to Temple's success. Above all, he thundered, "I would have him a Free Man."

Such comments must have made William wince, for their message was unmistakable. Still, he generally refrained from striking back or even acknowledging his father's pointed barbs. And he remained stubbornly convinced that Benjamin had both the will and the ability to find the magic solution that would reconcile the differences between England and America. He thought his father was the one colonial agent whose opinion Whitehall [the seat of the British government] respected. . . .

William's faith in his father was not as naïve as it appears in hindsight. He knew Benjamin had always harbored a deep and abiding love for the empire. True, the elder Franklin's criticisms of Parliament and the ministry had grown harsh over the years. But William had endured enough of his own quarrels with Whitehall to know that the ministry was capable of making serious errors. Moreover, he had sworn obedience to the king, not to Parliament. So long as his father remained loyal to the Crown, William did not foresee the possibility that he and Benjamin would go their separate ways.

Unfortunately for William, Benjamin Franklin's views of the king's role in imperial affairs was beginning to change. In this instance, he was ahead of most of his American compatriots. The colonists had always insisted that their quarrel was with a Parliament that had been corrupted by a venal ministry. At least in public, they refused to blame the king for their differences with the mother country. By the summer of 1773, however, Benjamin Franklin was finding it increasingly difficult to maintain a belief in the king's innocence. He was also beginning to argue that the colonists owed no absolute obedience to the monarch. When the first settlers came to America, he said, they voluntarily agreed to obey the English sovereign. It went without saying that their descendents had the right to reverse that voluntary decision to obey the king should circumstances warrant it. Even worse from William's perspective, Franklin blamed the king himself for the colonists' continued differences with England. "Between you and I," he confided to his son, speaking especially of the Tea Act, "the late Measures have been, I suspect, very much the King's own."

It is easy to imagine William Franklin groaning aloud when he read these comments, but it would be a mistake to assume that he comprehended their full import. Indeed, for a long time Benjamin himself was not prepared to follow his own arguments to their logical conclusion. Moreover, so long as the vast majority of Americans retained their loyalty to the king, and so long as the elder Franklin kept his darkest thoughts to himself, William did not think he needed to worry unduly about their consequences.

In 1774, however, after his ordeal before the [English Ministry's] Privy Council [where he was wrongly accused of inciting the Boston Tea Party and other acts of rebellion in that city], Benjamin's mood changed dramatically. . . . He was angered even more when the government stripped him of his post office position. To most people, even to his sister Jane, he hid his anger behind a mask of bland indifference. But when he wrote to William, just two days after he had been fired, Benjamin revealed his pain. It was a terse message, for he was too distraught to discuss his experience in any detail. Nevertheless, his expectation was clear. He assumed that William would resign his position as governor to protest his father's treatment. William now had no chance of being promoted, he pointed out, and his present position was poorly funded and likely to remain so. "I wish," he said, "you were settled on your Farm. 'Tis an honester and a more honourable because a more independent Employment."

While William sympathized with his father, he had no intention of leaving a position that was his sole source of income, identity, and purpose. Moreover, he was not a man who abandoned his obligations lightly. . . . Benjamin's letter came as a shock. It revealed how far his father had moved from England's corridors of power. Not only had the elder Franklin's usefulness to the governor come to an end, but he could now prove to be a detriment. Still, William had no more desire to turn his back on his father than he did to abandon the king. Thus, he simply did nothing. . . .

When news of the Boston Tea Party reached London, the government reacted harshly, displaying its determination to flex its muscles and reassert its authority in Massachusetts. At the end of March 1774, Parliament passed the Boston Port Act, closing Boston Harbor to all shipping until the East India Company had been reimbursed for its losses. News of the Port Act reached America in May, and the Massachusetts committee of correspondence responded immediately, asking the other colonies to suspend all trade with England. Merchants in New York and Philadelphia, however, did not view the proposed boycott with enthusiasm. They favored an inter-colonial meeting where delegates from all the colonies could discuss their differences with England. While Boston's political leaders were unhappy with what they saw as a delaying tactic, they reluctantly agreed to support the proposal for a continental congress. William tried to use the prospect of the congress to lure his father home [from England]. Everyone, he said, valued Franklin's experience and wanted him to attend. Unfortunately, in the same letter, William discussed his views of the Boston Tea Party, suggesting that the Bay Colony would be wise to pay the East India Company for the damages it had sustained. Not only would such compensation accord with the principles of "strict Justice," but it would be smart politics as well. It made sense for Massachusetts inhabitants to "do Justice before they ask it of others. Their making reparations to those whom they have injured would besides give greater Weight to their Representatives and do Credit to their Cause."

In September, when Benjamin replied to William's letters, he exploded. In a less contentious time, he had called his son a "thorough government man." But then, he had promised to make no attempt to "convert" him. He was no longer able to maintain a philosophical attitude toward his son's politics. He was deeply hurt by William's apparent indifference to his own public humiliation and pained by the implication that he had outlived his usefulness in London. The fact that the governor seemed more disturbed by Boston's rioters than he was by England's attack on colonial rights also disturbed the elder Franklin.

Thus, he lashed out. "I do not," he wrote with obvious sarcasm, "so much as you do, wonder that the Massachusetts have not offered Payment for the Tea." Although he himself had once proposed that Boston reimburse the East India Company for its losses, he now claimed that America owed England nothing. Rather, Parliament owed the colonies money for the "many Thousand Pounds" it had "extorted" from America over the years. But "you," he said in a tone that revealed the width of the chasm separating him from his son, "who are a thorough Courtier, see every thing with Government Eyes."

Clearly, Franklin had no immediate plans to return to America. To the contrary, despite his occasional fulminations and bitter outbursts, he still entertained some hope that he might be of use in persuading Parliament to soften its stance toward the colonists. Until Parliament passed the Boston Port Act, Franklin had remained surprisingly optimistic about the prospects for reconciliation. . . . But when the government began to take measures to punish the Bay Colony, Franklin's position hardened. The Port Act had been bad enough. Even worse were the three reform bills that Parliament passed in late May and early June. Known collectively, with the Port Act, as the Coercive Acts, the legislation envisioned a total restructuring of Massachusetts government. Parliament directed local authorities to find convenient quarters for royal troops and allowed the governor the right to transfer trials to England or to another colony if he thought local juries would be prejudiced against the government's case. It also gave the governor the right to appoint his council and to appoint or remove sheriffs and judges at his own discretion. Finally, it allowed the governor to forbid all town meetings except the annual one to elect officers. . . . In effect, Massachusetts existed under martial law. . . .

Franklin's on again, off again, contacts with various government emissaries lasted through the first part of March 1775. But at least by the middle of February, it was clear that Whitehall would not consider any limitations on Parliament's right to legislate for or to tax the colonies, nor would the ministry abdicate its power to alter colonial governments at will. That being the case, there really was nothing more to say. Franklin lost his normally cheery perspective. He was having a hard time sleeping. And he began to worry that nothing, not even the colonial boycott, would force the ministry to back down. . . .

Benjamin Franklin did not realize the extent of his son's commitment to the king. . . . The governor did more to help the ministry than offer his suggestions for solving the imperial crisis. As early as June 1774, he began systematically to compile and forward all news about events in New Jersey to Whitehall. By September, as the Continental Congress got under way, he started to amass information about colonial disorders everywhere. He sent [Lord] Dartmouth [President of the Ministry's Board of Trade] letters bulging with newspaper clippings describing the activities of the various committees of correspondence. He documented colonial attempts to organize extralegal provincial assemblies. He also enclosed Joseph Galloway's descriptions of the activities of the Continental Congress, whose meetings were held in secret. Franklin was, for all intents and purposes, acting as a self-appointed spy for the English government. He was fully aware of the implications of his activities. Much of the news came from sources who trusted his discretion, men who had no idea that their conversations ended up in Dartmouth's hands. It was just as well they didn't know, Franklin explained candidly, "lest they might be deterred from giving me Information." There were still many colonists who did not know how committed to serving the king he was, and William obviously needed to keep it that way. . . . He remembered all too well how [Massachusetts Royal Governor] Thomas Hutchinson had suffered when the contents of his private letters had been revealed to the public. The stakes were higher now, and he had no wish to incur the hostility that would surely accompany a public airing of his own letters. Thus he marked nearly every letter he sent to London "secret and confidential."

With each letter he sent, Franklin reiterated what would become a constant theme of all loyalists until the end of the Revolutionary war. The Continental Congress, he maintained, did not speak for most colonists. To the contrary, nearly everyone privately decried the actions of those radicals who had somehow seized the reins of power and were running roughshod over the moderate majority. "Few," he insisted, "have the Courage to declare their Disapprobation publickly, as they well know, if they do not conform, they are in Danger of becoming Objects of popular Resentment." Franklin, like loyalist leaders throughout the continent, did not recognize the depth or breadth of American anger. Moreover, he found it impossible to imagine that honest men might disagree with him. Thus, by definition, he believed that opposition leaders had their own agenda, an agenda that did not serve the interests of the people they so insidiously claimed to represent.

Had Benjamin Franklin known what his son was doing, he would have been devastated. At the beginning of 1775, Benjamin had written to Joseph Galloway. Rumor had it, he warned, that both Galloway and John Jay, a delegate to the Continental Congress from New York, were acting as spies for England. "I do not believe this," he said, "but I thought it a Duty of Friendship to acquaint you with the Report." He would have been incredulous had he known that his own son was involved with what, from his perspective, was a dishonorable business.

He would have been equally angry by the contents of William's letters. For years he had railed against Americans who claimed that colonial opposition to English policy was the province of a "small Fraction." Indeed, he had often written to William arguing that the colonists' "Discontents were really general and their Sentiments concerning their Rights unanimous, and not the Fiction of a few Demagogues, as their Governors us'd to represent them here." He professed to believe that these false depictions of colonial sentiment were largely responsible for the ministry's refusal to heed American demands. So long as English leaders believed that America was divided, that support for Boston was confined to a few well-organized and noisy hotheads, they would stand firm. . . .

When Benjamin Franklin sailed for home in the spring of 1775, he was nearly seventy years old. Angry and bitter, he had probably already accepted the reality that few other Americans were willing to face. Independence was inevitable. Only the timing was at issue. In America he began a round of activities that would have exhausted anyone half his age. He knew, he explained, that he was an old man whose most productive years were behind him. What fortune he possessed would have to support him for the rest of his life. He no longer expected to make any contribution to the world of science that would compare with the day he and William had brought the lightning from the skies. He intended to devote what time he had left to preserving his country's liberties. He only hoped that he could persuade his son to join him in his last adventure.

William was waging his own war for the hearts and minds of New Jersey's legislators when his father arrived in America. He was trying to hold his colony together and to fend off—or at least ignore—all the extralegal committees and congresses that were taking over the country and turning his own world upside down. He was also fighting for his very life, as he began to fear that he would be captured by his enemies and led "like a Bear through the Country." As he saw other governors abandon their posts, fleeing to the safety provided by the king's troops, he occasionally considered following their example. But like his father, William Franklin was a stubborn man. Benjamin had often declared that he would never voluntarily relinquish any position. "I shall never ask, never refuse, nor ever resign an Office," he said. For, as he had once observed to his son, "One may make something of an Injury, nothing of a Resignation." Thus both Franklins stuck to their respective positions, refusing even to sit out the growing controversy on the sidelines. Neither man would shrink from his duty as he saw it. King and country, father and son, were about to go their separate ways. . . .

Benjamin and William Franklin did not meet again until after the Revolution. [In June 1776, William was removed as governor of New Jersey] and remained a prisoner at Connecticut for more than two years, first at Wallingford and then at Middletown. At first, his accommodations were tolerable, and as a gentleman he was allowed to roam the countryside at will. Unfortunately, he used his freedom to render covert aid to the British army, granting pardons to the farmers he met on those not so innocent rides on the outskirts of town. Consequently, at the beginning of May 1777, the defiant prisoner was removed from his lodgings in Middletown and marched forty miles to Litchfield, where he remained in solitary confinement for nearly eight months. There, in his cramped and dirty lodgings, his captors watched him constantly, denying him the use of pen or paper and allowing him almost no contact with the outside world. By this time, most colonial leaders saw Franklin as a threat to their cause.

Benjamin did not lift a hand to secure his son's freedom or even to make his imprisonment more comfortable. Rather, he viewed William's predicament with singular detachment and only reluctantly offered his daughter-in-law [Elizabeth] any financial support. Indeed when he sent Elizabeth sixty dollars to help meet her barest expenses, he brusquely reminded her that many others suffered more than she did. By now, he had only two passions. He wanted to win the independence that America had declared in July 1776. And he was determined to keep [his grandson] Temple from embracing the loyalist doctrines that permeated the air the boy breathed whenever he visited [Elizabeth]. . . . Benjamin Franklin devoted the war years to the service of his country. His universal reputation as a scientist and political philosopher preceded him to Paris, and he was treated with respect, even awe, by some of France's most renowned luminaries. So long as he remained in France [as American ambassador], Franklin played the role of modest republican for all it was worth. Still, he lived a life of opulence that would have surprised, even disappointed, many of the leaders whose clause he so ably represented. In fact, Franklin was perfectly suited to his new role. A seasoned politician who was adept at the gamesmanship that characterized diplomatic activity in the eighteenth century, he enjoyed the intrigue in which he was involved, even while he was a shrewd, indeed tough, bargainer.

For William Franklin, the American Revolution was neither so pleasant nor so rewarding. He was finally released from Litchfield jail in October 1778, at the age of forty-eight. He emerged a bitter man. His wife had died while he was in captivity. . . . Franklin left Connecticut for the protection of British-controlled New York at the end of October 1778. His property had been confiscated, his salary discontinued, his health nearly broken. He had already paid a heavier price for his loyalty than any other colonial governor. Still, he did not yet join the some eighty thousand loyalists who fled the country.

Instead, Franklin became an unofficial spokesman for all loyal Americans, speaking out against [British] General Henry Clinton's lethargic war effort, seeking help for needy refugees, and interceding on behalf of loyalist prisoners of war. In 1780, he became president of the Board of Associated Loyalists, an American paramilitary outfit that organized and equipped loyalist units and planned guerrilla raids on rebel strongholds. . . . After the defeat of General Cornwallis at Yorktown in 1781, the war, for all practical purposes was over. Lord North resigned from the ministry to be replaced by the Earl of Rockingham. Parliament began to press for negotiations that would bring an end to the hostilities between England and its former colonies. William Franklin's Associated Loyalists tried to keep those hostilities alive, ordering the capture and execution of rebel officer Joshua Huddy in a vain effort to disrupt peace negotiations between the British and American forces. Benjamin, from his post in France, worked with John Jay and John Adams to negotiate to end the war. . . . Perhaps not surprisingly, it was Benjamin Franklin who fought hardest against the British request that the new American government compensate the former loyalists for the losses they sustained as a result of the war.

While Benjamin celebrated his and America's victory, his son left his native land in the fall of 1782 for the life of an exile in England, the cloud cast by the execution of Joshua Huddy still hanging over his head. Once in England, he tried to influence the peace negotiations, lobbying especially hard for provisions that would benefit American loyalists. In this, as in so many other efforts in these years, he was basically unsuccessful. Only after the Peace of Paris had been signed did William make an effort to patch up the differences between him and his father. The war was over. He had lost. Now it was time to let bygones be bygones, to "revive that affectionate Intercourse and Connection which till the Commencement of the late Troubles had been the Pride and Happiness of [his] life." He refused to apologize for his part in the war. "I uniformly acted from a Strong Sense of what I conceived my Duty to my King and Regard to my Country," he said. . . . Still, he begged his father for a "personal interview," hoping that now that he had "broken the ice," he and Benjamin might be friends once more.

Benjamin was unmoved. "Nothing," he said, "has hurt me so much and affected me with such keen Sensations as to find myself deserted in my old Age by my only Son; and not only deserted, but to find him taking up Arms against me, in a Cause wherein my good Fame, Fortune and Life were all at Stake." Had William taken a neutral position, he might have forgiven his son. He could not tolerate an active loyalist.

The two men saw one another only once after the war. In 1785, as Benjamin was preparing to leave for home . . . they met briefly at Southampton [in England]. The hurried visit was not cordial. Benjamin persuaded William to sell Temple his New Jersey lands for a paltry two thousand pounds sterling. He also insisted that he turn over some property he owned in New York in lieu of a debt of fifteen hundred pounds he still owed his father. His business with

William at an end, Benjamin returned to America. This would be the last time he would cross the Atlantic.

Questions for Discussion

1. Which policies of the British government, and responses to them by American colonists, were most important in driving Benjamin and William Franklin—and ultimately all rebels and loyalists—apart?
2. Why did the Franklins and other Americans distinguish between their attitudes toward policies of Parliament and their loyalty to the king? What was the significance of this distinction?
3. Describe the reasons William Franklin and other Americans at the time would have become loyalists. Describe why Benjamin Franklin and other Americans at the time would have become rebels. Which Franklin do you find most convincing? Why?

For Further Reading

Bernard Bailyn, *The Ordeal of Thomas Hutchinson* (1974); Carol Berkin, *Jonathan Sewell: The Odyssey of an American Loyalist* (1974); H. W. Brands, *The First American: The Life and Times of Benjamin Franklin* (2000); Jay Fliegelman, *Prodigals and Pilgrims: The American Revolution against Patriarchal Authority, 1750–1800* (1982); Barbara Graymont, *The Iroquois in the American Revolution* (1972); Walter Isaacson, *Benjamin Franklin: An American Life* (2003); Winthrop Jordan, "Familial Politics: Thomas Paine and the Killing of the King, 1776," *Journal of American History* 60 (1973–1974); J. A. Leo Lemay and P. M. Zall, eds., *The Autobiography of Benjamin Franklin* (1981); Jerrilyn Marston, *Kings and Congress: The Transfer of Political Legitimacy, 1774–76* (1987); Edmund Morgan, *Benjamin Franklin* (2002); Janice Potter, *The Liberty We Seek: Loyalist Ideology in Colonial New York and Massachusetts* (1983); Simon Schama, *Rough Crossings: Britain, the Slaves and the American Revolution* (2006); Stacy Schiff, *A Great Improvisation: Franklin, France, and the Birth of America* (2005); Randall Sterne, *A Little Revenge: Benjamin Franklin and His Son* (1984); Gordon Wood, *The Americanization of Benjamin Franklin* (2004); Melvin Yazawa, *From Colonies to Commonwealth: Familial Ideology and the Beginnings of the American Republic* (1985).

Southern Women and the American Revolution

Mary Beth Norton

Both the crisis leading up to the Revolution and the War for Independence itself altered the lives of American women. In the eighteenth century, politics, war, and diplomacy were exclusively male pursuits. But in the crisis-packed decade leading up to the open break between Great Britain and the colonies, many American women suddenly found themselves drawn into the male world of political conflict.

For example, the American boycott of goods taxed by the Townshend Act passed by Parliament in 1767 could not have succeeded without the active support of women colonists. In Boston, hundreds of housewives, the main purchasers of most day-to-day consumer products, publicly announced their decision to boycott tea, a widely used commodity taxed under the Townshend Act. In 1774, women in North Carolina signed an agreement to do the same. And hundreds of women in various colonies organized "spinning bees" to make homespun clothing rather than purchase British-made cloth.

Important though these activities were, they were not a dramatic departure from traditional female roles. Women involved in boycotts were making a political statement, but did so within the context of their "normal" feminine roles and behavior. That changed for some women with the onset of the war. Around 20,000 women were with the Continental Army during the War for Independence. While most simply accompanied their husbands (not an unusual practice in that century), others served in a variety of capacities. Some cooked and did laundry for General Washington's troops; others nursed the wounded. A few took a more active role in the struggle. "Molly Pitcher" of New Jersey (her real name was Mary Ludwig Hays) became famous for hauling

This print depicts Revolutionary War heroine Molly Pitcher at the battle of Monmouth in 1778. What features of the reproduction provide clues about the impact of the War for Independence on women's place in American society?

pitchers of water to American forces during the battle of Monmouth in 1778. She also loaded the cannon manned by her husband after he was wounded. When Margaret Corbin's husband was killed at the battle of Fort Washington in 1776, she took charge of his cannon; she surrendered it only when she herself was wounded. A few women disguised themselves as men and saw combat, and both patriot and loyalist women acted as couriers and spies.

Some slave women fled to the British lines to escape servitude and served in regimental units; others defiantly refused to work for their masters. It is impossible to know how many women were victims of sexual violence during the war, but sexual and other assaults against women, including Native American females, were committed by soldiers on both sides.

The American Revolution was an ideological struggle as well as a war for independence. And it is doubtful that the social, economic, and political status of American women benefited much from the stirring words of the Declaration of Independence. "All *men* are created equal" was a radical statement in the eighteenth century. But it meant "men" and only men—and white men at that.

There was one example of political inclusion for white women as a result of the democratic ideals promoted by the Revolution. During the 1780s in New Jersey, women who owned the required amount of property were allowed to vote in local elections. Except for widows and some unmarried females, this still excluded most women. Once they married, American women forfeited ownership of their property to their husbands. Nonetheless, for more than two decades some women in New Jersey did vote. In 1807, however, the state legislature disfranchised all women, as well as free black men.

In the next essay, Mary Beth Norton describes the experiences of southern women during the Revolution. Her essay is important for a number of reasons. For one, Norton portrays the ways of life of different classes of women—poor, middling, elite, and enslaved—before and during the war. In addition, Norton suggests that a war-ravaged South came through the struggle determined to recreate a male-dominated, slavery-based plantation economy. According to Norton, this left black and white southern women in even more subservient positions than their counterparts in the North.

Source: Mary Beth Norton, "What an Alarming Crisis Is This?: Southern Women and the American Revolution," in Jeffrey J. Crow and Larry E. Tise, eds., *The Southern Experience in the American Revolution* (Chapel Hill: University of North Carolina Press, 1978), pp. 203–234.

Before one can assess the impact of the Revolution on southern women, one must begin by outlining the patterns of women's lives in the South in the years prior to the war. . . . For the purposes of this analysis, it is best to distinguish three separate types of households in which southern women led quite different lives: first, the rural homes of the poorer and "middling" parts of the white population; second, the urban households inhabited by members of the same group; and third, the large, multiracial households (whether rural or urban) that contained both the wealthiest whites and the black Americans who served them, the latter usually constituting a numerical majority of the family.

Because poorer and middling southern women frequently were illiterate, or if able to write, rarely were called upon to do so, historians seeking to study their lives must turn to the accounts of observers and the records of their dealings with governments to gain insight into the conditions of their existence. In rural areas, such an investigation shows, white women worked in the fields or tended livestock in addition to caring for their houses and children. When Oliver Hart, a lonely South Carolinian separated from his wife by the war, day-dreamed about her, he told her he saw her "on my Farm, busying yourself with your Poultry, traveling the Fields, admiring the Flocks and Herds, or within, managing the Dairy." That his characterization of his wife's role was accurate is revealed not only by the statements of such persons as the tutor Philip Vickers Fithian, who noticed white women planting corn in Virginia fields, but also by the contents of claims submitted by female refugees after the war to the loyalist claims commission in London. Rural women demonstrated a wide-ranging knowledge of farm tools and livestock, while admitting their ignorance of many aspects of their husbands' financial affairs. Their knowledge, in effect, revealed the dimensions of their lives. The Georgian Janet Russell, for example, mentioned that she regularly milked thirty-two cows and noted that she counted the sheep on her farm "a few days before she came away." She and other rural southern loyalist women submitted claims documents that included long lists of the dishes and utensils they handled daily, of the spinning wheels they occasionally operated, of the foodstuffs they prepared and stored, of the livestock they helped to feed, and of the clothing, linens, and furniture that were their prize possessions.

The lives they led were hard and exhausting, with little respite or relief. The Reverend Charles Woodmason, an itinerant Anglican clergyman who traveled extensively in the Carolina backcountry, commented that the people there ate "fat rusty Bacon" and corn bread; lived in "open Logg Cabbins with hardly a Blanket to cover them"; and wore but scanty clothing and no shoes or stockings. He noted that the women were "so burthen'd with Young Children" that they could not "attend both House and Field," thus confirming the work demands made on rural women and recognizing that in many cases they were unable to meet them. One wonders how many rural white women were like the mother of a boy (the fourth of eight children) born on a Shenandoah Valley farm in 1769, whom he described thus: she "from my earliest recollection was weak & sickly . . . confined principally to her bed for the last two or three years of her life."

In the towns, there were no crops to plant, no herds of livestock to attend (though there might be a cow or a few chickens), and as a result the lives of women of the "middling sort" who resided in urban areas were somewhat different. They prepared the food, but instead of cultivating crops in the fields they raised produce in small kitchen gardens or purchased it at city markets. They cared for numerous children, but the children might attend small schools run by women much like themselves for part of the day. They spun some wool and linen thread, but were more likely to buy their cloth at local stores. They also were more likely to engage in business activities on their own. In rural areas, the only way women could make money was by taking in travelers or by doing some spinning and weaving for wealthier neighbors, but in towns women could work alongside their husbands in taverns or shops or run independent businesses. In Charleston, for example, William Brockie sold "Fruit & Garden stuff" and his wife Mary was a mantua [women's gowns] maker; Katherine Williamson ran a grocery store while her husband Robert "worked at his Trade as a Bricklayer"; the widowed Janet Cumming made 400 pounds annually as the most respected midwife in town; Eleanor Lestor took over her husband's liquor store after his death; and Mary and Robert Miller together kept a tavern. Most of these women . . . represented only a small proportion of the overall female population, but they led quite independent lives. When all the women just described became loyalist refugees, their experiences in coping with manifold business problems stood them in good stead, as shall be seen.

The lives of the wealthiest group of southern white women differed markedly from those of the poorer and middling sort. Foreigners and northerners almost invariably described well-to-do southern women as "indolent" because of the combined effect of "their living in so warm a climate and being surrounded by such a multitude of slaves." But appearances were deceiving to a certain extent. Such women were freed from the more monotonous and onerous household duties by the labor of slaves, but in exchange they had to superintend large and complex families. One Virginia wife, complaining of how she and her husband could not leave home, told a friend that she and her female neighbors were "almost in a State of vegetation" because they constantly had to "attend to the innumerable wants" of their multiracial households. Appropriately, these women were commonly described as "good managers" or "remarkable Economists." The skills they developed were those of command and of personnel management rather than of handwork and of "making do" with less than ample supplies of food or clothes.

They learned the habit of command early. In her diary, one little Virginia girl complained about the laziness of her black washerwoman and raged about a male slave who killed a cat: "a vile wretch of new negrows, if he was mine I would cut him to pieces, a son of a gun, a nice negrow, he should be kild himself by rites." A four-year-old North Carolina girl was described by a doting cousin as "strutting about in the yard after Susanna (whom she had ordered to do something) with her work in her hand & an Air of as much importance as if she had been Mistress of the family." As adults, such women were entirely capable of directing the many-faceted activities of a plantation household. Eliza Lucas's 1742 description of how she spent her days is instructive here. Arising at five o'clock, she read till seven, saw "that the Servants are at their respective business," then ate breakfast. Afterward she practiced music, studied, and taught her younger sister until dinner time. She again turned to her music, then to needlework, and finally in the evening once again read or wrote. Although Eliza Lucas may have been more insistent on early rising than her female contemporaries (she recorded that at least one woman neighbor warned that the practice would age her unnecessarily), the diaries and letters of other wealthy southern women show a similar daily pattern: giving orders to servants in the morning, doing needlework in the afternoons, and reading, writing, or playing music at various times during the day. . . .

And what of the black women whose labor made all of this possible? Their lives differed in obvious ways from those of whites, most notably, of course, in the inescapable fact of their servitude. But married women of all descriptions in the colonial South were, in a legal sense, "slaves" to their husbands, and white female servants sometimes worked alongside black women in both house and field. The tasks female slaves performed were equivalent to, if not exactly the same as, those done by the poorer and middling whites: they worked in the fields, prepared food, cared for children, and spun thread. But, significantly, specific individuals did not do all of these tasks, for the sheer size of plantation households meant that the work of slave women could be specialized in a way that that of poor white women could not. During her lifetime, a slave woman probably would serve her master and mistress in several capacities: as a youngster, she might spin or mind smaller children; as an able-bodied woman, she might work in the fields; as an older woman she might again spin, work as a house servant, or be a nurse or a midwife to both blacks and whites. But she would not engage in these tasks simultaneously. And on occasion a young girl would be singled out "to bring up in the House," or would show such aptitude for a particular job that she would be assigned to that task alone (as was Mulatto Milly, the "principal spinner" on John Natley Norton's quarter in Fauquier County, Virginia). As a result, slave women living on large plantations had opportunities to acquire a level of skill that their white mistresses did not, and this may have contributed to the development of such self-confidence as that exhibited by "Miss Charlotte," an East Florida slave who in 1769 reacted to a dispute between two whites over who owned her, one of them reported, by "living with neither of us," but instead going "about from house to house," saying "now she's a free woman.". . .

Whether black or white, rich or poor, however, the lives of most colonial southern women can be summed up in one word: "circumscribed." All were tied down by the care of their families. The nature of that care varied, as did the size and racial composition of the households, but the women bore responsibility for the day-to-day familial routine. They rarely traveled, and the demands of their regular duties seldom allowed them to venture outside their domestic sphere, though the shape of that sphere varied according to their race, place of residence, and economic status. Foreign travelers noted this quality in southern women: Maryland females, observed an Englishman in 1745, had "an Air of Reserve and somewhat that looks at first to a Stranger like Unsociableness," but was rather the "effect of living at a great Distance from frequent Society and their Thorough Attention to the Duties of their Stations." A Venezuelan commented nearly forty years later on North Carolinians that the "married women maintain a monastic seclusion and a submission to their husbands such as I have never seen . . . their entire lives are domestic. Once married, they . . . devote themselves completely to the care of family and home."

It does not take much imagination to realize that women with little experience outside the confines of their households would find being in the midst of a disruptive civil war an unnerving experience. In the years after 1775, and especially in 1778 and thereafter, southern women had to cope with a myriad of unprecedented problems: armies on the march, guerrilla bands, runaway inflation, shortages of food and other supplies, epidemics spread by military movements—all in the absence of their husbands, fathers, brothers, and sons they had long been told to look to for guidance. It was not an easy time.

Paradoxically, in light of the reputed paucity of resources for black history, it is easier to assess the impact of the Revolution on southern black women than on their white counterparts. This is essentially because to slaves the war was a chance—a slim one, admittedly, but still a chance—for freedom. The Revolution, furthermore, by depriving planters of the British manufactured goods on which they previously depended, also caused a significant rise in the production of cloth within plantation households. Thus some slave women were afforded the opportunity to develop new skills of spinning and weaving, and, by implication, perhaps gained somewhat greater independence and self-confidence. . . .

Far more dramatic than the opening of this skilled occupation to slave women were the direct consequences of the war itself and, in particular, the results of British military policy regarding blacks. In November 1775, in an attempt to bolster his sagging cause, Lord Dunmore, the last royal governor of Virginia, issued a proclamation offering freedom to all blacks and indentured servants who would join him to fight the rebellion. Although only an estimated eight hundred slaves responded to Dunmore's call immediately, southern whites were terrified by the implications of the offer. One commented, "Hell itself could not have vomited any thing more black than his design of emancipating our slaves." In July 1776, Robert Carter called together the black residents of his Coles Point plantation (which was dangerously situated on the Potomac) and suggested that Dunmore intended to sell those who joined him to West Indian planters. Carter's argument apparently dissuaded potential runaways at that time, but when the British army returned to Virginia in 1781 thirty-two of the Coles Point Negroes absconded during one nine-day period. Throughout the South, the story was the same: everywhere, the redcoats attracted slaves "in great numbers," according to the contemporary historian David Ramsay.

Although a majority of runaways were male, women apparently sought freedom in greater numbers during the war than in peacetime. Jefferson noted twenty-three who "joined British" in his farm book, twelve of whom were women, and one of whom took her three children with her. The South Carolinian John Ball listed the names of fifty-three runaways to the redcoats in his plantation accounts; of these, only fifteen were adult women (many of whom left with their children), but none returned voluntarily, whereas as least ten men did. A woman named Charlotte may have instigated a mass escape. She originally fled on 10 May 1780, but "was brought home." A week later, however, she left again in company with fourteen other slaves, none of whom appears to have returned. That the sex ratios among runaways from the Jefferson and Ball plantations were not unusual is suggested by the lists of black evacuees prepared by British authorities at the end of the war. One Savannah list of 1,956 slaves is 41 percent male, 36 percent female, the remainder being children; and of the 3,000 blacks recorded as leaving New York City in 1783, 914 (or approximately 30 percent) were women.

Even when the blacks did not run off, all was not well from the owner's point of view. Thomas Pinckney reported to his mother Eliza that the only slaves left on his Ashepoo plantation after a British raid in May 1779 were pregnant women and small children, who "pay no Attention" to the overseer's orders and "who are now perfectly free & live upon the best produce of the Plantation." Mrs. Pinckney had similar problems with her slaves at Belmont: she wanted them to come to her daughter Harriott's Santee plantation, she told

Tom, but they were "attached to their home and the little they have there [and so] have refused to remove." She concluded that if the blacks wished to join the British, neither she nor anyone else could stop them, "for they all do now as they please everywhere." More than a year later she complained of how she had been "Rob'd and deserted" by her slaves, remarking that it was impossible even to raise money by selling them because the "slaves in this country in gen[era]l, have behaved so infamously and even those that remain'd at home so Insolent and quite their own masters that there are very few purchasers" who would take them.

Not all of the slaves who joined the British found freedom. Smallpox and camp fever were endemic in the British encampments, and many thousands of southern blacks died from those and other diseases. Of the runaways from Jefferson's plantations, only three (two men and a woman) seemed to have joined the enemy and survived in freedom. Five more initially fled to the British, "returned and lived." The other fifteen died with the British or after they returned home, and Jefferson recorded the deaths of eleven more slaves as a result of disease caught from the returnees. Blacks who were the property of loyalists also ran the risk of being returned to their masters, and after the war it appears that some of the Negroes who were evacuated with the British army to the West Indies were sold as slaves. But although the British formally agreed at the evacuation of Charleston and in the provisional peace treaty of November 1782 that they would not carry away slaves belonging to Americans, the army proved extremely reluctant to return to servitude blacks who had sought its protection. One South Carolina planter, all of whose slaves were in Charleston with the redcoats, was reduced in autumn 1782 to the futile hope that "they will not have transports enough to carry the negroes off." In all, the British carried with them approximately four thousand from Savannah, six thousand from Charleston, and four thousand from New York City. After the war, white southerners estimated their total losses in slaves at more than fifty-five thousand.

If the British army attracted black Americans like a magnet, it repelled white Americans with similar force and efficiency. Everywhere the army went, fighting followed, and wherever there was fighting civilians, rebel and loyalist alike, left their homes to find places of greater safety. In January 1779, a South Carolinian told his brother, "the poor Georgians are flying over into this State, by Hundreds; many of them leaving their All behind." A few months later, as the British advanced northward, the people of his own state were experiencing "ravaging" and "Havoc." That year the revolutionaries successfully resisted the British invasion, but Charleston and much of South Carolina fell to royal forces in 1780. The victory did not bring peace to the province; quite the contrary. David Ramsay later recalled that after the surrender of Charleston, "political hatred raged with uncommon fury, and the calamities of civil war desolated the State." Then it was North Carolina's turn, and Virginia's. In 1781, Cornwallis's incursion in to the latter state sent "every body scampering," to use the words of the young Yorktown girl Betsy Ambler. "What an alarming crisis is this," she wrote to a friend as she and her family fled before the advancing redcoats. "War itself, however distant, is indeed terrible, but when brought to our very doors . . . the reflection is indeed overwhelming."

In later years Betsy described her mother as having been especially "afflicted" by the family's repeated moves during the war; throughout the South white women had to endure similar hardships. Not only were many widowed by the war (reputedly there were 1,200 to 1,400 widows in the sparsely populated Ninety-Six district of South Carolina alone), but also they frequently had to face marauding troops and irregulars by themselves, since their husbands, fathers, and brothers were absent serving with one army or the other. Isolated in the countryside, groups of women and children gathered together for protection: at least twice during the war, for example, female friends of the Pinckney family sought refuge at Daniel and Harriott Horrey's Santee plantation, and the wealthy widow Eliza Wilkerson, who lived in the sea islands south of Charleston, wrote of seeing "crowds of helpless, distressed women, weeping for husbands, brothers, or other near relations and friends, who were they know not where, whether dead or alive." According to Mrs. Wilkerson, when the British moved through her neighborhood en route to Charleston in 1779, there were "nothing but women, a few aged gentlemen, and (shame to tell) a few skulking varlets" to oppose them.

Mrs. Wilkerson had a frightening encounter with some British raiders, and her reflections on her experience are enlightening. For months she had assured herself that "our weak sex, 'incapable of wrong, from either side claims privilege of safety,'" but a visit from "abusive" plunderers accompanied by armed Negroes disabused her from that notion. After the raiders had left with their booty, Mrs. Wilkerson found that she "trembled so with terror, that I could not support myself," and in the privacy of her room, she "gave way to a violent burst of grief." In the aftermath of the attack, she recorded that "we could neither eat, drink nor sleep in peace; for as we lay in our clothes every night, we could not enjoy the little sleep we got. The least noise alarmed us; up we would jump, expecting every moment to hear them demand admittance. In short, our nights were wearisome and painful; our days spent in anxiety and melancholy."

For most well-to-do slaveholding whites like Mrs. Wilkerson, such troubles were unprecedented. Raised in luxury, accustomed to the constant attention and service of slaves, many were unprepared to cope with the situation in which they found themselves and they recognized their own lack of resiliency. After the war, once-wealthy southern loyalist women frequently referred to the fact that they had been "accustomed to the Indulgence of Fashion & Fortune," had been "nurtured in the Lap of Affluence," or had been "born and bred to Affluence and indulgences of the tenderst Nature," when each explained her lack of success in handling "difficultys of which she had no experience in her former life."

Contrast to this the behavior of southern women who had previous experience in handling "difficultys," many of whom were of the poorer or middling sorts. They, too, encountered problems of unprecedented magnitude, but they—especially the urban businesswomen—seemed to land on their feet more often than their wealthier neighbors, and they were more willing to take the initiative and to act positively instead of sitting back passively waiting for the worst to happen.

Thus in 1780 a rural North Carolina woman impulsively followed her husband's militia unit to a battlefield, where she cared for the wounded of both sides until she learned he was unhurt. A Maryland carpenter's wife, whose drunken husband had enlisted on a privateer, physically resisted the marines who came for him and caused such an uproar by calling the recruiting officer "every vile name she could think of" that her husband was allowed to remain at home. Eleanor Lestor, the widowed Charleston shopkeeper, hid British sailors in her house and spoke "freely" against the rebel cause, and another "she-merchant" from Charleston, Elizabeth Thompson, assisted British prisoners of war, carried letters through the lines, and drove a disguised British spy through the American camp in her own chaise. Other women like these followed their husbands to the armies of both sides and, though they lost many of their meager possessions, managed to surmount innumerable difficulties.

The amazing saga of Susannah Marshall is a case in point. She and her loyalist husband William ran a tavern and boarding house in Baltimore before the war, until the rebels forced him to flee to the West Indies. She continued to operate their business, though the rebels looted the house, quartered troops in it, and prevented her from collecting from her debtors. In 1776 she chartered a ship to sail to Norfolk to join Lord Dunmore, but he had left the area by the time she arrived. Sailing back up Chesapeake Bay to Head of Elk, she there acquired another tavern and the local ferry concession. Allowed to leave the state in 1777, Mrs. Marshall invested her money in a cargo of foodstuffs, chartered another ship, and once again set sail. En route to the West Indies her ship was captured by the Americans, then recaptured by a royal cruiser. Since the cargo had been in the possession of the rebels, it was forfeited under British law, and Mrs. Marshall salvaged nothing. Finally, she made her way to England, only to learn that her husband had died and to have her petition for a loyalist pension rejected by the authorities. Undaunted, she went to work as a nurse to support her family and in 1789 at last was awarded a permanent allowance by the British government.

Susannah Marshall's tale doubtless was unique. But southern loyalist and patriot women alike saw their husbands murdered before their eyes, traveled hundreds of miles to escape one set of partisans or the other, [and] endured repeated plunderings of their homes and farms. . . . At the end of the war many were left with little more than the knowledge that they had managed to live through it all. . . .

It is hardly surprising that in later years Betsy Ambler Brent, whose words supplied this essay with its title, entertained mixed feelings about the Revolution. The same event that has brought "independence and prosperity to my country," she mused in 1809, had involved "my immediate family in poverty and perplexity of every kind." Striving to discover the beneficial effects of the war, she found them not in public occurrences but rather in her own personal development: speaking of herself and her younger sister, she commented, "The only possible good from the entire change in our circumstances was that we were made acquainted with the manners and situation of our own Country, which we otherwise would not have known; added to this, necessity taught us to use exertions which the girls of the present day know nothing of. We were forced to industry to appear genteely, to study Manners to supply the place of Education, and to endeavor by amiable and agreeable conduct to make amends for the loss of fortune."

Surely Mrs. Brent's characterization of the war as requiring "exertions which our girls of the present day know nothing of" could have come from the pen of any other southern woman who had lived through the Revolution. Less wealthy families did not find their circumstances as greatly altered by the war as did the Amblers, but other southern women had had similar experiences. Accordingly, during and after the war the more highly educated and reflective among the white women began to raise questions about the social role to which they and their northern counterparts long had been confined. The fact that they did so constitutes an important consequence of the Revolution for American women; when coupled with the opportunity for freedom that the war offered to black families, it shows that, contrary to what historians usually have maintained, women did not simply "quietly sink back in their places and take up the old endless routine of their existence" after the war.

Some colonial women always had railed against male condescension. One thinks, for example, of the poet Anne Bradstreet's defense of her literary capacities against carping male critics, or of Esther Edwards Burr's almost equally well-known "smart combat" with a Princeton tutor who had "mean thoughts of Women." Such female outbursts were of a piece with the raging of a North Carolina girl in 1784 against me who "treat women as Ideiots" instead of recognizing them as "reasonable beings." Such anger was not new, even if it was perhaps more commonly expressed in the aftermath of the Revolution. But a great deal was new in other issues raised by women during the 1770s and 1780s. Abigail Adams's correspondence with her husband John and her friend Mercy Otis Warren contains often-quoted examples of such ideas; what is less well known is that southern women expressed similar thoughts. The Virginian Hannah Corbin, for example, asked her brother Richard Henry Lee whether she, as a widow holding only a life interest in an estate, rightfully could be taxed by the state on its values, since she could neither vote nor alter the property in any way. . . .

Such sentiments were not unusual, if not exactly commonplace, in the writings of American women in the 1780s. But, strikingly, only north of the Mason-Dixon Line did they have a significant impact. There men began to respond to the women's concerns and to expand their notions of what constituted women's sphere, to provide increased educational opportunities for women, and to publish (if not always agree with) women's statements on their own behalf. In the South no comparable developments occurred. There women expressed their sentiments privately, to each other and their husbands, but they did not find men responsive to the issues they raised. The key question is why, and to find the answer it is necessary to return to a discussion of the impact of the war in the South.

By all accounts, the South suffered more from the Revolution than did the northern and middle states. The phases of the war fought on southern soil were both more destructive and more prolonged than those experienced by any northern region other than the immediate vicinity of New York City. The war in the North (with the same exception) largely concluded with the evacuation of Philadelphia in summer 1778, and so by the time the peace treaty was signed in autumn 1782 even the hardest-hit northern area had time to recover. Not so the South. Long after Yorktown, guerrilla warfare continued throughout the Carolinas in particular, and not until after peace was officially proclaimed could recovery begin. Plantations had been laid waste, farms neglected, houses and fences left in disrepair, for far too long a time. Navel stores and indigo, two of the South's most important prewar exports, were now denied the bounties they had received when America was part of the British Empire. Britain began to tax American rice and tobacco, thus necessitating a search for new markets and subjecting those products to increased competition in Britain itself. . . .

The impact of this devastation upon society and social attitudes was incalculable. In the less-affected North, the post-war period could be one of experimentation with new ideas and social forms. Slaves could be emancipated, women could be educated, egalitarianism could be instituted in theory, if not in practice. But not in the South. There efforts were directed simply at rebuilding what had been lost, at conservatively reconstituting colonial society rather than at creating a new republican way of life. And so a Virginia planter in 1780 refused even to pay lip service to egalitarian rhetoric when he criticized the "little people": "Do they know that a Gentleman is as necessary in a State, as a poor Man, and the poor as necessary as the Gentleman"? he asked. "So it must be! Through all generations—for if we were all equal, one hour, nay one minute, wou'd make a difference according to mens Genious & Capacity. . . ."

In rebuilding colonial society, in putting their resources into reconstructing an agricultural economy based on slavery, white southern males were ensuring, consciously or not, that the lives of their wives and daughters would continue to be determined by the nature of their households. Southern men were reinforcing a patriarchal society centered on an expanded household economy. In the North, the household became progressively less important in the economy as the years passed, as factories began to produce items formerly manufactured within the household, and as men increasingly worked outside the home. But in the South the household retained, perhaps in certain areas expanded, its significance, as slavery gained an ever-tighter grip on the southern economy. Where the optimal family continued to be large and multiracial, and where the husband continued as the head of an increasingly important household, the wife's role necessarily contracted or remained the same.

Questions for Discussion

1. Summarize the author's description of the daily lives of female slaves along with poor, "middling," and elite white women. Despite these differences, what does the author claim linked the destinies of these women?
2. How did each group of women fare during the War for Independence?
3. How did slaves respond to British offers of freedom during the war? How many slaves left for the British lines? What was their fate?
4. The South suffered far more destruction during the War for Independence than the North. According to the author, how did this difference affect the future of women, patriarchy, and the future of the family in each region?

For Further Reading

Joy Day Buel and Richard Buel Jr., *The Way of Duty: A Woman and Her Family in Revolutionary America* (1984); Judith Van Buskirk, "They Didn't Join the Band: Disaffected Women in Revolutionary Philadelphia," *Pennsylvania History*, 62, no. 3 (1995); Edith Gelles, *Portia: The World of Abigail Adams* (1992); Joan R. Gundersen, *To Be Useful to the World: Women in Revolutionary America, 1740–1790* (1996); Ronald Hoffman and Peter J. Albert, eds., *Women in the Age of the American Revolution* (1989); Linda Kerber, *Women of the Republic: Intellect and Ideology in Revolutionary America* (1980); Cynthia Kierner, *Beyond the Household: Women's Place in the Early South* (1998); Holly Mayer, *Belonging to the Army: Camp Followers and Community During the American Revolution* (1996); Mary Beth Norton, *Liberty's Daughters: The Revolutionary Experience of American Women: 1750–1800* (1980); Gordon Wood, *The Radicalism of the American Revolution* (1992); Alfred Young, *Masquerade: The Life and Times of Deborah Sampson, Continental Soldier* (2004); Rosemarie Zagarri, *A Woman's Dilemma: Mercy Otis Warren and the American Revolution* (1995).

8

Pioneers on the Western Farming Frontier

John Mack Faragher

"Those who labour in the earth are the chosen people of God," wrote Thomas Jefferson in his book *Notes on the State of Virginia* published in 1785. Jefferson's lavish praise for those who farmed was tied to his vision of the young country's future. He believed the American experiment in freedom could succeed only as long as the majority of its people earned their livelihoods from agriculture. In Jefferson's view, the farmer who owned enough land to be self-sufficient—to satisfy the basic material needs of his family through his own labor on his own land—was the backbone of American freedom. The owner of a "family farm" was independent: he worked for himself and had a material stake in the orderly functioning of society. He was free as well from the whims of an employer. Jefferson also idealized rural life. Because farmers lived in a rural setting—where clean air and wide-open spaces seemed almost to breed morality—Jefferson believed they were more likely to possess the virtues necessary for responsible citizenship in a free society. By contrast, for Jefferson cities were arenas of moral corruption and social disorder.

Jefferson's views about the moral value of rural life may have been fanciful, but his emphasis on the economic importance of farming corresponded with American reality. When he was elected president in 1800, more than 80 percent of Americans earned their living in agricultural pursuits. The country's population was rapidly expanding, as was the appetite of its people for more and cheaper land on which to farm. That was one reason Jefferson engineered the Louisiana Purchase in 1803. By adding 830,000 square miles of territory to the United States, much of it suitable for farming, Jefferson hoped to create what he called an agrarian "empire for liberty." He hoped

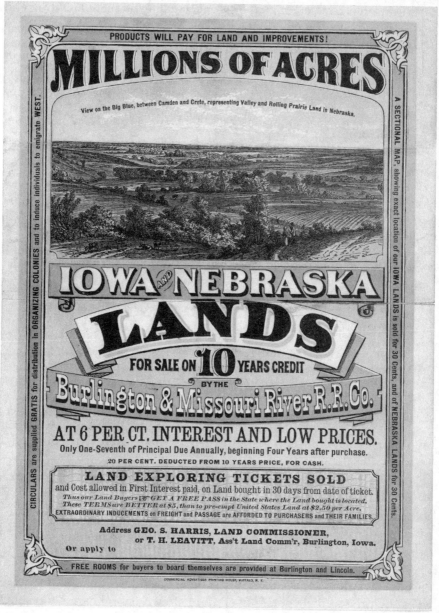

This circular advertising the dream of land ownership was printed after the Civil War. But the same dream animated the farming pioneers of Illinois described in this article. What strikes you most about the advertisement? How does it relate to the issues raised in the article? Does it anticipate more recent issues concerning home ownership and easy credit?

America would remain a nation of farmers and avoid manufacturing and large cities. Instead of building factories, Jefferson urged Americans to import most of their manufactured goods from Europe.

In the next selection, John Mack Faragher describes the lives of pioneer farming families in the central Illinois frontier around the time it became a state in 1818. Today we refer to this part of the country as the Midwest, but at that point in the country's history, Americans called it the "West." Most of the settlers who came to Sugar Creek, Illinois, had migrated west from Tennessee and Kentucky.

Jefferson tended to portray the lives of farmers in idyllic terms. But Faragher brings to life the day-to-day grind and the back-breaking labor it took to carve a living from the soil in a raw, frontier community. He shows that farmers were less self-sufficient economically, and more dependent on market forces, than Jefferson assumed. He also describes the techniques of farming they employed, as well as the division of labor among men, women, and children.

In some ways, Faragher's portrait of life in a midwestern farming community supports Jefferson's beliefs. These farmers *were* relatively independent, and most succeeded. But there were plenty of failures as well. Either way, however, life in a pioneer community could cause strains for families. It was often a lonely experience for women, a violent one for men, and an endless, back-breaking life of work for both.

Source: John Mack Faragher, *Sugar Creek: Life on the Illinois Prairie* (New Haven, CT: Yale University Press, 1986), pp. 96–113, 151–155.

"The whole stock of the first settlers generally consisted in their two hands," English immigrant and agricultural reformer Morris Birkbeck observed of his Illinois neighbors in 1817; "there is, properly speaking, no *capital* employed in agriculture."

Thirteen years later Illinois editor James Hall admitted that "our husbandry is yet in a rude state." Most farmers farmed with simple, home-manufactured tools. "My father knew of every crooked root, and every stick of timber which could be fashioned into some tool or implement of use," William Riley McLaren remembered, "for everything from an ox-yoke to a hay or grain rake was made of wood and by hand." Well into the 1840s, according to Moses Wadsworth, Sugar Creek farmers continued to break timber soil with wooden plows, harrow fields with tree limbs, and thresh wheat by driving their horses over grain strewn on the barn's threshing floor. Inventories of farm property, included in the probate records of Sugar Creek farmers, show that before the 1850s, tools remained essentially unchanged from those of colonial times. Along with poor roads and resulting high farm-to-market costs, primitive hand tools restrained the commercial development of agriculture.

But most agricultural reformers blamed the state of western agriculture on what they considered the backward attitudes of farmers. After a trip through central Illinois in the 1830s, Timothy Flint concluded that "agriculture improvement comes at a slow pace. The people are not given to experiments, they continue to farm in the beaten way." The Sangamo [central Illinois farm country], wrote one northeastern emigrant to the creek, was "destitute of any energy or enterprise among the people, their labors and attention being chiefly confined to the hunting of game." Another Yankee complained that when the snow began to fall in December of 1830, inaugurating what was forever after remembered as the "Winter of the Deep Snow," "it found most of the corn standing on the stalks. The fall had been so warm and wet that the farmers had a better reason than common to indulge the careless habits of leaving their corn in the field, to be gathered as they wanted it." One farmer, born in the 1820s near Drennan's Prairie, later condemned the "slovenly" practices of his neighbors, who left their cornstalks standing all winter, then fired their fields to clear them for plowing in the spring. Unbeknownst to this critic, or even to the farmers he criticized for that matter, this practice, long used by the Indians, helped to return essential nutrients to the overworked and under-manured soil. But lack of "enterprise," "slovenly" and "careless habits," and "the beaten way" seemed to account for the backwardness of western farming.

Undoubtedly, many of these "common" farmers did think differently about the nature of their work than progressive "agriculturalists" did. "Moon farming," for example, was commonplace in the backcountry. Potatoes, radishes, turnips—all root crops, in fact,—ought to be planted in "the dark of the moon," otherwise they would go to seed; it was believed that corn should be planted as the moon waxed full, for "the light of the moon" would spur the plant to greater growth. Girdling of trees was best accomplished during the new moon of August, was the correct setting of fence posts. "The moon is a wonderful worker of miracles," wrote James Hall; "philosophers assign to her the regulation of tides, and rustics endow her with absolute supremacy over the land. No saint in the calendar was ever consulted so often, or with such entire faith. . . . By her changes all farming operations are regulated, seed is sown, fences are made, and children weaned, when the moon is propitious; and by the same rule, I presume that a maiden who should be courted when the *sign was in the heart* would melt sooner than at any other period." Carl Sandberg, reflecting on his youth in rural Illinois, thought he understood the compelling power of such superstitions: "the worker on the land, who puts in crops and bets on the weather and gambles in seed corn and hazards his toil against so many whimsical, fateful conditions, has a pull on his heart to believe he can read luck signs, and tell good luck or bad luck to come, in dreams of his sleep at night, in changes of the moon, in the manners of chickens and dogs, in little seeming accidents that reveal the intentions and operations of forces beyond sight and smell.". . .

Within the limits established by prevailing attitudes and available technology, a family—a farmer, his wife, and their half-grown children—on a model eighty-acre Sugar Creek farm could achieve a subsistence living. In 1840 the livestock of an average Sangamon farmer included several score of hogs, a dozen head of cattle, oxen, and milch cows, a small flock of sheep, and assorted poultry. Families raised vegetables and root crops in their gardens, flax or cotton in the "patch," perhaps apples or peaches in a small orchard. Farmers "made a crop" on fifty or sixty enclosed acres, producing averages of 1,100 bushels of Indian corn, 150 bushels of oats, and 50 bushels of wheat. . . . The existing state of the means of production limited capitalist agriculture but allowed most families to achieve a minimum of modest sufficiency, so farmers directed their energies to production for domestic use, placing the security of their families first.

That commitment of energy took its toll. Men's hands hardened from gripping farm handles, their legs bowed from tramping over the clods turned up by the ploughshare; women's hands cracked, bled, and developed corns from the hard water of the family wash, their knees grew knobby from years of kneeling to grit corn or scrub puncheon [wooden] floors. "We had to work very hard clearing ground for to keep soul and body to-gether," remembered [Dennis] Hanks. Yet an English immigrant living south of Sugar Creek wrote his brother in 1841 that an "industrious family," through such labor, could provide nearly all its own food and fodder, and he praised the settlers' ability to "manufacture most of their own clothing, soap, candles, and sometimes sugar."

This labor nearly all came from within the family. Since land was available and free for the using, few men were willing to work as wage laborers. Only a small number of families could afford the cost of a hired hand anyway. "Labour is scarce and highly remunerated," wrote Patrick Shirreff, an English traveler through the Sangamo in 1835; "in a country where Nature is so bountiful and land so abundant and cheap, the wages of labour must necessarily be high." So farming required families. . . .

Lucinda Casteen emigrated [from Kentucky] to central Illinois with her husband and children in 1831, accompanied by her unmarried brother, Isham, who farmed an adjoining claim. In letters to her mother, Lucinda regularly worried about Isham: she rarely saw him, he worked too hard, was too single-mindedly ambitious, and drank too much. But it was his unmarried state that most troubled his sister. How could he manage, Lucinda wondered, without a wife? Isham had "come so well provided in cloths" that he was not yet wanting for weaving; Lucinda herself had somehow found the time amid her busy rounds to make him a suit of jane, and did all his sewing and mending. Isham hired a woman from the neighborhood to do his washing for two bits a month, and "he expects his neighbor's wife to milk for him." "He gets it all tolerably well done," she wrote, yet it was troubling, her brother living alone like that. Isham needed a wife, and when he married in 1838, Lucinda rejoiced in spite of her jealousy over her new sister-in-law's monopoly of her brother's time.

As Timothy Flint wrote in the mid-twenties, "a vigorous and active young man needs but two years of personal labour to have a farm ready for the support of a small family." "It will be to your interest to come or go where you can have a home of your own," Lucinda Casteen counseled her younger sister, still in Kentucky; "but never give your hand or heart to a lasy [sic] man." Marriage created new farm households, and each new household created a new workplace. If high levels of fertility constituted the first traditional feature of family life in Sugar Creek, the intimate and direct connection between the reproductive and productive lives of farm families constituted the second. The times yoked childbearing and work together.

The demand for farm labor helps to account for fertility patterns, for large families were a distinct advantage in the struggle to win a living from the land. Since there was no certain supply of labor outside the family, wrote one Midwesterner, "the rule was, that whoever had the strength to work, took hold and helped." Children were an economic necessity, and choices about fertility could not be divorced from the requirements of production. "In this fine country, which literally flows with milk and honey," a traveler commented, "man is the only growth that's wanted"; settlers were taking care of the problem, for "every log Cabin is swarming with half-naked children. Boys of 18 build huts, marry, raise hogs and children at about the same expense."

Children contributed their full share to this domestic economy. "The first day of March found every able-bodied boy back on the farm whether school was out or not," one settler recalled. "School was a mere incident of minor importance, while 'the call of the wild' or 'back to the farm' was imperative. There were rails to make, fences to build, grubbing to do, lands to clear, and the thousand and one other things to do, to prepare for a crop." Boys mucked out [cleaned] barns, made hay, cleared and gleaned fields, hoed, husked, and plowed, so that by the ages of ten or twelve they had assumed most of the working responsibilities of full-grown men. Daughters learned the many small tasks connected with the preparation of yarn and cloth, as well as the finer arts of the needle and, by following mothers through their endless round of chores, quickly learned women's work. Lucinda Casteen wrote her mother that "our school at home"—the chores and housework that her girls had to perform to keep the place running—absorbed all her daughters' time and kept them from "ABC school." "I fear we can't go on regular [school schedule]," she despaired, "but I think of sparing them 4 hours a day if possible."

The work of children was important, but it was the work of farm wives that made the difference between the success or failure of productive strategies. Besides bearing and caring for a large family of children, besides preparing at least three large meals every day, besides cleaning, washing, ironing, and mending, women produced an abundance of goods without which a family found it hard to survive. In gardens they raised sweet corn, pumpkins, beans, and potatoes, as well as a wide variety of green vegetables, medicinal herbs, flax, and even cotton. Through long evenings they carded, worked at omnipresent spinning wheels, wove cloth, and tailored garments for the family. In henhouse or farmyard they tended flocks of chickens and geese, collected eggs, set hens, plucked down, and strangled roosters for the pot. In the dairy they fed and milked cows, and later, on porch or in pantry, they churned butter and sometimes made cheese. Farm wives produced towels, blankets, and quilts, as well as pickles, cider, dried fruit, soap, candles, and nearly every other thing that made the difference between a hovel and a home.

Wives frequently assisted men in the fields as well. "The farmer himself and one or two big boys made up the laboring strength of the farm," wrote one Midwesterner; but he readily acknowledged that under the press of weather or season "the wife or older daughter would be called on to help, and sometimes they would assist in planting and hoeing the corn, raking the grain or hay in harvest." In a typical case of cooperation, Mary and David McCoy, young Sugar Creek emigrants of the 1820s, plowed their fields together—he pushing the plow, she driving the oxen, as their firstborn slept in a box strapped to the plow beam. When illness or accident disabled farmers, farm women picked up the burden of field work that could not wait. Nor did convention restrict a girl's work to the household and barnyard. "In the planting of corn, which was always done by hand," wrote a local resident, "the girls always took a part, usually dropping the corn, but many of them covering with a hand-how." In the springtime, on many farms, "the father would take his post at the plow, and the daughter possession of the reins." Folk beliefs that certain crops benefited from cooperative planting by men and women suggests the importance of joint farm work. Certain superstitious farmers sowed flax seed by throwing it against the backsides of wives who walked ahead with their skirts jacked up, and folklorists of the Ozarks have reported a similar custom of the flax patch, in which husband and wife worked the field together stark naked while chanting the line "Up to my ass, an' higher too!"

But farmers could not exist entirely outside the market. Every farm family needed salt, gunpowder, and iron, and desired rope, harness, crockery, coffee, and other manufactured commodities; the proprietors of small country stores set up to meet this demand. In 1819, a young Massachusetts emigrant took over a cabin near the junction of Lick and Sugar creeks and began supplying families along the creek with farm essentials, patent medicines, and locally produced whiskey, a large stock of which he regarded as "indispensable" to conducting a good business. Traveling peddlers from New England, their wagons loaded with notions, began to cover central Illinois almost as soon as the settlers arrived. In 1833, for example, Ezra Barnes left Hartford, Connecticut, headed for the Illinois country with a wagonload of clocks and other manufactured goods, and by November was selling his wares to farm wives along Sugar Creek. After two years of making friends in the Sangamon, he bought land, married a local girl, and began farming along the creek; but other peddlers took his place.

Sugar Creek families before the late 1840s were able to produce a reasonable level of subsistence, but they had a harder time generating the income needed to pay for manufactured commodities. . . . The stories told by settlers of their attempts to market their small "surplus" in Springfield [Illinois] were intended to illustrate their failure. Because of its bulk, corn was never a market crop. When prices reached a peak in 1836, one local farmer hired a wagon to haul twenty bushels to the Springfield market; but the best price he could get, five cents per bushel, did not even cover the cost of hauling. Another man, anxious to raise cash to finance a move north, found it impossible to sell his corn crop at any price so bartered it for a barrel of whiskey, swapped the whiskey for a steer, and finally sold the steer for ten dollars. Barter remained the preferred way of doing business in Springfield before the late-1840s. . . .

Farm wives seemed to have less difficulty finding a ready market for their surplus production of butter, eggs, and homespun, although these commodities, too, brought miserably low prices. In 1850, when the federal census for the first time collected precise production statistics, Sugar Creek women produced over twenty-six thousand pounds of butter, an average of nearly 180 pounds per household, a rate of production that was low compared to the "butter belts" around eastern cities but still impressive considering that such a quantity over the course of a year required each farm wife to milk at least five cows twice a day, in addition to making the butter itself. One woman remembered "selling butter at 5 cts per lb., and that churned in a bowl, with a spoon, as a churn was not to be found." Other women used the dasher-churns [hand-mixers] frequently itemized in estate inventories. Because not every family produced its own butter, a local market existed for the fresh product, and women preserved the surplus in brine, trading it with local merchants, who shipped it to St. Louis, Chicago, or Detroit.

Households consumed most of their homespun, just as they consumed most of their butter. "We raised cotton, picked it out of the burr, then picked out the seeds with our fingers, then card and spun it, then wove it into cloth making gingham dress goods (of which it took about four yds to make a dress), bed spreads, etc.," Sugar Creek settler Ann McCormick remembered. . . . But a vigorous local trade existed in homespun. When she moved to the Sugar Creek area with her husband and four children in 1825, Charlotte Jacobs remembered that "I brought with me three cows, and my husband brought five hounds," but they were without pigs. "The first hogs we had," she reported, "I bought twelve shoats, and paid for them with linsey and jeans of my own make." In other reminiscences women reported weaving hundreds of yards of cloth for trade. At the general store in Springfield in the 1820s, women's commodities figured prominently as items of trade: homespun jean, linen, and cotton cloth were the fabrics most commonly accepted for store goods, with beeswax, honey, and butter next in importance. Storekeepers also traded in wild herbs. In the 1820s and 1830s, Mahala and Sarah Ernest dug ginseng in the timber with which to barter; over the years the insatiable demand for "seng," which many considered an aphrodisiac, nearly wiped the plant from the local flora. As farmers concentrated their attention on the hunt, most farm wives handled the family trading for "boughten goods."

There is no precise way to measure the relative contributions of men and women to the surplus production of the family farm. Even from this distance, however, the mutual dependence of the farmer and his helpmate seems clear, for butter, cloth, and other women's goods, as well as field crops, measurably added to the ability of farmers not only to practice self-sufficiency but to enter the market. Moreover, many families required income to make payments on their land and to invest in seed, livestock, or tools. Industrious farmers sold not only field crops but furs, fence rails, and whiskey; they toiled as day laborers in the fields of well-to-do neighbors and sweated during hard winters in the lead mines of Galena, in northern Illinois, all in an effort to raise the money needed to buy land. The greater the surplus that women could introduce into the market for household and farm necessities, the more men could dedicate their surplus labor to investment.

The labor of some women contributed more directly to the process of accumulation, just as Charlotte Jacob's homespun helped to stock her family farm with hogs. In the 1830s, one wife produced butter that her husband hauled all the way to Chicago, where he purchased farm equipment with the proceeds. Phoebe Russell Twist, from Seneca Falls, New York, used her talents to make cheeses that her husband regularly carted to St. Louis, saving the earnings until they raised enough to buy their first eighty acres. Since few women from the upland South made cheese, Phoebe may have sold some of her cheddars locally; she must have accumulated some savings, for in 1833 she bought sixty-six acres of timberland in her own name. Accumulation may have taken second place to consumption, but western families placed a high priority on purchasing the land they worked, and success in that pursuit, like success in self-sufficiency, depended upon the contributions of both sexes.

But mutuality, so necessary in production, did not extend to the ownership of farms. Men constituted 93 percent of Sugar Creek owners on the county tax lists of the mid-1830s and nearly 99 percent of the owners identified on the first published county plat map of 1858. From 1823, when Sangamo lands first came on the market, to the 1850s, when the last quarter-sections passed into private ownership, men composed 98 percent of the over twenty-six hundred individuals who filed federal land claims. In Sugar Creek, as elsewhere, men and women jointly worked farms, but it was the men who owned farm property.

Women labored under legal disability, for by the laws of Illinois, in accord with the English common-law doctrine of coverture, a married woman lost the rights she enjoyed as a single woman (a *femme sole*) to own or manage chattel or real property, or to enter into contracts without a co-signature. A husband gained the rights to manage estates brought into the marriage by his wife and, upon the birth of a child, to will any such property to *his* heirs as he saw fit (another legal principle known as curtesy). In the words of Sir William Blackstone, whose eighteenth-century *Commentaries on the Laws of England* became the standard guide to the common law for the American bar, "by marriage, the husband and wife are one person in law; that is, the very being or legal existence of the woman is suspended during the marriage, or at least is incorporated and consolidated into that of the husband; under whose wing, protection, and cover, she performs every thing." In 1836, first-term [Illinois] legislator Abraham Lincoln made a back-handed statement of this principle when he declared that "I go for all sharing the privileges of government who assist in bearing its burdens. Consequently, I go for admitting all whites to the right of suffrage who pay taxes or bear arms (by no means excluding females)." Some have quoted this statement to applaud Lincoln's "advanced views" on the "woman question," but surely he was commenting tongue-in-cheek, for at the time women neither paid taxes *nor* bore arms—their husbands did. Illinois laws for women changed little before the passage of married women's property acts in the 1860s. . . .

Few Sangamon settlers left us their impressions of the condition of farm women. . . . The testimonies of visitors to central Illinois in the years before the Civil War offer a more direct and forceful assessment of farm women. The most articulate of these observers was Frances Trollope, a remarkable Englishwoman who lived for several years during the late 1820s and early 1830s in the frontier town of Cincinnati. Western women married "too young," she believed, and early, frequent pregnancy aged them prematurely.

> It is rare to see a woman in this station who has reached the age of thirty, without losing every trace of youth and beauty. You continually see women with infants on their knee, that you feel sure are their grand-children, till some convincing proof of the contrary is displayed. Even the young girls, though often with lovely features, look pale, thin, and haggard. I do not remember to have seen in any single instance among the poor, a specimen of the plump, rosy, laughing physiognomy among our cottage girls.

Mrs. Trollope may have exaggerated the health and contentment of English lasses, but James Fenimore Cooper, after several years abroad, where women commonly married in their mid- to late twenties, concurred that "these early marriages, which are the fruits of abundance, have an obvious tendency to impair the powers of the female, and to produce premature decay."

Trollope's book on American manners sold well in America, although her comments provoked hostile reactions from Americans, who have never taken well to foreign criticism. But, as Mark Twain observed later in the century, on most matters Trollope simply told the truth. She wrote of her shock at the enormity of the workload reported by a backwoods wife: she "spun and wove all the cotton and woolen garments of the family, and knit all the stockings. She manufactured all the soap and candles they used, and prepared her sugar from the sugar-trees on the farm. All she wanted with money, she said, was to buy coffee, tea, and whiskey, and she could 'get enough any day by sending a batch of butter and chicken to market.'" "The life she leads," Trollope concluded of the western woman, "is one of hardship, privation, and labour." Margaret Fuller, touring Illinois in the early 1840s, agreed that women's work was "disproportioned to their strength, if not to their patience." And Sangamon immigrant Charles Clarke wrote home to New England that "a man can get corn and pork enough to last his family a fortnight for a single day's work, while a woman must keep scrubbing from morning till night the same in this country as in any other."

Trollope admired the proud independence of farm women but was disturbed by the "wild and lonely situation" in which they found themselves. She and others condemned the open-country pattern of western settlement that prevented women from visiting friends or neighbors, and she viewed their isolation as a major disability. Harriet Martineau, another famous English visitor, watched a lone woman paddling a canoe against the swift current of the mighty Mississippi, probably, she wrote tongue-in-cheek, "to visit a neighbor twenty or thirty miles off. The only comfort was that the current would bring her back four times as quickly as she went up." In Sugar Creek, neighbors often lived miles apart; Mary Jane Drennan Hazlett recalled that, "although the people were sparsely settled we would visit ten or fifteen miles distant and call them neighbors." But distance and the responsibilities of work on the farm kept women at home most of the time. Trollope's backwoods farm wife, "in somewhat of a mournful accent," told the visitor "'tis strange to us to see company: I expect the sun may rise and set a hundred times before I shall see another *human* that does not belong to the family," and a central Illinois pioneer woman wrote that "three visits were all that I made out of our neighborhood for the first four-and-a-half years."

Isolation robbed women of the company and companionship of female peers. Most young women moved directly from their parents' to their husbands' houses, where they assumed heavy responsibilities at a young age. The absence of a period of semi-independence, when young women might build relationships with each other before the pressures of marriage began, contributed to a pattern of female dependency. This was Mrs. Trollope's most telling criticism. "In no rank of life," she wrote, "do you meet with young women in that delightful period of existence between childhood and marriage, wherein, if only tolerably well spent, so much useful information is gained, and the character takes a sufficient degree of firmness to support with dignity the more important parts of wife and mother. The slender, childish thing, without vigour of mind or body, is made to stem a sea of troubles that dims her young eye and makes her cheek grow pale, even before nature has given it the last beautiful finish of the full-grown woman." Harriet Martineau believed that in rural America "every woman is married before she well knows how serious a matter human life is," with the consequence that wives were lacking in strong intellectual and moral character. "It is unquestioned and unquestionable," she concluded, "that if women were not weak, men could not be wicked. . . ."

[Woman's] place remained domestic, largely "invisible" to the world at large. Pubic life was dominated by men and their rituals. The public culture . . . was, in the words of another historian of the Sangamo, "ultra-virile."

Consider drinking and drunkenness. Farm women consumed their share of alcohol, but it was the men who regularly engaged in public boozing. One early settler remembered that at the Sangamon general election of August 1822 tavern-keepers lined up their wares on benches outside the log-cabin Springfield courthouse. Present were "white men," as well as "Indians and darkies, they of course not being allowed the right of suffrage," but all got equally drunk. "The white men sang songs, the Indians and darkies danced, and a general public frolic occurred. Every candidate had to fill his portmanteau [traveling bag] with whiskey, and go around and see and treat every voter with the poisonous stuff, or stand a chance of being defeated." Whiskey was ever present in Sangamon society. [Abraham] Lincoln noted in an 1842 temperance address: "government provided it for soldiers and sailors, and to have a [log] rolling or [cabin] raising, a hunking or hoe-down, anywhere without it, was *positively insufferable*." It was, as one settler wrote, a "universal custom" to serve corn whiskey—plenty of it—at all public gatherings, customary for the captain of the local militia to treat the company after the drill, customary for candidates to campaign, as the Sugar Creek Whigs complained, with liberal donations of "ardent spirits. . . ." More than one Sangamo pioneer told of postponing his cabin raising until he could afford to supply the thirsty neighborhood. William McLaren recalled raisings where fifty or sixty men consumed "fiery red whiskey" until their faces were "swollen up like bitten with a hundred wasps." Indeed, accidents caused by drunkenness presented the greatest danger at raisings. To supply this demand many farmers added distilleries to their farms. . . .

Drunk or sober, public fighting was another common occurrence. Moses Wadsworth wrote that on election and muster days "nearly every boy in the precinct, old enough to ride a horse, accompanied the fathers and brothers, and all spent the day. Liquor was usually available, and drunken men and fights were often witnessed. "You needn't be tryin' to bullyrag and scrouge [crowd] me unless you're spilin' for a fight," one citizen shouted to another, "and if you are, I reckon you'll find me an owdacious scrouger that'll just bodiacerously split you right open down the middle." "You onery low-down dog," his opponent shot back: "ye needn't try to get shet of me with all your tomfool brag. I'll knock you into a cocked hat soon'r'n ye kin say Jack Robinson." Samuel Williams remembered that at a muster "some of the men became very boisterous, and several of them stripped to the pants for a fist fight." In electoral contests between partisans, verbal jousting frequently broke into violence. In the 1838 congressional contest, John Stuart got Stephen Douglas into a headlock and the "Little Giant" bit his opponent's thumb so hard that he left a scar. Through the 1840s, gangs of neighborhood toughs frequently fought out their electoral differences with their fists as well as their votes. At the polls in 1840, Sugar Creek Democrat Dr. Alexander Shields challenged a leading county Whig to fisticuffs, no holds barred. "His fist was soft; my head was hard, and by the time he raised some five or six knots, his fist was useless. I caught him and drew him down upon me, and then reached to get him by the throat; and my thumb landed in his eye," but before he could pop his victim's eyeball from its socket, Whigs pulled the fighters apart, and the dispute ended with the opponents paying fines for disorderly conduct to the local justice. Men also loved cockfighting, bull-baiting, and other blood sports. One of the farmers' favorite amusements at log rollings, William McLaren recalled with delight, "was to round up a chip-munk, a rabbit, or a snake, and make him take refuge in a burning log-heap, and watch him squirm and fry," or, at communal hunts, "to skin a wolf alive and watch his antics."

Not all men drank themselves into oblivion or fought like dogs, of course, but male culture generally accepted such conduct as a regular occurrence of public life. Westerners argued that this spirit of robust competition produced an egalitarian community within which no man was better than another. Caroline Kirkland overheard an Englishman loudly complaining of the lack of respect westerners showed traveling gentlemen. "Respect!" retorted the tavern-keeper, "why should I show more respect to any man than he does to me? Because he wears a finer coat? His coat don't do me any good. Does he pay his taxes any better than I do? Is he kinder to his family? Does he act more honestly by his neighbors? Will he have a higher place in heaven than I shall?"

Western men did demonstrate an undeniable familiarity. It was common, for example, for a man to "take a seat on the knee of a friend, and with one arm thrown familiarly around his friend's neck, have a friendly talk, or a legal or political consultation." Men also thought nothing of rolling up together around campfires to keep each other warm, or sharing the few available beds of frontier hotels. One Sangamon lawyer told of two colleagues, Campbell and Benedict, who shared a bed on the circuit until one, feeling greatly put upon by the other's bed behavior, finally objected. "Confound you," exclaimed Campbell, "I have lain with you, but I never did *sleep* with you." Nevertheless, that night Benedict returned from an evening at the tavern, "got undressed, even to the taking off of his drawers," then "jumped into bed and began to fondle" his mate. Campbell had "armed his heel" with one of his spurs for just such a contingency, however, and jabbed it into Benedict's flanks. "Jesus!" Benedict cried as he flew out of bed and across the room, "the fellow has taken me for his blamed old horse." Such familiarity, one settler wrote, "would have shocked our English cousins, and disgusted our Boston brothers," but in the West men found it perfectly acceptable. . . .

"Women of that day attended none of the rough and exerting sports of men," wrote settler James Haines; they "cultivated the joys and pleasures of the hearth and home." Traveling through northern Illinois in the early 1840s, essayist and feminist Margaret Fuller expressed a somewhat different sensibility concerning this contrast between the vigorous male public life and the mundane household existence of women. Farm women "found themselves confined to a comfortless and laborious life," she wrote, "while their husbands and brothers enjoyed the country in hunting or fishing." A quarter-century later an aging western farmer fondly recalled the cabin raisings, log rollings, and other occasions for "swapping work," the public politics, militia musters, and road duty, the freedom to "roam and fish, or hunt as we pleased, amid the freshness and beauties of nature"—in short, the "virile" public life of the antebellum era. "There was excitement in all this—a verve and scope, a freedom, and independence and abandon, suited to our rougher nature and coarser tastes." "But," he pondered, "how was it with our wives: From all these bright, and to us fascinating scenes and pastimes, they were excluded. They were shut up with the children in log cabins."

Questions for Discussion

1. How did Thomas Jefferson's vision of the family farmer compare with farm life described in this essay? Given all the difficulties of succeeding as a farmer, why do you think so many Americans found that life so attractive?
2. What impact did farming have on the size of the rural family and on the daily routines of its members?
3. Jefferson hoped family farmers would be self-sufficient. According to this essay, to what extent were Illinois farmers self-sufficient? In what ways were they dependent on the marketplace? What were the roles of men and women in the production of surplus farm products?
4. What was coverture? What were its consequences?
5. What was the impact of frontier conditions on the daily lives of women? Of men?

For Further Reading

Carol Billingsly, *Communities of Kinship: Antebellum Families and the Settlement of the Cotton Frontier* (2004); Don Doyle, *The Social Order of a Frontier Community: Jacksonville, Illinois, 1825–1870* (1978); John Mack Faragher, *Women and Men on the Overland Trail* (1979); Cheryl Foote, *Women of the New Mexico Frontier, 1846–1912* (1995); Stephen Hahn and Jonathan Prude, eds., *The Countryside in the Age of Capitalist Transformation: Essays in the History of Rural America* (1985); Katherine Harris, *Long Vistas: Women and Families on Colorado Homesteads* (1993); Robert V. Hine, *Community on the American Frontier: Separate But Not Alone* (1980); Cathy Luchetti, *Children of the West: Family Life on the Frontier* (2001); Leo Marx, *The Machine in the Garden* (1964); Marilyn F. Motz, *True Sisterhood: Michigan Women and Their Kin, 1820–1920* (1983); Sandra L. Myres, *Westering Women and the Frontier Experience, 1800–1915* (1982); Linda Peavy and Ursula Smith, *Women in Waiting in the Westward Movement: Life on the Home Frontier* (1994); Glenda Riley, *Frontierswomen: The Iowa Experience* (1981), *Building and Breaking Families in the American West* (1996), and *Women and Indians on the Frontier, 1825–1915* (1984); Lillian Schlissel, *Far From Home: Families of the Westward Journey* (1989); Emily Werner, *Pioneer Children on the Journey West* (1995).

9

From Farm to Factory
The Beginning of Industrial Labor

Barbara Tucker

Just as Thomas Jefferson hoped the new nation would remain agricultural and rural, his archrival Alexander Hamilton was equally intent upon promoting manufacturing and urban development. Hamilton believed that if America diversified its economy it could become a world power. To do so, it needed factories and cities as well as farms and countryside.

As the nation's first Secretary of the Treasury, Hamilton championed policies that helped create its first large-scale manufacturing enterprises. In 1790 Hamilton convinced President Washington and Congress to establish a national bank. Among other things, he envisioned the bank as a means of financing new manufacturing enterprises. Also, Hamilton wanted both the federal and state governments to give "bounties," in the form of tax credits and other incentives, to entrepreneurs. In his famous 1791 *Report on Manufactures*, Hamilton predicted that factories and cities would promote economic development, encourage large-scale immigration, and inspire technological innovation. Factories would also provide employment for "persons who would otherwise be idle." Hamilton was referring to women and children: "women and Children are rendered more useful and the latter more early useful by manufacturing establishments, than they would otherwise be."

On all counts, Hamilton's predictions were uncannily accurate. A year before his *Report on Manufactures*, Samuel Slater, an English immigrant, constructed the nation's first textile mill in Pawtucket, Rhode Island. By 1800, Slater's company employed more than 100 hands—most of them women and children. Over the next two decades Slater opened numerous cloth

In the essay, Barbara Tucker points out the prevalence of child labor in early-nineteenth-century textile mills. This photograph, of two fifteen-year-old sisters working in a Massachusetts textile mill in 1911, indicates that child labor remained common in American industry into the twentieth century. Why?

manufacturing mills, where he employed entire families, many of whom lived in his company-owned houses. In 1813, Francis Lowell started the Boston Manufacturing Company in Waltham, Massachusetts. Lowell's textile company hired mostly young, unmarried women from the farms of northern New England. By 1840, 40,000 people, most of them women, worked in the Massachusetts textile mills alone. America's industrial revolution was underway.

In the next essay, Barbara Tucker describes the world of work experienced by the first generation of factory hands in Slater's mills. It is important to keep in mind that these individuals were pioneers in the transition from farm to factory labor. Tucker shows how Slater attracted farm families to his mills by assuring them that the patriarchal authority of the traditional farm family would be reproduced in his factories.

For example, Slater would hire an entire family, including the mother and children, but their wages were turned over to the father. Also, in the early years of his operation, Slater allowed parents to play a role in determining their children's working conditions, just as they had on the farm. But as Tucker shows, over time management gained control of working conditions, and wages were paid to the individual rather than the family. By the middle of the nineteenth century, the transition from a system of labor largely controlled by the family to a capitalist economy, in which wages and working conditions were set primarily by the employer, was nearly complete.

Source: Reprinted from *Barbara M. Tucker: Samuel Slater and the Origins of the American Textile Industry, 1790–1860.* © 1984 by Cornell University. Used by permission of the publisher, Cornell University Press.

In the first decades of the nineteenth century, young children, adolescent boys and girls, and unmarried women comprised approximately three-fourths of the industrial labor force. From the outset, few people opposed the employment of young people: quite the contrary, society condoned and encouraged it. H. Humphrey, noted author of child-training books, expressed the prevailing attitude toward the employment of children when he wrote:

> Our children must have employment—must be brought up in habits of industry. It is sinful, it is cruel to neglect this essential branch of their education. Make all the use you can of persuasion and example, and when these fail interpose your authority. . . .
> If he will not study, put him on to a farm, or send him into the shop, or in some other way provide regular employment for him.

And Matthew Carey, a well-known political economist, praised manufacturing as an excellent form of youthful employment: "The rise of manufacturing establishments throughout the United States, elevated thousands of the young people of both sexes, but principally the females, belonging to the families of the cultivators of the soil in their vicinity, and from a state of penury and idleness to competence and industry." Usefulness was still the yardstick by which society measured an individual's worth, and factory work allowed otherwise unemployed or underemployed people to make profitable use of their time and to benefit the community.

The young labor force of Union Mills in Webster [Rhode Island] was typical. In 1840 thirty children and adolescents worked in the carding department under the direction of an overseer and several second hands. Approximately two-thirds of the workers there were female; 52 percent were children from nine to twelve years of age, 31 percent were from thirteen to fifteen years, and the remainder were sixteen or older. In the spinning department, the gender ratio approximated that of the carding room. Children as young as eight were introduced to the factory system through employment in this department. Of the twenty-five laborers employed there, 32 percent were from eight to twelve years of age, 44 percent were from thirteen to fifteen, and the remainder were sixteen or older. An overseer and a second hand monitored the labor of the spinning-department employees.

One of the largest rooms in the factory was the weaving department, and there young women, not children, dominated the labor force. At Union Mills in 1840 sixty-nine women wove either full or part time. With the exception of two young sisters, Mary and Sophia Strether, aged eleven and twelve, all of the women employed in the weaving department were between the ages of fourteen and twenty-four. Although some hand-loom weavers remained on the payroll, most of the cloth produced by Samuel Slater and Sons in 1840 was woven by machine.

Most of the people employed at Union Mills belonged to kinship groups. During the early years of industrialization family labor dominated the factory floors. Slater employed only a few people who had no kin working for a Slater enterprise or who did not live in the factory colonies; such employees were men who assumed skilled and supervisory positions and girls and unmarried women who tended power looms. . . .

Under the family system of labor, householders exercised considerable power within the factory, influencing the composition of the labor force, the allocation of jobs in the various departments, the supervision of hands, and the payment of wages. Bargaining between labor and management over the employment of children and labor conditions began before the youngsters entered the mills. On behalf of their children, householders negotiated a contract with Samuel Slater. Casual and verbal compacts at first, these agreements became more formal over time. Although written contracts certainly were initiated earlier, the first set of formal agreements found in the Slater company records are dated 1827; the last are dated 1840. Drawn up in February and March and effective from April 1, the annual contracts made between householders and Samuel Slater listed the names of kin employed, their rate of pay, and any special conditions pertaining to their employment. Typical of these agreements was one signed by John McCausland in 1828:

> Agreed with John McCausland for himself & family to work one year from Apr. 1st next as follows viz:—
>
> Self at watching 5/6 pr night = provided that any contract made with Saml. Slater for the year shall be binding in preference to this—
>
> Self to make sizing at 9/- pr. week
>
> Daughter Jane—12 pr. week—
>
> Son Alex.—7/per week—
>
> Son James—5/pr. week
>
> Each of the children to have the privilege of 3 months Schooling and Alex to be let to the mule spinners if wished.

Education and training provisions were commonly included in the contracts. Parents sought release from factory employment so that their children could attend school from two to four months annually, and permission was granted for both boys and girls to attend class. For their sons, householders sometimes sought further concessions. Like John McCausland, many parents wanted their sons to learn a skilled trade such as mule spinning, an occupation that commanded both prestige and high wages. . . .

While these contracts limited labor turnover and guaranteed Slater a steady supply of workers, they also ensured that parents would retain their position as head of the kinship unit and that children would not gain economic independence. Children looked to their parents to protect their interests. All children employed in the factories had to be sponsored by a householder; with few exceptions before 1830, Slater did not look beyond the kinship unit for labor.

Parents also determined in which department their children would work and the conditions under which they would do so, although this is not stated specifically in the contracts. Family members often worked in the same department, attending machines side by side. Mule spinners hired and paid their sons, nephews, or close family friends to piece [work] for them, and weavers hired kin to assist them at their machines. In 1840 Asa Day, a blacksmith employed by Union Mills, Webster, placed his daughters, Francis and Caroline, aged nine and thirteen, in the carding room. John Costis's six children, who ranged in age from nine to eighteen, also worked there, while the four Drake youngsters, aged ten to sixteen, worked together in the spinning department. In the weaving room, sisters often tended looms near one another. Mary Strether worked beside her older sister, Sophia; the Boster sisters, the three Faulkner girls, and the Foster and the Fitts sisters also worked there.

Parental concern did not end with the formal agreement. Although Samuel Slater established strict rules and regulations for the smooth, efficient operation of the factory, and although he demanded that workers be punctual, regular in attendance, industrious, and disciplined, he nevertheless bowed to parental pressures and allowed householders appreciable influence over the supervision of hands and the payment of wages.

The organization of the factory floor in the Slater mills was a reflection of the dominant position of the male householder. Within each department, the supervisory hierarchy came to reflect the hierarchy of the home. All the positions of authority, from the second hand to the overseer, were filled by men. Although female labor was predominant in the industrial labor force, no woman filled a managerial position. Like children, women were the subordinates, not the supervisors. The pre-factory family hierarchy, in which authority and power were vested in the husband, was transferred from the home to the new industrial order. The factory system did not challenge paternal authority; it perpetuated it. . . .

The wage scale adopted by Samuel Slater also recognized the customary status held by the householder as the primary provider for the family and further enhanced paternal authority. In the 1830s and 1840s rates paid to unskilled and semiskilled male workers ranged from $0.65 to $1.00 per day, more than twice the rates paid to adolescents and unmarried female operatives and three to four times the rates paid to children. . . .

Until the 1830s householders received a daily ration of spirits or wine as part of their payment. This was a cherished custom, one not easily relinquished by laboring men. For generations the consumption of liquor by workingmen and artisans had been an accepted part of life in New England.

During the working day, laborers had received a ration of gin, rum, or cider brandy, often totaling as much as a gallon per month. . . . Liquor was such an accepted part of the work routine in factory villages that the building of a road, the mending of a fence, or the construction of a building, even a church, would have been unthinkable without the rum ration. In the 1820s, during the construction of the first Methodist church in Webster, the pastor had to purchase several gallons of rum for his workmen. Believing that an explanation was due his congregation, the pastor said "This item of rum was produced for medicinal purpose to be given to the men who were injured when a gale of wind blew off the rafters as the workmen were putting on the roof. Mr. Abbingine Marsh of Charlton had a leg broken and sustained other injuries. Several others were also injured." Under the Slater system, the practice of dispensing liquor to employees eventually perished. . . .

The conditions of labor observed in Slater's communities represented a compromise between the demands of householders and the requirements of the new production system. Within the new industrial order, the traditional status of the male and female householder as provider and protector of the family was preserved. By providing householders with socially acceptable forms of task-oriented labor, by allowing parents appreciable influence over the conditions under which their children worked, and by paying house-holders all wages earned by their families, Slater eased the transition of hundreds of families from farm to factory. Yet their control was limited.

Negotiations between householder and management encompassed a variety of issues, but one area in which factory families had little influence was the scheduling of work. Samuel Slater set the operating schedule of the factory. In the 1820s and 1830s hands worked six days each week, from twelve to fourteen hours each day. During the winter months operations began at daylight and continued until 8:00 p.m., while during the summer laborers worked from 5:00 a.m. until 7:00 p.m. Within the mill the long workday was broken by two meal breaks, one lasting approximately thirty minutes and another between thirty and forty-five minutes. The factory bell, the only time mechanism found in the mills, signaled the beginning and end of each meal break, summoned hands to the factory in the morning, and tolled the end of each workday. . . .

Industrial discipline posed some of the gravest problems faced by early factory masters, who had to devise various methods to teach people the so-called habits of industry: regularity, obedience, sobriety, steady intensity, and punctuality. . . . In part Samuel Slater and other manufacturers supported religion because they viewed it as a form of social control which facilitated the discipline of workers. The dictums and discipline advanced by the church became part of the foundation of a work ethic, and as such they served to train, discipline, and control workers. This was the case in Webster, where the Methodist church educated a whole generation in the dictates of their religion. The written tracts, hymns, sermons, and other literature used in the church all advanced the same messages: obedience, deference, industry, honesty, punctuality, and temperance. The lessons prepared the young operatives for ultimate salvation and also trained them to be good, obedient factory hands. In Webster the Methodist Sabbath school was the principal agency through which these lessons were taught. . . .

This Sabbath school owed its origin to Samuel Slater. Like his mentor, Jedediah Strutt, Samuel Slater established Sabbath schools in each of his industrial villages. Based on the British system he had observed, these schools were to "condition the children for their primary duty in life as hewers of wood and drawers of water." Through these Sunday schools, Samuel Slater sought to foster attitudes toward right and proper conduct that would make children good citizens and good workers. A hymn from Dr. Isaac Watt's songbook sung by the children in Slatersville [Rhode Island] and Webster [Rhode Island] began:

> *Why should I deprive my neighbor*
> *Of his goods against his will?*
> *Hands were made for honest labour,*
> *Not to plunder or to steal.*

When churches became firmly established in Webster and Slatersville, Slater disbanded his Sunday school and relinquished moral education and industrial training to the churches.

In transferring moral education to religious bodies, Slater could be confident that the church would continue to inculcate virtues and beliefs sympathetic to the new industrial order. In Webster, for example, the men who ran the Sunday school were the same men who supervised local factory operations. For twelve to fourteen hours each day, six days each week, children worked under Charles Waite and William Kimball, and on the seventh day they listened while the same men interpreted the scriptures. . . .

Values taught in the Sunday schools proved favorable to factory discipline. One of the first lessons taught to children concerned obedience. This was the first law of childhood, the first rule of the church, and the regulation deemed indispensable for the smooth, efficient operation of the factory. Sabbath school teachers stressed this dictum and condemned all children who disobeyed those in authority, whether at home, at school, or in the factory. One lesson used to instill this particular value might have been introduced to children in the following way: "As you sit here now, listening to me," the Sabbath school teacher might begin,

> can you remember any disobedient habit of yours, that make the father and the mother unhappy, when they look at you and see how fast you are growing, without growing better? Is it true that you have had a bad temper, and do not love to be controlled? . . .
> Is it true that you have grown, but that you have not grown out of any of these habits: just as bad as ever, just as disobedient, just as wicked with the tongue as ever?

Punctuality, a cornerstone of any work ethic, also received considerable attention from the Methodists. They were concerned about time. In an era when people were accustomed to family time and to task-oriented labor, Methodist children were being taught: "Be punctual. Do everything exactly at the time." In his reports to the company, factory agent and Sabbath school administrator Charles Waite often stressed the need for punctuality: "Punctuality is the life of business whether in the counting house or the factory." The severe style of life demanded of the faithful allowed no place for carefree play, laughter, or harmless pranks. "No room for mirth or trifling here," began a child's hymn on amusement titled "And Am I Only Born to Die?" Children were constantly warned that "life so soon is gone," that although

> We are but young—yet we must die,
> Perhaps our latter end is nigh.

All hymns carried a similar warning: children should "sport no more with idle toys, and seek far purer, richer joys," devote themselves totally to Christ, and obey the teachings of the church.

Many values, including punctuality, attention to duty, and seriousness of purpose, were neatly summarized in the Webster Sabbath school constitution, which was drawn up by local church officials. The constitution was in fact a code of conduct similar to that maintained in the factory. In part the constitution required all children "to be regular in attendance, and punctually present at the hour appointed to open school. To pay a strict and respectful attention to whatever the teacher or Superintendent shall say or request. To avoid whispering, laughing and any other improper conduct." Altogether these values became the moral foundation for a strict work ethic. But one element essential to the successful operation of this ethic was missing: internal self-discipline.

As a work ethic these dictums and values would have been much less effective had not the church also taught self-discipline, self-restraint, and self-regulation of behavior. All efforts were made to internalize values in order to create an inner discipline that would control and limit the child's behavior. Children were taught to "do good" instinctively and to develop an internal drive toward right and proper conduct. In effect, they became their own taskmasters; conscience rather than rewards and punishments directed their actions.

To achieve this end, Sunday school teachers linked proper conduct to grace or, to put it conversely, disobedience to damnation. An exchange used to close an infants' class made the connection explicit:

> TEACHER: Do you know who belong to Satan's army? Say after me—
>   All who tell lies, all who swear and cheat; all who steal; all who
>   are cruel.

In the child's mind, to cheat, to steal, to lie, or to misbehave in any way was to violate God's law, lose grace, and risk damnation. And such a risk was unthinkable. The songs published in *Hymns for Sunday School* describe hell in forceful and emotional terms:

> *There is a dreadful hell,*
> *And everlasting pains;*
> *There sinners must with devils dwell,*
> *In darkness, fire, and chains.*

Images of everlasting punishment and fears of eternal damnation worked to ensure a strict and steady compliance with the values advanced by the church.

The Sabbath school trained Webster child workers well. In the factory, children quickly learned to obey all orders, for to disobey was to feel anxious and to risk censure or eternal damnation. Corporal punishment, fines, and the ultimate discipline—dismissal—were largely absent, and in fact unnecessary when children readily and willingly, not to say cheerfully, obeyed the dictates of second hand and overseer. Operations almost always ran smoothly. Supervisors faced few disciplinary problems such as absence, theft, inattention to duties, or general mischievous behavior. The instructions children received in the Sabbath school were largely responsible for the exemplary behavior.

The tenets of the church were reinforced by lessons learned in the home. In the area of discipline the responsibility of the parents was widely recognized. . . . In communities such as Webster and Slatersville, the home became another training ground for a generation of factory hands. Lessons taught there stressed the implicit, unquestioning obedience and deference to authority deemed necessary for good family government, for a well ordered society, and for the successful operation of the factory system. In antebellum New England familiar values, expressed through child-rearing practices and reinforced by religious tenets, operated to create tractable hands. . . .

The values taught in the home were those required by industry: they served to make both dutiful, respectful children and submissive workers. Even the most liberal authorities on child-rearing practices, such as Lydia M. Child, cautioned parents that "implicit obedience is the first law of childhood," that "whatever a mother says must always be done." Other writers concurred. John Abbott, described by one historian as the Spock and Seuss to the people of the Civil War generation, went a step further and joined disobedience with wickedness. In *Child at Home* he wrote: "Think you, God can look upon the disobedience of a child as a trifling sin? . . . It is inexcusable ingratitude."

> The only path of safety and happiness is implicit obedience. If you, in the slightest particular, yield to temptation, and do that which you know to be wrong, you will not know when or where to stop. To hide one crime, you will be guilty of another; and thus you will draw upon yourself the frown of your maker, and expose yourself to sorrow for time and eternity.

All commands had to be immediately and cheerfully obeyed. Children were expected to respond to orders with glad and happy hearts. Again John Abbott: "Obedience requires of you, not only to do as you are bidden, but to do it with cheerfulness and alacrity"; and Theodore Dwight, Jr.: "Children should be obedient—must be obedient, habitually and cheerfully."

If obedience was the first law of childhood, then deference was the second. Children quickly realized their subordinate position within the patriarchal family. Mothers taught that father was the head and ruler of the household, that he stood before them as God's representative on earth, and that, as supreme earthly legislator, he exercised complete control over their every action. According to Humphrey, "children must early be brought under absolute parental authority, and must submit to all the rules and regulations of the family during the whole period of their minority, and even longer, if they choose to remain at home." Once again religious injunctions were employed. Humphrey warned: "Now to disobey your parents, is to dishonor them. This you have done, and in doing it, you see you have broken God's holy law. We can forgive you, but that will not lessen your guilt, nor procure forgiveness from your heavenly Father. You must repent and do so no more."

Lessons taught at home, reinforced by tenets learned from the scriptures, became the moral foundation for a disciplined labor force. Workers found little difference between disciplinary patterns in home and factory. Both home and factory were paternalistic, and both were controlled by men who expected unquestioning compliance with all commands. Children merely transferred their values and behavior patterns from the home and the church to the factory: old values were easily accommodated by the new institution.

At the turn of the nineteenth century the family system of labor had served the needs of both employers and employees. Economic and social circumstances peculiar to the era had brought about this conjunction of interests. Yet this system lasted barely one generation. With the growth of the market economy, and with increasing competition from foreign producers, the interests of workers and managers diverged. Management attempted to salvage its own economic position in part at the expense of labor by dismantling rights long accorded householders and workers.

The dissolution of the traditional family system of labor occurred over several decades. Efforts to change customary worker prerogatives proceeded slowly and in a piecemeal fashion. Although labor and management disagreed on some issues, patriarchy initially remained the context in which issues were decided. Nevertheless, the unmistakable force of events moved against familial influence. Slowly the firm chipped away at traditional rights, advancing and retreating on issues as events and the economic situation dictated. By the 1850s little remained of the labor system established by Samuel Slater at the turn of the century. . . . The householder was stripped of his influence within the factory, and Slater dealt separately with individual workers. . . .

Changes under way within the factory system would have important consequences for the family system of labor. It was difficult for the Slater family to achieve a higher level of economic rationality while householders continued to influence factory operations. Disciplinary policies, placement procedures, and conditions of labor, customarily part of the domain of householders, were in conflict with the rational organization and operation of the factory floor. Authority could not remain divided between householder and factory master. By the 1830s management appeared to be ready to sacrifice the moral discipline associated with the family and the church in order to maintain more extensive control over the individual workers. Privileges once accorded the householder in the factory came under scrutiny and began to be dismantled as economic factors became the primary influence in the actions of management. . . .

Among the first issues addressed by the Slater family was the work schedule. The Slater family introduced Sunday and overtime work and members of the same family began working different shifts. Some children worked extra hours on Tuesdays and Wednesdays, others on Thursdays and Saturdays; householders and older boys worked on Sundays. Mothers could not be certain when all members of the family or unit would be together. Sunday lost significance as the traditional day for family as well as for religious communion. Further inroads against tradition followed. Morning and afternoon breaks, which had long been periods for workers to meet and chat with kin, to exchange gossip with fellow workers, even to slip out of the mill and dash home to run errands, were abolished. Agents complained that workers took advantage of the breaks, that they stretched the allotted fifteen minutes into forty-five or sixty minutes. By eliminating rest periods, Slater forced more work from his laborers.

Parental supervisory prerogatives also came under attack. Samuel Slater and Sons assumed the power once vested in mule spinners to hire, pay, discipline, and dismiss piecers [piece workers]. A mule spinner no longer had the right to hire and supervise his sons or to teach them his trade. Parents were also forbidden to enter the mill and supervise their children while they were in the overseer's charge. Householders who objected to this regulation were fired. Peter Mayo's entire family, for example, was discharged because he attempted "to control his family whilst under charge of overseer and disorderly conduct generally." Economic incentives and penalties began to replace traditional forms of control within the factory. To encourage acceptable standards of work and behavior, the stick-and-carrot approach was introduced. Black marks were recorded against weavers for shoddy work and fines for tardiness, absence without leave, or disorderly conduct were deducted from their wages, while good work was rewarded by extra allowances.

A further assault against long-standing practices occurred when manufacturers abandoned the family wage system and began to pay wages directly to individual workers. Initiated in the mid-1830s, this method of payment was first introduced in the weaving department, but when parents complained, the former system was restored. In the early 1840s the firm tried once again, and this time it succeeded. By 1845 each worker received his or her wages. On settlement day in 1845 Daniel Wade, a watchman, and his two adolescent daughters, Laura and Elmira, both weavers, received separate pay slips. Children could now dispose of their own income. With the introduction of the new pay system, contracts were eliminated.

When the householder collected all wages, he controlled the available income and distributed it according to his priorities. With this new arrangement, however, economic power shifted in part to children and adolescent workers, and the householder's domination of the family was threatened. Parents had to negotiate with each child over the disposal of his or her wages. With economic independence, with jobs available in Webster and elsewhere, children, charges, and boarders could move out of the family home and take up residence in local boardinghouses or leave the community altogether. By this time the company operated two large factory boardinghouses, one that accommodated fifty-six men and women and another that housed twenty-eight people. Local residents also took in lodgers.

Families began to drift apart. . . . Within the factory the family unit was broken down; individual laborers rather than the work unit, became the focus of the factory agent, who dealt directly with each member and no longer communicated through the householder. With this development the cash nexus began to replace traditional forms of control, and authority passed increasingly from the householder to the factory agent. Economic considerations formed the basis for the new relationship between Slater and the operatives.

While Slater checked the power of the householder, he also tried to introduce new policies that would increase the productivity of his labor force. The workday was stretched another fifteen, twenty, or thirty minutes, depending on the whim or the needs of the factory agent. It should be remembered that few workmen had clocks, and that a factory bell summoned hands to work, signaled breaks for lunch and dinner, and tolled at quitting time. But factory time invariably fell behind true time, and agents exacted extra work from hands. This was the case not only in the Slater mills but throughout southern New England. At the Hope factory in Rhode Island, operatives started work approximately twenty-five minutes after daybreak and did not leave for home until the factory bell signaled the end of the day at 8:00 p.m. But as the *Free Inquirer* reported, 8:00 by factory time "is from twenty to twenty-five minutes behind the true time." Many manufacturers defended this practice, arguing that "the workmen and children being thus employed have no time to spend in idleness or vicious amusements." Forced to maintain the production schedules set by the manufacturer and to cut costs where possible, supervisors lengthened the workday to obtain additional labor from hands.

To increase production further, the stretch-out and the speed-up were intensified. Slater crowded more and more machines into already cramped spinning, carding, and weaving rooms and assigned additional machines to each worker. In the weaving department, for example, the number of looms attended by each weaver was increased steadily from two to three to four and then to six. Not only did the hands operate more machines, but the machines were run at higher speeds. Initially the speed-up was management's response to the pressure of weavers who worked on a piece-rate basis (approximately 20 cents a cut for weaving 4-by-4 sheeting and shirting), who could increase their earnings only by producing more cloth. In 1837 [Slater supervisor] Alexander Hodges complained to the head office: "The weavers are being uneasy about the speed being slow and some of the new ones will leave. I think we had better put on a little in order to keep the best of them nothing short of this will answer as the mills in this vicinity have advanced the prices." Soon, however, the speed-up became a method to increase production. Writing to Union Mills in 1855, [Slater accountant Ezra] Fletcher confided, "As soon as the supply of good weavers can be obtained . . . the increased speed of looms will show itself by increased quantity." Piece rates remained constant at the earlier level. The speed-up and stretch-out were introduced into almost every room in the factory, without an appreciable increase in pay.

Supply and demand factors, new technology, education laws, and factory acts worked together by the 1850s to transform the labor force employed at Samuel Slater and Sons. The route pursued by the firm led toward an autonomous worker, one who was cut off from his or her family and looked to the factory system for opportunity, support, and survival. The labor force had been streamlined; the family unit, tied to a firm social base, was replaced by an individual tied to the wage economy.

Questions for Discussion

1. On balance, Thomas Jefferson hoped the American future would lean toward an agricultural way of life; as Secretary of the Treasury, Alexander Hamilton geared his policies toward creating—again, on balance—an urban-industrial society. Whose vision do you think was best for the country?
2. Children as young as eight years old were employed in the Slater factories. How did Americans justify the widespread use of child labor?
3. Describe the "family system of labor." In what ways did it benefit the employer? How did it benefit the family?
4. What were Samuel Slater's motives in providing religious instruction for children who worked in his mills?
5. Over time, the family system of labor declined. Why? With what consequences?

For Further Reading

Priscilla F. Clement, *Growing Pains: Children in the Industrial Age, 1850–1890* (1997); Thomas Cochran, *Frontier of Change: Early Industrialism in America* (1981); Elisha Douglass, *The Coming Age of American Business: 1600–1900* (1966); Thomas Dublin,

Women at Work: The Transformation of Work and Community in Lowell, Massachusetts, 1826–1860 (1979); Steven Dunwell, The Run of the Mill (1978); David Hawke, Nuts and Bolts of the Past: American Technology, 1776–1860 (1988); Joseph Kett, Adolescence in America, 1790 to the Present (1977); Bruce Laurie, Artisans into Workers: Labor in Nineteenth Century America (1988), Working People of Philadelphia, 1800–1860 (1980); Shirley Marchalonis, The Worlds of Lucy Larcom, 1824–1893 (1989); Linda S. Peavy and Ursula Smith, Frontier Children (1999); Jonathan Prude, The Coming of Industrial Order: Town and Factory Life in Rural Massachusetts, 1810–1860 (1983); Jacqueline S. Reinier, From Virtue to Character: American Childhood, 1775–1850 (1996); W. J. Rorahbaugh, The Craft Apprentice: From Franklin to the Machine Age in America (1986); Bernice Selden, The Mill Girls: Lucy Larcom, Harriet Hanson Robinson, Sarah G. Begley (1983); Christine Stansell, City of Women: Sex and Class in New York, 1789–1860 (1986); Anthony F. C. Wallace, Rockdale: The Growth of an American Village in the Early Industrial Revolution (1978); David Zonderman, Aspirations and Anxieties: New England Workers and the Mechanized Factory System, 1815–1850 (1992).

10

A New Economy and a New American Family

Steven Mintz and Susan Kellogg

In the half-century following the American Revolution another significant transformation in American life took place: a new American family came into being. During the colonial era, when the vast majority of Americans earned their livings from farming, the family was a "comprehensive" institution with a wide variety of responsibilities. It not only raised children but was responsible for their education. The colonial family was an economic institution as well: men, women, and children did the planting, harvesting, and most other work necessary to sustain its members. Very few individuals worked for wages or did steady labor beyond the boundaries of the family farm. The family was also a welfare institution: it had primary responsibility for taking care of the sick and the aged. And as we saw in Chapter 3, for most colonists it was a patriarchal institution: fathers and husbands were expected to exert final authority in family matters.

As Steven Mintz and Susan Kellogg point out in the next essay, by the mid-nineteenth century the increasingly urban and industrial texture of American society helped create a new American family. It had four prominent features that made it very different from the traditional family. First, the new family lived in or near cities. It was part of the gradual shift from countryside to city and from family farming to wage labor described by Barbara Tucker in Chapter 9. Instead of supervising the labor and lives of his wife and children, the father in this setting left the household and went off to work. If he was middle class, he might work in the banks, publishing houses, and other commercial establishments that blossomed in the city; if he was working class, he left each morning for the factories, butcher shops, and other sites of manual labor. But

This lithograph is titled "The Good Husband: The Fruits of Temperance and Industry." Note the husband is leaving for work (his hat lies on the sofa to the right), while his wife is dressed for, and engaged in, what Mintz and Kellogg describe as "middle-class domesticity." How does the illustration portray issues raised in Chapter 10?

the point is he left the home, leaving his wife in charge of the day-to-day management of the household and of raising their children. This is a major reason patriarchy declined as an ideology during this time. Although men continued to monopolize political and economic power in American society, control of the household increasingly shifted to women.

This led to a second and related new feature of the family. Images of women and men became divided into starkly separate spheres. The ideal breadwinner-husband not only worked outside the home, but was characterized by a tough-minded masculinity suited to the often ruthless worlds of political and economic competition. His wife, by contrast, was seen as innately sensitive, morally upright and, therefore, not able to survive in the competitive jungle beyond the home. Women, then, were destined to be wives, mothers, and homemakers. Their lives were supposed to revolve around making the home a tranquil, loving refuge for their husbands and children. The idea that women home and family (private life) was a haven from the slings and arrows of society (the public sphere) carried an implicit message about American society. It was as though Americans had divided their world in two: the private one of love, nurture, and trust and the public one of impersonal, no-holds-barred competition for money, power, and status.

This new family—called by some the "democratic" or "companionate" family (and, ultimately, the "Victorian" family of the nineteenth century)—had a third quality, one that made it similar to today's middle-class family. It was child-centered and dedicated to the nurturing, education, and upward mobility of its children. Instead of sending their children to work at an early age, as poor and working-class families would continue to do well into the twentieth century, the middle class sent them to school. The principal social role of the new middle-class family, by sharp contrast with the traditional family, was essentially reduced to a single function: raising children—and not only raising children, but focusing on their development in a manner that would ensure their success in school and in future careers. This desire to focus on children (along with the fact that urban families did not need children to provide labor, as farming families did) led urban, middle-class families to practice birth control.

A final characteristic of the new family was that it placed a premium on love and romance. Now a woman and man were supposed to "fall" in love before considering marriage. This was also in sharp contrast to traditional marriages where love, if it came at all, developed after marriage.

It is important to keep in mind that the Victorian family first appeared among the urban middle class in the northeastern part of the nation. Over time, its values would be idealized as the model of family life in America. But it was never the only model. Nevertheless, it met the needs of those who lived within the nation's rapidly changing economic and demographic landscape.

Source: Steven Mintz and Susan Kellogg, *Domestic Revolutions: A Social History of American Family Life* (New York: Free Press, 1988), pp. 44–47, 49–58, 60–64.

During the seventeenth century, the family had been seen as the foundation of the social order and the center of institutional life. It was "a little church," "a little commonwealth," "a school," the cornerstone of church and state and a microcosm of the larger society. This conception of the family reflected the fact that colonial conditions had broadened the family's functions and responsibilities. Not only was the colonial family responsible for the care of children, it was also the basic unit of economic production, the center of religious observance, and the institution charged with primary responsibility for education and for the care of the ill and the elderly.

By the beginning of the nineteenth century, a radically new definition of the family had emerged. Instead of being viewed as an integral component of the network of public institutions, the family was beginning to be seen as a private retreat. The term "family" generally referred not to the household or kin group but to the smaller and more isolated nuclear, or conjugal, family—the unit made up of the father, mother, and their children. It was a place for virtues and emotions threatened by the aggressive and competitive spirit of commerce, a place where women and children were secure and where men could escape from the stresses of business and recover their humanity.

The family, which seventeenth-century colonists believed to be governed by the same principles of hierarchy and subordination as the community at large, was, according to a flood of early-nineteenth-century books and articles celebrating the sanctity of hearth and home, governed by values fundamentally different from those that held sway in the outside world. The values of independence, self-reliance, and ambition were appropriate for the marketplace and government, but within the home, a wholly different set of values reigned supreme: love, mutuality, companionship, selflessness, sacrifice, and self-denial. No longer a microcosm of the larger society, the family was now a counterweight to acquisitive values and a refuge from materialistic corruptions.

The new attitude toward the family was a reflection of a more general shift in sensibility that sentimentalized the home as a bastion of harmony and higher moral and spiritual values. It was also a reaction to the nation's rapid material and geographic expansion, which led men and women to place a high premium upon the family, which worked for order and cohesion amidst vast social and economic change. An increasingly commercial and market-oriented economy demanded a new work discipline that required less emotionality on the job and more impersonal relations with other workers or customers. The home became the primary arena for feelings of affection, vulnerability, and belonging. . . . By the end of the eighteenth century and the beginning of the nineteenth, the American family had been transformed from a public institution whose functions were primarily economic into one whose major role was to rear children and provide emotional support for its members.

The roots of the transformation that had taken place in the American family lay in enlightened philosophical, religious, political, and economic ideas about the rights of the individual. In the years just before the American Revolution, a flood of advice books, philosophical treatises, and works of fiction helped to popularize revolutionary new ideas about child rearing and the family. . . . The burgeoning literature on the family explicitly rejected the older conception of marriage as an economic transaction between two families based on property considerations in favor of marriage as an emotional bond between two individuals. As such, neither parental permission nor parental approval were prerequisites for a happy marriage. Rather than choosing spouses on economic grounds, young people were told to select their marriage partners on the more secure basis of love and compatibility. In a survey of all extant colonial magazines published during the thirty years preceding the Revolution, one issue out of four contained at least one reference to "romantic love" as the proper basis of marriage; during the next twenty years, the number of references to romantic love would triple. Affection, compatibility, and reciprocated love, readers were told, were the only lasting adhesives that would bind spouses together. Personal happiness, not wealth or a desire to please parents, should be the primary motive behind the decision to marry. . . .

Within marriage the older ideals of patriarchal authority and strict wifely obedience were replaced by new ideals of "mutual esteem, mutual friendship, mutual confidence." According to one popular English guide published in 1762, in an ideal marriage, husbands regarded their wives not as "domestic drudges, or the slaves of our pleasures, but as our companions and equals." This shift to a new companionate conception of marriage was accompanied by an open recognition that personal happiness was a primary goal of marriage and a union's success or failure should be judged by its ability to provide love. It was a commonplace of the eighteenth-century novel that the choice of a spouse should be based exclusively on mutual affection and that loveless marriages lacked legitimacy. . . . It needs to be stressed that the new ideal of marriage did not imply sexual equality or a blurring of gender boundaries. The new companionate ideal of marriage was based on the idea that husbands and wives were interdependent partners, joined in a "reciprocal union of interest."

A new attitude toward children was an essential element in the emerging mid-eighteenth-century conception of the family. Childhood was depicted as a stage in the life cycle, and the child was described as a special being with distinctive needs and impulses. Drawing on [John] Locke's view of the child as a *tabula rasa*, or "blank slate" which could be imprinted in an infinite variety of ways, and on [Jean-Jacques] Rousseau's conception of children as naturally social and affectionate, novelists and child-rearing experts told their readers that the primary object of child rearing was not to instill submission to authority but to develop a child's conscience and self-government. Earlier in time, community leaders had held that the primary task of parenthood was to restrain children and make these innately sinful creatures obedient to external authority. Increasingly, however, parents were told that self-government was a necessity. . . . Childhood, previously conceived as a period of submission to authority, was increasingly viewed as a period of growth, development, and preparation for adulthood. . . .

The early nineteenth-century spread of a new conception of the family as a private and protected place was closely tied to a broad process of social and economic change that transformed the economic functions of the family. This economic process is usually termed "industrialization," but in fact, changes in the family's economic roles were already under way several decades before the significant growth of factories. This process would eventually deprive married women of earlier "productive" roles and transform them into housewives, prolong the length of childhood and produce a new stage of youth called "adolescence," and create the demographic transition through which families began to reduce their birthrates.

Throughout the seventeenth and eighteenth centuries, more than 90 percent of the population lived on farms, and most households were largely self-sufficient. Craftsmen with specialized skills produced the small number of items difficult to make at home, such as hats, iron implements, men's clothing, saddles, and shoes, but most other necessities were produced in the home. Families, sometimes assisted by neighbors, erected their own houses, produced their own food, made their own furniture, dipped their own candles, tanned their own leather, spun their own wool, manufactured their own cloth, and sewed their own garments, but not men's. Even in the Chesapeake and Southern colonies, where from an early date many farms and plantations produced such cash crops as indigo and tobacco, most households were largely self-sufficient in the production of food and clothing.

Inside the home, the husband, the wife, and their older children were all expected to play important productive roles. Typically a father and his elder sons took charge of the fields, while a wife and her daughters took care of the dairy cows, the poultry, and spinning, knitting, weaving, and fabricating cloth. The wives of urban craftsmen might also manage the shop, keep accounts, and supervise apprentices. Because production was integrated with familial activity, servants, apprentices, and paid laborers usually lived in their master's house.

The expansion of a market-oriented economy during the eighteenth century reinforced the older conception of the family as a cooperative economic enterprise. The need for a cash income led many households to participate in various "putting out" systems of production. Urban merchants and village storekeepers supplied individual households with the raw materials to make such articles as thread, cloth, textiles, beer, cigars, and shoes. A wife and her older children might supplement the family budget by spinning yarn, making lace, sewing dresses, or setting up a tavern or inn in their home. Under these circumstances, married women and children had clearly defined economic functions and made a readily measurable contribution to the family economy.

During the first decades of the nineteenth century, however, the family as a largely self-sufficient economic unit began to disappear. Instead of producing most of the items necessary for subsistence, a growing number of farm families began to specialize in the production of grain or cotton and use the cash proceeds they obtained from the sale of crops to buy necessities. Especially in the Northeast, fewer families produced their own food, cut their own clothing, or made their own candles and soap. Hand stitching of garments or shoes at home was replaced by factory production using power looms and sewing machines. Economic specialization began to extinguish the domestic industries that had employed large numbers of married women and children. . . .

By the middle of the nineteenth-century, the older pattern in which husbands, wives, and children worked together as participants in a common economic enterprise had been replaced by a new domestic division of labor. The middle-class husband was expected to be the breadwinner for the family. Instead of participating in domestic industries, the middle-class wife was expected to devote herself fulltime to keeping house and raising children. Psychologically the daily lives of men and women became more separate and specialized. For a growing number of men the place of work shifted

from the farm or household to counting houses, mills, factories, shops, and offices, where work was defined by wages and a clearly demarcated working
day. Women's work, in contrast, was unpaid, unsupervised, and task-oriented.
It took place in a segregated sphere of domesticity, which became dissociated
from the masculine, more literally productive world of income-earning work.
As a result, work and family life came to be viewed as two distinct and separate
endeavors.

The displacement of economic partnership from the matrix of family
life contributed to a fundamental demographic change: a marked lowering
of the birthrate. Before 1800 marriage was followed by a repeated cycle of
pregnancy and childbirth. A woman might bear her first child at the age of
twenty-three and continue to bear children at two-year intervals until she
was forty-two. This twenty-year span of childbearing consumed more than
half of a woman's married life, since a typical husband died at the age of
forty-six. A woman devoted most of the years of her marriage to productive
labor and to bearing or rearing children. As a new child arrived, older children were often fostered out as servants or apprentices or sent out on their
own on a seasonal basis to work as hired laborers or to attend school.
Between 1800 and 1860, a drastically different pattern of family life gradually emerged. By the middle of the nineteenth century, women were bearing
fewer children and lengthening the interval between births by birth control.
Instead of bearing seven or eight children, most women were having five or
six. By the end of the century, women had further reduced the number of
children born to three or four, spaced them closer together, and ceased childbearing at earlier ages. At the same time, older children were staying at
home with their parents longer. Increasingly, child rearing, not childbearing,
became the most time-consuming aspect of a woman's life.

The gradual imposition of limits on the birthrate is one of the defining
characteristics of the "democratic" family that emerged in early nineteenth-
century America. During the seventeenth and eighteenth centuries, a typical white woman bore seven children, one or two more than her West
European counterpart. By the late eighteenth century, before a comparable
decline began in most Western European countries, some groups, like the
Pennsylvanian Quaker, were already making conscious and effective efforts
at contraception. In all parts of the United States, fertility had begun a sustained decline by 1810, and by the end of the century, birthrates had been
cut in half.

The sharp decline in birthrates is a phenomenon easier to describe than
to explain. The drop in fertility was not the result of sudden improvements
in contraceptive devices. The basic birth control techniques used before the
Civil War—such as coitus interruptus (withdrawal), douching, and
condoms—had been known about in earlier times but had previously been
employed haphazardly and ineffectively. Nor was the imposition of limits
on the birthrate a result of urbanization. Although fertility fell earliest and
most rapidly in the urban areas of the Northeast, the decline in fertility

occurred in all parts of the country—in rural as well as urban areas and in the South and West as well as the Northeast.

In part the reduction in fertility reflected the growing realization among parents that in an increasingly commercial and industrial society, children were no longer economic assets who could be productively employed in household industries or bound out as apprentices or servants. Instead children required significant investment in the form of education to prepare them for respectable careers and marriages. The emergence of a self-conscious middle class concerned about social mobility and maintaining an acceptable standard of living encouraged new limits on family size.

The shrinking size of families was not merely a matter of economics; it also related to a more enlightened view of women and children. The drop in fertility reflected the changing relationship between husbands and wives and the growing concern with child development. So long as women were regarded essentially as chattel and child rearing simply as a process through which children were taught to submit to authority, there was little impetus to reduce the number of births. But when husbands took an increasing interest in their wives' welfare and parents showed increasing concern about forming their children's character and drawing out their latent abilities and potentialities, a reduction in fertility seemed not only desirable but essential. Smaller families permitted parents to improve the quality of their child's upbringing by allowing them to invest more time and energy as well as more financial resources in each child.

By 1831 . . . demographic, cultural, and economic changes had converged to produce a new configuration of roles within the middle-class family.

During the late-eighteenth and early-nineteenth centuries, roles within the family were sharply redefined to meet the radically altered requirements of the workplace. The model husband and father was solely responsible for earning the family's livelihood; he was expected to earn the income that supported the family and to provide for his wife and children after his death. The ideal wife and mother devoted her life exclusively to domestic tasks; she was expected to run an efficient household, provide a cultured atmosphere within the home, rear moral sons and daughters, display social grace on public occasions, and offer her husband emotional support. And children, particularly in urban, middle-class homes, were expected to be dutiful dependents who were to devote their childhood and adolescence to learning the skills necessary for the demands of adulthood.

Alexis de Tocqueville [a French student of American life who visited the United States in the early 1930s] likened the differentiation of roles within the family to the broader process of specialization and differentiation taking place in the economy as a whole. In the economic sphere, specialization maximized efficiency and productivity. In the domestic sphere, role differentiation also served the function of efficiency; each family member had a proper "place" that was appropriate to his or her age and gender and contributed in his or her own way to the family's effective functioning.

The father earned income outside the family, the wife ran the domestic sphere, and children might help around the house or supplement the family's income by taking on odd jobs. As in a factory, the roles assigned to each family member were interdependent, distinct but complementary.

Today many people believe that the division of roles in the nineteenth-century family represents an ideal. But even in the nineteenth century, the family roles of father, mother, and child were already characterized by a series of latent tensions. Although the democratic family was idealized as a place of peace and a haven from the strains of modern life, it was not immune to internal stress and conflict. From its inception in the latter part of the eighteenth century, the family's roles were characterized by a series of underlying contradictions.

In sharp contrast with the contemporary image of the early-nineteenth-century father as the patriarchal head of his household, nineteenth-century observers emphasized the relative weakness of paternal authority in America. Foreign travelers and native commentators shared the opinion that the paternal role was characterized by an informality and permissiveness unknown in contemporary Europe or America itself earlier in time.

During the seventeenth century, it had been an almost unquestioned premise that the father, as head of his household, had a right to expect respect and obedience from his wife and children. A father's authority over his family, servants, and apprentices was simply one link in the great chain of being, the line of authority descending from God. Fatherhood was associated with sovereignty. The centrality of the father's position within the colonial household was reflected in child-rearing manuals, which—up until the middle of the eighteenth century—were addressed to fathers and not to mothers, and also in family portraits, which, prior to 1775, uniformly showed the father standing above his seated family.

By the middle of the nineteenth century, the scope of the father's authority had, to a limited degree, been constricted—a transition clearly evident in art, with family portraits, for the first time, showing all members of the family members on the same plane, and in child-rearing manuals, which began to be addressed to mothers, not to fathers. In the realm of law, the father's prerogatives began to be restricted as well. As early as the 1820s, married women began to gain legal control over their own personal property and earnings, and the right to enter into legal contracts and to bring lawsuits. A number of states gave courts discretion to grant mothers custody of younger children. Fathers increasingly were expected to acquiesce in the early independence of their sons, and child-rearing experts openly criticized those who persisted in meddling in their children's lives after they had grown up.

The ability of the father to transmit his "status position" to his children declined. By the early nineteenth century, families were finding it increasingly difficult to pass on their status by bequeathing land or a family craft to their offspring. The practice of partible inheritance, in which the paternal estate was divided into equal portions for all the children, made it difficult for farm or artisan families to pass on farms or family shops over time. An increase in opportunities for non-agricultural work, and the replacement of land as a primary medium of value by more portable forms of capital, further reduced the dependence of grown sons upon their parents.

As the father's economic role changed, a new set of images of fatherhood began to emerge. Instead of referring to a father's sovereign right to rule his household, the late-eighteenth- and early-nineteenth-century literature on the family spoke about a father's paternal duties. Foremost among these was responsibility for his family's economic well-being. But a father was expected to be more than an economic provider. He also had a duty to provide love and affection to his wife and moral and religious training to his children, and he had ultimate responsibility for putting down disobedience or disrespect on the part of his offspring. The father's authority, which had once rested on control of land and craft skills, had become increasingly symbolic. Where the mother represented nurturance, selflessness, and devotion to others, the father was the symbol of public and external conceptions of authority. He was referred to as a "moral force" or a "governor" because his role was to prepare a child for a life of disciplined independence.

The early nineteenth century witnessed a radical redefinition of women's roles. A profusion of women's magazines, novels, poems, and sermons glorified the American woman as purer than man, more given to sacrifice and service to others, and untainted by the competitive struggle for wealth and power. This set of ideas, known as the "cult of true womanhood," extolled the American wife and mother as the personification of four primary virtues: piety, submissiveness, purity, and domesticity. A torrent of articles with titles such as "Woman, Man's Best Friend" and "The Wife, Source of Comfort and Spring of Joy" depicted women as inherently more virtuous and less selfish than men. This conception of womanhood was sharply at odds with the image that had held sway earlier. Well into the eighteenth century, womanhood was associated with deviousness, sexual voraciousness, emotional inconstancy, and physical and intellectual inferiority. Now, in a sudden reversal of opinion, there was a growing consensus that only women, through their uplifting influence over the home and children, could be a source of moral values and counterforce to commercialism and self-interest. . . .

At the same time, during the first decade of the nineteenth-century, unmarried women between the ages of fourteen and twenty-seven received unprecedented opportunities to work outside the home as schoolteachers and as mill girls or to remain at home in their parents' increasingly affluent households. A growing number of women achieved leadership positions organizing religious revivals, engaging in missionary work, establishing orphanages and almshouses, and editing religious publications. Many middle-class women achieved a public voice in such reform movements as temperance and antislavery and succeeded in communicating with a wider public as journalists and authors. Rising living standards, increased access to education, and unprecedented opportunities to work outside the home increased women's expectations for self-fulfillment and contributed to a new outlook on marriage.

Tocqueville and other European commentators were struck by a seeming paradox in American women's lives: Compared to their European counterparts, young American women experienced a high degree of independence and freedom. . . . But the lives of American wives seemed more restricted. Their daily lives were largely circumscribed "within the narrow circle of domestic interests and duties" beyond which they were forbidden to step. European travelers were struck by the rigid social division between married men and women; they noted, for example, that at social gatherings women were compelled by public opinion to separate from men after dinner.

This discrepancy between the relative independence of girlhood and the "extreme dependence" and heavy duties of wifehood would exert a direct effect on women's attitudes toward marriage. During the colonial period, marriage was regarded as a social obligation and an economic necessity, and few women or men failed to marry. But beginning in the mid-eighteenth century, the number of unmarried men and women increased and a growing number of women elected to remain single. Marriage became a far more deliberate act than it had been in the past. It was an enormous responsibility. As Catherine Beecher, an early-nineteenth-century educator and author of the nation's most popular books on household management put it, "the success of democratic institutions" depended "upon the intellectual and moral character of the mass of people," and "the formation of the moral and intellectual character of the young is committed mainly to the female hand. The mother forms the character of the future man . . . the wife sways the heart, whose energies may turn for good or for evil the destinies of a nation."

By 1830 a new conception of childhood began to emerge. . . . As the economic role of children began to shift from producer to consumer, childhood began to be viewed as a distinct stage of growth and development in which a young person was prepared for eventual emergence into adulthood. Techniques of child rearing changed too. There was a growing consensus that the object of child rearing was not to break a child's will through intense moral or physical pressure but to shape his or her character in preparation for the temptations of life. The primary purpose of child rearing became the internalization of moral prohibitions, behavioral standards, and a capacity for self-government that would prepare a child for the outside world. According to innumerable guidebooks, tracts, and domestic novels dealing with the "art and responsibility of family government," the formation of character was best achieved not through physical punishment or rigorous instruction in moral and religious precepts, but by emotional nurture, parental love, and the force of parental example. Obedience remained a primary goal, but a growing number of experts believed that techniques designed to provoke guilt, such as confining children to their rooms, withholding love, or expressing parental disapproval, would be more effective in securing obedience than would physical punishment. . . .

According to a growing number of writers, child rearing was a task for which women were uniquely suited. A reason for the shift from father to mother as primary parent was the belief that children were more effectively governed by persuasion than coercion and by rewards than by punishments (a belief that ties in with the growing conviction among laissez faire economists that laborers could be encouraged to work harder by rewarding rather than by punishing them). Women were perceived as more likely than men to entice obedience from their offspring. Physical discipline or corporal punishment, the province of fathers, was increasingly viewed as producing at best outward conformity; at worst it provoked obstinacy or a sense of bitterness. But persuasion held out the hope of bringing about a basic change in a child's character. The emphasis placed on moral influence tended to enhance the maternal role in child rearing, since mothers were believed to have a special talent for instilling self-control. Whereas paternal authority was associated with fore and fear, female influence connoted love and affection.

By the middle of the nineteenth century, the realities of a middle-class upbringing differed dramatically from the pattern prevalent half a century before. Instead of shifting back and forth between their parents' home and work experiences as members of other households, a growing proportion of children were continuing to live with their parents into their late teens and twenties. One justification for this new practice of keeping children at home longer in life was the growing belief that "adolescence" (previously a rarely used term) was a particularly unsettled phase of life during which children were deeply in need of parental protection and supervision. Drawing on (Jean-Jacques) Rousseau, a growing number of educators and advice writers argued that the years surrounding puberty were a period of rapid physical growth and moral, sexual, and psychological upheaval during which youngsters were particularly vulnerable to the corruptions and temptations of the adult world. This was no time to send youngsters out on their own. As one expert put it, "Early departure from the homestead is a moral crisis that many of our youth do not show themselves able to meet. It comes at a tender age, when judgment is weakest and passion and impulse strongest.". . .

Banners, barricades, and bayonets are often thought of as the stuff of revolutions, but sometimes the most important revolutions take place more quietly—and so successfully that when they are over, few even realize that they ever took place. Such was the transformation that took place in American family life between 1770 and 1830—as profound and far-reaching as the political revolution then reshaping American politics. This period witnessed the emergence of new patterns of marriage, based primarily on companionship and affection; a new division of domestic roles that assigned the wife to full-time care for the children and to maintain the home; a new conception of childhood that looked to children not as small adults but as special creatures who needed attention, love, and time to mature; and a growing acceptance of birth control in order to produce fewer children.

In many respects the new patterns of middle-class family life . . . represented a clear advance over family life in the past. A marked decline in childhood and adulthood mortality meant that family life was much less likely to be disrupted by the premature death of a child or a parent. Lower birthrates meant that parents were able to invest more material resources and emotional energies in their offspring. Rising living standards and a shrinking family size allowed many middle-class women to raise their expectations for self-fulfillment.

There can also be little doubt that the new patterns of family life were well adapted to the changing conditions of society. The inward-turning, child-centered, middle-class family was well matched to the object of teaching children the complex tasks demanded by an increasingly urban and commercial society. Within the home, parents would instill skills that children would need as adults: qualities of independence and self-direction, a capacity for self-discipline, an ability to suppress instinctual desires, and sensitivity to the needs and feelings of others. The sharp separation of the husband's and wife's roles fitted well with the process of economic specialization that was separating "domestic" and "productive" tasks and taking production and the father out of the home. Finally, this new style of family was well suited to providing men with an emotional haven from the world of work.

And yet, for all its many benefits, this new style of family life also involved certain costs. The patterns of family life that began to appear in the late eighteenth century often proved in practice to be a source of conflict and personal unhappiness. One underlying source of strain lay in the disparity between women's rising expectations for self-fulfillment and the isolation of married women within a separate domestic sphere. Young women were raised in a society that placed a high value on independence. Growing numbers of women attended school, earned independent incomes as mill girls, teachers, and household servants, and were allowed to manage courtship largely free of parental interference. On marriage, however, a woman was expected to "sacrifice . . . her pleasures to her duties" and derive her deepest satisfactions from homemaking and childbearing and rearing. The latent contradiction between woman's preparation for self-fulfillment and her role as the family's key nurturing figure often resulted in enormous personal tension, sometimes manifested in the classic nineteenth-century neurosis of hysteria.

Another source of tension derived from the increasing isolation of the family. By the early nineteenth century, the American family had been deprived of a range of traditional economic, social, and ideological supports. The family had lost its economic autonomy and was increasingly dependent on the vagaries of the marketplace. Parental authority had lost the reinforcement of local churches and courts and a system of apprenticeship. The middle-class family existed in a society that rewarded independence and self-reliance and tended to isolate domestic ideals—deference, obedience, and loyalty—from broader economic and political values. Yet, at the very time that the family had been detached from traditional economic roles and external supports, it had acquired awesome new emotional and psychological responsibilities. It was charged with primary responsibility for properly rearing children and providing its members with emotional sustenance. Even before the Civil War, men and women of diverse persuasions agreed that the family should be a source of affection, nurturance, and companionship. Already the family was beginning to acquire an overload of expectations it often proved incapable of meeting—a failure apparent in the gradually rising divorce rates.

One more source of stress grew out of the prolongation of childhood dependence. Middle-class children left home, married, and entered the professions at later stages than their eighteenth-century counterparts. The erosion of traditional productive roles for young people within the household further sharpened the split between childhood and adulthood. It exacerbated the difficulties children faced in asserting independence in the home and compounded the difficulties they faced in transforming childhood emotional bonds into acceptable adult forms. Prolonged residence with parents provided the basis for a previously unimaginable degree of emotional closeness between children and parents, but it also increased dependence and resentment.

Questions for Discussion

1. Describe the social and economic changes that created the modern family. How did it affect men? Women?
2. Why did the family become a more private and intimate place as American society became more impersonal and competitive?
3. Why did patriarchy decline as the new family appeared? Did the decline of patriarchy inevitably lead to enhanced status for women?
4. How did the modern family lead to what the authors call a "new conception of childhood"?
5. In your opinion, on balance, was the new family an improvement over the traditional one?

For Further Reading

Norma Basch, *Framing American Divorce: From the Revolutionary Generation to the Victorians* (1999); Nancy Cott, *The Bonds of Womanhood: "Women's Sphere" in New England, 1780–1835* (1977), *Public Vows: A History of Marriage and the Nation* (2000); Carl Degler, *At Odds: Women and the Family in America from the Revolution to the Present* (1980); Stephen Frank, *Life with Father: Parenthood and Masculinity in the Nineteenth-Century American North* (1998); Robert Griswold, *Family and Divorce in California, 1850–1890: Victorian Illusions and Everyday Realities* (1982); Michael Grossberg,

Governing the Hearth: Law and Family in Nineteenth-Century America (1985); Hendrik Hartog, *Man and Wife in America: A History* (2000); Sylvia Hoffert, *Private Matters: American Attitudes Toward Childrearing and Infant Nurture in the Urban North, 1800–1860* (1989); Anya Jabour, *Marriage in the Early Republic: Elizabeth and William Wirth and the Companionate Ideal* (1998); Jan Lewis, *The Pursuit of Happiness: Family and Values in Jefferson's Virginia* (1983); Sally McMillen, *Motherhood in the Old South: Pregnancy, Childbirth and Infant Rearing* (1990); Ellen Rothman, *Hands and Hearts: A History of Courtship in America* (1984); E. Anthony Rotundo, *American Manhood: Transformations in Masculinity from the Revolution to the Modern Era* (1993); Mary Ryan, *Cradle of the Middle Class: The Family in Oneida County, New York, 1790–1865* (1981); Carroll Smith-Rosenberg, *Disorderly Conduct: Vision of Gender in Victorian America* (1985); Peter Sterns, *Anxious Parents: A History of Modern American Childrearing* (2003); Barbara Welter, *Dimity Convictions: The American Woman in the Nineteenth Century* (1976).

Irish Immigrant Women and Their Men in New York City

Carol Groneman

The extraordinary growth of its economy, an inadequate supply of labor, and the private decision of many families to have fewer children made the United States a magnet for immigrants in search of opportunity. From the 1830s through the 1850s, 4.5 million immigrants arrived on American shores. And for the first time in the country's history, the majority of them were not English-speaking Protestants from Britain. About 1 million of them came from Germany. But by far the greatest number of immigrants came from British-dominated Ireland. The Irish accounted for approximately 40 percent of immigrants during this period. Many spoke their native Irish language of Gaelic rather than English; the vast majority of them were Catholic, not Protestant.

The largest surge of immigration from Ireland occurred between 1845 and 1855, when 1.5 million Irish landed in America. They were fleeing the Great Famine. A fungus—*Phytophthora infestans*—destroyed the potato crop that was the main source of nutrition for the majority of Ireland's 8.5 million people. But the fungus was not the sole source of the starvation and hunger-related diseases that killed between 1 and 2 million people. Absentee British landlords, seeking greater profits from their holdings in Ireland, were partly responsible. They consolidated their farmlands, shifting from grain production to more profitable livestock grazing. In the process, they not only forced hundreds of thousands of Irish tenant farmers onto smaller plots of land (or evicted them altogether), but made them more dependent on the potato

The first and second frames of this mid-nineteenth-century cartoon show an Irishman (in top hat on the left) and a Chinese man devouring "Uncle Sam." What does the third frame show? Why would many Americans of the time find it the most disturbing consequence of immigration?

for nourishment. (More potatoes could be harvested per acre than any other crop grown in Ireland.) Policies of the English government, especially those requiring the export of Irish grains and livestock to British markets, were also responsible for the famine, which further increased the tragic dependence of the Irish on the potato. In 1845 the potato fungus struck, and the starvation began. The tragedy would continue for a decade. The British government's aid to the Irish, whom the English despised for ethnic and religious reasons, was equal parts grudging and inadequate.

Although most of the Irish immigrants were peasants from rural areas, the majority of them congregated in America's cities. Between 1840 and 1860, they helped swell the urban population. For example, during those years, New York City's population nearly tripled, from 312,000 to 813,000; Boston's population increased from 93,000 to 177,000. Largely unskilled, the Irish took the lowest paid, most dangerous jobs. And they lived in dilapidated, crime-ridden, garbage-strewn, congested neighborhoods, such as the notorious

Five Points district on the Lower East Side of Manhattan. Neither, to say the least, were the Irish welcomed by America's Protestant majority, many of whom were passionately anti-Catholic. In Boston, Philadelphia, and New York, rioting Protestants burned Irish schools and churches.

Yet, as Carol Groneman emphasizes in the following essay, it is important to keep in mind that the Irish were not passive victims of poverty and prejudice. There was another side to the story. Like scores of immigrant groups before and since, the Irish came to America hungry, poor, and desperate—but they also came with powerful cultural and family values. Those values sustained and nourished them while they struggled to find a place in their new homeland. And some of those traditions and values would gradually become part of the American social fabric, changing and enriching the nation's culture.

Groneman's article is important because she shows that the history of American immigration is a two-way street. America changes immigrants and their values, but immigrants change America and its values as well.

Source: Carol Groneman, "Working-Class Immigrant Women in Mid-Nineteenth-Century New York: The Irish Woman's Experience," *Journal of Urban History* 4, no. 3 (May 1978), 255–274.

The beginnings of mass immigration in the pre-Civil War decade would profoundly affect both American society and the men and women who came here. The transition from a pre-modern to an industrializing nation in this and later decades coincided with the entrance of predominantly pre-industrial agrarian peoples of diverse European backgrounds. While physically "uprooted," these immigrants brought with them distinct patterns of behavior, of work, family, and leisure which continued to mold their responses and adaptations to the circumstances of their new life. . . .

Focusing on Irish women's experiences in pre-Civil War New York City, we will look in more detail at some of these cultural continuities— namely work, leisure patterns, and family life—which added coherence to their lives in an alien and changing world.

Let us look at the Irish lassie in mid-nineteenth-century New York, at least as she was viewed by an upper-class contemporary: the attire of "Lize," the wife or sweetheart of a Bowery b'hoy [a young, flamboyant, working-class male],

> Was a cheap but exaggerated copy of the prevailing Broadway mode; her skirt was shorter and fuller, bodice longer and lower; hat more gaudily trimmed; handkerchief more ample and flauntingly carried; corkscrew curls thinner, longer and stiffer; her gait and swing were studied imitations of her lord and master.

Who were these Irish young women who came here in such great numbers during this period? Why had they come? What were their expectations?

How did their past experiences affect the choices they made both in Ireland and in America?

The story begins not here but in Ireland. The backdrop for the tragedy of rural Ireland was painted in the late eighteenth and early nineteenth centuries when several factors converged: increased use of land for tillage rather than pasture because of higher grain prices, a consequent breakup of large pastures into small farms, an increased reliance by the peasants on the potato as the only source of food, the decline of domestic industries, and a phenomenal growth in population. Because there was simply no other way to feed one's family in rural Ireland for most of the peasantry, land on which to grow potatoes was an absolute necessity. Holdings had been increasingly subdivided over generations so that by 1841 the majority of the rural population held, but did not own, fewer than five acres. Contemporary reports indicated that many of these small holders lived in wretched poverty, existing mainly on potatoes, and desperately in need of work to pay their rent. Seasonal migration to harvest crops in the English and Scottish countryside became traditional for many men and some women during this period.

The impulse toward permanent emigration to British Canada or America was already present in the early nineteenth century among the small farmers, weavers in the declining linen and wool industry, servant girls, and city workers in general who could save the money necessary for passage. The one million Irish who emigrated to the United States between 1815 and 1845 would provide the possibility for the much greater emigration following the Great Famine of 1846–1849. Even in this early emigration, and particularly after 1830, women formed a higher proportion of those leaving Ireland compared to migrants from other European countries, a trend that would continue throughout the nineteenth and early twentieth centuries. By 1845 one-half of the total emigrants were women, partly because laborers left in family groups, but also because a growing number of single young women emigrated.

This eagerness to leave their beloved country can be accounted for in several ways. Marriage in Ireland had continued to fall throughout this period. The subsistence level at which peasants lived encouraged them "to seek a partner to share their misery," for all a young couple needed to start life together was a tiny plot of land on which to grow potatoes and a mud hut which could be built with little difficulty. In a land where professional matchmaking was important only to a small class of peasants who owned land and had the money for a dowry for their daughters, most Irish girls had little hope that marriage would provide anything more than subsistence existence. As one young emigrant girl wrote to her parents from New York in 1850, "Oh how happy I feel . . . that it was not . . . destined for me to get married to some Loammum [lowly farmer] or another at home that after a few months he and I may be an Incumberance upon you or perhaps in the poor house."

The high proportion of female emigrants continued throughout the nineteenth and early twentieth centuries; in some years females even exceeded males. Robert E. Kennedy, in his demographic study of Ireland, has suggested that Irish women, relative to Irish men, had more to gain by emigrating. The freedom and independence promised by a paying job in a distant city was more attractive than the subordinate role of unpaid helper in her own family, he concluded, and convinced many young women to make the difficult break from home and family. Furthermore, young women were more certain of obtaining immediate employment and were particularly faithful in sending remittances to their families. It is possible that families, especially after the Famine, chose to send their daughters rather than their sons to the New World as the hope for insuring the family's future.

The work experience of women in an agricultural society like Ireland included the usual domestic chores connected with very small farms. As one Cork correspondent reported upon seeing a group of women preparing for departure to America, the women could not have been capable of anything more than "to churn, to feed pigs, work in dairies, or mind children." But his report was not completely accurate. Over one-fourth of the adult women in Ireland had some skill as spinners, weavers, seamstresses, and other cloth workers, predominantly in the cottage industries of the north and east of Ireland. As the woolen and cotton domestic industries declined in the early nineteenth century, some of these women migrated to Belfast and Dublin, to the industrializing cities of Scotland and England, or to the United States and Canada.

Approximately one-quarter of a million women (one-tenth of the adult female population) worked as domestic servants in the 1840s. These women came from laborers' or the very poorest cottiers' families. As one farmer's wife commented:

> I would be glad to get my little girl into a house where she could learn something and earn something; but sure, as for three or four pounds a year, she can earn that at home, and more, in the fields, at the wheel, the needle or the straw plait, and Mrs. Mullin's [the local gentry] food isn't much better than our own.

Domestic servants were relatively better off economically than those women who remained with their families since they received wages and lived in the houses of the gentry or substantial farmers. Even so, in the spring, when they received their wages and the emigrant ships left port, some took advantage of the possibility of going to America or Canada.

In general, women did not hire out as agricultural laborers, although approximately 8,000 migrated yearly in the early 1840s to Scotland and England for the harvest. Whole families immigrated to the industrializing towns and cities of Scotland and England. Some 60,000 Irish-born women lived in Scotland in the early 1840s, and the labor force in the Scottish cotton mills was composed chiefly of Irish girls. In England, Irish women could be found working in the mills, as domestic servants, as peddlers, hucksters, and lodging-house keepers.

Over half of the 300,000 adult women who emigrated from Ireland between 1851 and 1855 listed an occupation with British government officials. Approximately 10,000 indicated that they were spinners, weavers or other cloth workers; 22,000 had been domestic servants; and over 120,000 said they were agricultural workers. The latter figure was predominantly women who worked on their families' small plots of land, as well as the increasing number of women hiring out as agricultural laborers after the Famine. While most of these women would not work on farms in America, many of them would perform work somewhat similar to their work in Ireland as domestic servants, peddlers, or boarding-house keepers. Work in the textile mills of Belfast and Glasgow may have prepared some women for work in the textile mills of New England, but most of their experience as spinners and weavers in their family homes would not be comparable to the piece-work and sweating system of the Boston and New York City tenements.

Upon arrival in America, most immigrants sought out relatives or fellow country folk with whom to stay. A job had to be found within a few days because few women came with any surplus cash and most had families who were counting on their remittances. Irish women worked in a variety of occupations, including umbrella, paper box, and flower makers, book binders, printers, peddlers, store keepers, and in the needle trades, but the majority were domestic servants. Given the increasing demand for servants in expanding middle-class households and in the hotels and boarding-houses of the growing city, it is not surprising that Irish girls chose this kind of work. Over 25% of the Irish working population of the city were domestic servants, compared to less than 15% of Germans, Welsh, Scottish, French, and Swiss workers. I use the word "chose" cautiously because of the limited opportunities in other fields. However, factory work in the clothing industry of the city had been developing since the 1830s, and the amount of skill required would not have been prohibitive. But domestic service offered a greater possibility of saving the few dollars a month one earned because room and board were supplied in addition to the $4.00 to $8.00 per month wages. These few dollars were absolutely crucial as remittances to their families in Ireland, either to help pay the rent on the few acres of potatoes or to bring other members of the family to America. Out of the meager wages of servants and other Irish workers in the city, over $20 million was remitted to Ireland in the decade following the Famine.

About one-third of Irish women under 30 years of age worked in the needle trades. Some had probably learned the rudiment of the trade in Ireland, and the Irish tailor and tailoress teams in New York City were possibly the children of the Irish weavers and spinners of the early nineteenth century. The 1853 investigation by the New York *Tribune* vividly described the appalling conditions of the "Needlewomen of New York" and the shops which paid them about 8 cents to make a shirt. Since finishing three shirts was a hard day's labor, the *Tribune* estimated that a woman needle worker, taking into consideration the time expended to obtain and return the goods and other journeys to secure her pay, could conceivably receive about 50 cents for an entire week's labor. "Though some thousands of females in different callings—milliners, dressmakers, shop-assistants—make between $3.50 and $6.00 a week which could be considered a living wage," stated the *Tribune*, "there are hundreds of women tailoresses and seamstresses who have an average yearly income, if fully employed, of only $91." Obviously, needle trade workers paid this nonliving wage either had several members of their family working or turned to other means of support: help from friends and relatives, the very limited funds from charitable agencies, or prostitution.

Of the 2,000 prostitutes questioned by William Sanger in 1855, over one-third of them were Irish-born, almost half had been prostitutes for less than one year, about 40% were married or widowed, and almost half had children. Most listed their former occupation as domestic service or needle trades. As Sanger himself suggests, prostitutes were working women who moved into the trade when faced with periods of unemployment. "Those who follow an employment faced at intervals," he stated, "are mostly women whose trades are uncertain, and who are liable at certain seasons of the year to be without employment. Then real necessity forces them on the town until a return of business provides them with work." A prostitute put it more succinctly when asked why she followed the profession: "M. T. answered, 'I had no work, no money, and no home.'" S. F., a widow with three children, stated that she could earn only $2.00 weekly at cap making, but could not get steady employment even at those prices. One might assume, particularly since almost half had been prostitutes for less than one year, that the opportunity for other employment might find prostitutes moving out of the trade and returning to their former work. As Judith and Daniel Walkowitz have shown in their study of prostitution in nineteenth-century England, "[Prostitutes] were not dehumanized vagabonds. . . . They were very much part of a lower-class community, and their general social and economic profile did not differ significantly from that of the rest of the poor in those districts." A look at the most notorious slum in nineteenth-century America, New York City's predominantly Irish Five Points [on the Lower East Side], supports their conclusions.

One middle-class reporter believed than in the Five Points "nearly every house and cellar is a groggery below and a brothel above. . . . In the doors and windows may be seen, at any hour of the afternoon or evening, scores of sluttishly-dressed women, in whose faces drunkenness and debauchery have destroyed every vestige of humanity." A social and economic profile, however, indicates that single young women living alone or in groups, who might have been prostitutes, shared the streets of the Five Points with a variety of working-class families, mainly laborers, but including some artisans and the usual assortment of grocery/liquor stores, pawn shops, and old-clothing stores found in poor neighborhoods. Neither the age distribution, the marital status, nor the household and family composition of these women was peculiarly deviant compared to available statistics on the city and on other poor neighborhoods.

While the occupational experience of single young women can tell us much about that segment of the community, we must also look at the experiences of their married sisters. In a study of one mid-nineteenth-century immigrant community, New York City's Sixth Ward [the location of the Five Points], evidence from the census manuscripts indicates that almost one-half of Irish households had at least one other member of the household, most often working wives, contributing to the family income. The major occupation of these married women, one which has often been overlooked by historians relying on the compiled census statistic, was taking boarders into their households. Fully 25% of Sixth Ward married women supplemented family income in this manner.

It is interesting to speculate on the amount of possible income these women sacrificed by working in the home. The Sixth Ward factories, for example, paid an average of $5.50 per week to women workers. Certainly lack of skills might have had some influence on the limited number of married women working outside the home. Many industrial trades, however, were easily learned within a few weeks' apprenticeship. The lower wards also offered the greatest number of industrial jobs, and many single women worked in the local factories, hotels, and laundries. Thus, we might hypothesize that the work Sixth Ward married women performed reflected more than limited opportunities—namely, an element of conscious choice. Women may have chosen this particular occupation because it allowed them to continue to function in their role as housewife and mother while also contributing to the family's support.

This is not an insignificant suggestion. A considerable body of historical literature insists that immigration and the alienation of the large city led to disruption and breakdown of the family. The evidence from a poor working-class area like New York City's Sixth Ward is all the more revealing because its residents, many of whom had fled the Irish famine, would have been particularly vulnerable to the processes of family disintegration. These traditionally family-centered Irish peasant women adapted to the economic pressures of urban life by combining their economic activity with the functions of childrearing and housekeeping. That Sixth Ward married women engaged in the occupation of taking boarders would suggest that this was a central means of coping with the multiple demands placed upon immigrant women in America. Even when forced by necessity to work, they did so in ways which would reinforce, rather than disrupt, their traditional familial values.

The long hours of work in the 1850s consumed a major portion of the day, but what did these women, recently arrived from the Irish countryside, do during their free time? Life in the urban slum was lived mainly on the streets, to escape the cramped, uncomfortable tenements. On a warm June Saturday night in the 1850s, crowds gathered in and around the little triangular park, rather winningly called Paradise Square, in the heart of the Five

Points. Threading their way through the crowd in front of the notorious Old Brewery across from the park might be Mary O'Neill and her sister Margaret returning home to Mulberry Street from work as umbrella makers in a local factory. They would probably have changed to dresses reserved for the Saturday night promenade along the Bowery. The center of working-class night life, parts of the Five Points on a Saturday night must have resembled a county fair in their home villages.

On Centre Street they would have passed by the apple stands, quoit [ring] games, peddlers, weighing machines, lung testers, and other penny catchers going full tilt. The row of booths on each side of the street, the colorfully-dressed women busy making their purchases or chatting and laughing, and the hearty kiss given when people met all describe both a fair in Killala, County Mayo in the 1840s as well as the heart of the working-class district in urban America in the 1850s. . . .

A night on the town for the O'Neill [sisters] and their boyfriends would include a visit to a saloon like D. Brennan's on the park or to the oyster cellars of Canal Street where for 6 cents they would consume vast quantities of oysters and beer. This might be followed by a visit to the Bowery or Olympic Theaters to see "A Glance at New York," a play featuring the John Bunyan-like character, Mose, modeled after a New York City fireman. They would have shared their gallery seats with "butcher boys . . . the mechanic and his family, the boy in red flannel shirt sleeves, the chop woman, the sewing girl, the straw braider, the type rubber, the paper box and flower maker, with a liberal sprinkling of undercrust blacklegs [strike breakers] and fancy men." Foot-stomping, clapping, hissing, shouts of encouragement greeted the "blood and thunder plays"—audience participation was as much a part of the show as the performance on stage.

There was other entertainment: Kit Burn's Sportsmen's Hall, where the sons of rural Ireland watched waterfront rats being pitted against a terrier; variety acts in the concert saloons, some including women pugilists; or, for the more bizarre, McGlory's Armory Hall where waiter girls were joined by a bevy of lithe-limbed waiter boys, both outfitted in short skirts and high red boots.

The evening would end with a visit to Harry Hill's or one of the many dance halls in the neighborhood. A room about 25 feet square, its white-washed walls garnished with wooden benches, a bar at one end and a raised platform for the musicians, usually several fiddlers and a tambourine man, provided dancing room for about one-dozen couples. The corners of the room filled with onlookers, paying 10 cents for admission and 3 cents for a glass of whiskey, waiting for the chance to enter the smiling, foot-stomping throng. As Charles Dickens recorded in an 1840s visit to a Five Points dance hall,

> [as the couples take the floor] instantly the fiddler grins, and goes at it tooth and nail, there is new energy in the tambourine; new laughter in the dancers. Single shuffle, double shuffle, cut and cross-cut, snapping his fingers, rolling his eyes, turning in his

knees, presenting the backs of his legs in front, spinning about on his toes and heels like nothing but the man's fingers on the tambourine . . . having danced his partner off her feet, and himself, too, he finishes by leaping gloriously on the bar-counter, and calling for something to drink.

The "breakdowns" described in the Five Points dance halls sound much like the description of rural Irish weddings in the years before the Famine. "First single parties dance reels, jigs, and doubles . . . the male partner 'shows off,' and the best idea we can give of it," commented Mr. and Mrs. Hall on an Irish wedding party in 1841, "is that it consists in striking the ground very rapidly with the heal and toe, or with the toes of each foot alternatively. . . . A stranger, not hearing the music, and seeing only the dancer, would be sure to imagine he was killing a rat; nor would it be very safe to have this dance performed by a stout fellow in a frail loft." These young people had brought their dances and music with them to America.

Just as in Ireland, young single women in America had relatively more independence than married women. Care of children was completely in the hands of the mother, but more than that, Irish recreation tended to be segregated along sex lines, particularly after marriage. While all members of a family, in America as in Ireland, attended crucial family events such as weddings, christenings, and wakes, the everyday recreation, visiting bars, theaters, dance halls, or the races, tended to be male only or single males and their girlfriends. The traditional function of such customs as dances and saints' festivals was matchmaking, and thus single girls were more likely to be in attendance. A young Irish man in the 1850s had more organized forms of recreation than did the women in his household. He might have been a member of the Sixth Ward Democratic Club, the Kenmare Hurlers, the semisocial and political clubs of the Five Points, like the Plug Uglies or the Dead Rabbits, the Lady Washington Engine Company or a militia unit.

Sabrina Conway Devlin of 213 Mulberry Street, 27 years old, married to an Irishman from County Sligo, her home county, and the mother of two children, belonged to no clubs or organizations. She had lived in America for nine years, and like many other fellow countrywomen she married a few years later in America than girls in Ireland. She would have between three and four children, probably one of whom would not reach adolescence. She faced the real possibility of being widowed young since her husband, James, a laborer, was subject to what the City inspector called "a high rate of deaths among the young male population due to industrial accidents." More than one-quarter of her countrywomen in New York City over the age of 50 headed their own households. The possibility for remarriage was lessened for Sabrina, compared to other immigrant women in the city, because of the higher proportion of Irish women to men in all age groups.

Like most Irish peasant women, Sabrina was used to a life of hard work and insecurity. Employment for day laborers was irregular and seasonal, and perhaps her husband spent several months a year away from his family working on the railroad gangs in upstate New York. These separations, although difficult, had been traditional in County Sligo, where she was born, and her father might have gone to harvest crops each year in England or Scotland. The irregularity of employment and the low wages meant that she would have to take in washing or sewing, and although there were not boarders in her house, her 18 year old brother probably contributed his wages to the family income.

What effect did the tension and strains of the immigration process, the new and alien urban world, and the developing industrialization of America have on the families and the Sabrina Conways of mid-nineteenth-century New York? Did the massive exodus from the Great Famine encourage a sundering of family ties? After settling in New York City, did the Irish—traditionally family-oriented, and in the pre-Famine period organized into nuclear family households—constitute a mass of disorganized, unattached individuals in the "alienating" atmosphere of a large port city like New York? We have one further fragment of evidence on Sabrina Conway: when her second son, James, was christened in 1855, the godparents included her brother, Patrick Conway, and her husbands' sister, Elizabeth Devlin. Although thousands of miles from their Irish homeland, the families of Sabrina Conway and James Devlin continued to fill their traditional roles. While family ties were strained by immigration and tensions were created by the movement into an urban, industrializing world, the Irish brought with them and maintained enduring cultural patterns and family and kin relationships. . . .

An analysis of the census manuscript schedules of this area [New York City] indicates that almost three-quarters of this Irish population came to America either in family groups or by the process of "one-bringing-another"; 86% of the population lived with at least one person related by blood or by marriage; the great majority of the population (93%) lived in households headed by a nuclear family, with only a small proportion living alone or with unrelated adults; large masses of unattached young Irish men and women did not create a separate class living outside organized family since only 5% lived in boarding-houses rather than boarding with a family; and 75% of the Irish over 60 years of age lived with relatives, indicating that the strong bonds of duty and affection toward parents were not broken by immigration. These statistics take on even more significance because they describe one of the poorest areas of New York City, home to the disreputable Five Points slum.

Let us turn from a consideration of numbers to a much more eloquent state of what these figures show. Margaret McCarthy, a young Irish immigrant, wrote to her "Dear Father Mother Brothers and sisters" in 1850:

> Come all you Together Courageously and bid adieu to that lovely
> land of our Birth, that place where the young and old joined

Together in one Common Union, both night and day Engaged in Innocent Amusement. But alas, I am now Told it's the gulf of Misery oppression Degradation and Ruin of every Discription with I am Sorry to hear of so Doleful a History to Be told of our Dr. Country. This Dr. Father induces me to Remit to you in the Letter 20 Dollars . . . until you might be Clearing away from that place all together and the Sooner the Better for Believe me I could not Express how great would be my joy at seeing you all here Together where you would never be at a loss for a good Breakfast and Dinner. . . .

Margaret McCarthy was only one of the millions of Irish immigrant women to come to America throughout the nineteenth century, but her response to her experiences was far from unique. Strong ties of duty and affection continued to endure in spite of the immigrant process. It might be said that the Irish were hardly breaking family ties by leaving Ireland—over five million Irish men and women emigrated during this period—they simply went to live with other members of their families or eventually managed to bring those temporarily left behind to join them in America.

Patterns of behavior, work, leisure, and family brought with them from Ireland continued to influence these immigrant women in mid-nineteenth-century New York. Their experiences in Ireland as farm laborers, domestic servants, seamstresses, hawkers, peddlers, and factory hands provided some preparation for their work experience in America. Family and kinship ties, while strained by emigration, continued to endure. Music, dance, and leisure patterns, while transformed on the streets of American cities, provided ties with their Old World experience. Uprooted physically from the land of their birth, their cultural roots continued to shape their responses and adaptation to their new environment. This process was true for the millions of immigrants and migrants to American urban centers throughout the nineteenth and twentieth centuries. Only by studying the complex interaction between the culture they brought with them and the society which they entered can we begin to understand the "many pasts" of America.

Questions for Discussion

1. Women formed a higher proportion of immigrants from Ireland compared with migrants from other countries. Why?
2. What skills did Irish women bring with them to the United States? How did they correspond with the job opportunities available in America?
3. Describe the lively street life of New York's Lower East Side. The author argues it was not totally alien to the young, recently arrived Irish immigrants. Why?
4. The author is suggesting that immigration not only made the Irish Americans, it made part of America Irish. Do you agree? Can this argument be applied to other groups of immigrants, before and during the twentieth century?

For Further Reading

Tyler Anbinder, *Five Points* (2001); Susan Campbell Bartoletti, *Black Potatoes: The Story of the Great Irish Famine, 1845–1850* (2001); Shirley Blumenthal and Jerome S. Ozer, eds., *Coming to America: Immigrants from the British Isles* (1980); Hasia R. Diner, *Erin's Daughters in America: Irish Immigrant Women in the Nineteenth Century* (1983); J. P. Dolan, *The Immigrant Church: New York's Irish and German Catholics, 1850–1865* (1975); Robert Ernst, *Immigrant Life in New York City, 1825–1863* (1949); William D. Griffen, ed., *The Irish in America, 1550–1972* (1973); Oscar Handlin, *Boston's Immigrants* (1968); John Higham, *Strangers in the Land: Patterns of American Nativism, 1860–1925* (1963); Dale T. Knobel, *Paddy and the Republic: Ethnicity and Nationality in Antebellum America* (1986); Kerby A. Miller, *Emigrants and Exiles: Ireland and the Irish Exodus to North America* (1985); Kerby A. Miller and Paul Wagner, *Out of Ireland* (1997); Cecil Woodham Smith, *The Great Hunger* (1962); Christine Stansell, *City of Woman: Sex and Class in New York, 1789–1860* (1986); Richard J. Stivers, *Hair of the Dog: Irish Drinking and American Stereotype* (1976); Doris Weatherford, *Foreign & Female: Immigrant Women in America, 1840–1930* (1986).

CHAPTER 12

Indian Removal
Cherokee Women and the Trail of Tears

Theda Perdue

By the 1820s and 1830s, the boom in cotton cultivation ran up against the scarcity of unclaimed land suitable for growing that crop. At that point, the eyes of land-hungry southern white people—and the strong arms of the federal and state governments—turned their attention to land owned by Indian tribes of the Southeast. The Cherokees, Creeks, Choctaws, and Chickasaws controlled tens of thousands of square miles of enormously fertile land in parts of Georgia, Alabama, Tennessee, Arkansas, and Mississippi. Various treaties between the United States government and these tribes guaranteed Native American sovereignty over this land. Nevertheless, for years whites, especially in Georgia, had lobbied the federal government to wrest the land from the Indians, peacefully if possible, by force if necessary. Presidents James Monroe and John Quincy Adams urged the Native tribes to sell their land. But neither president favored forced removal.

That changed with Andrew Jackson's election as president in 1828. Jackson was determined to remove all southern Native Americans to new lands west of the Mississippi. When the government of Georgia passed legislation that compromised the sovereignty of the Cherokee nation—that tribe owned 35,000 square miles of territory, much of it in Georgia—Jackson falsely claimed that the federal government lacked the authority to intervene on behalf of the Cherokee. Instead, he urged Congress to pass the Indian Removal Act, which he signed in 1830. In his State of the Union message to Congress that year, Jackson defended Indian removal by contrasting the ways of life of white Americans and Native Americans: "What good man," said Jackson, "would prefer a country covered with forests and ranged by a

In the top photo is prominent Cherokee, John Ridge, who favored the treaty of New Echota; in the bottom photo is the leader of the Cherokee, John Ross, who led the opposition to the treaty and the removal of his tribe. In justifying forced removal, President Andrew Jackson referred to the Cherokee as "wandering savages." How does that view square with the portraits of Ridge and Ross?

few thousand savages to our extensive Republic, studded with cities, towns, and prosperous farms, embellished with all the improvements which art can devise or industry execute, occupied by more than 12,000,000 happy people, and filled with all the blessings of liberty, civilization, and religion?"

When applied to the Cherokee, Jackson's words were ironic, among other things. The Cherokee of Georgia had incrementally adopted many ways of white culture. At the urging of presidents from George Washington to John Quincy Adams, many Cherokee men had turned away from hunting and took up farming. Some grew cotton, acquired capital, and enjoyed considerable prosperity; some even owned African American slaves. Many converted to Christianity. Nonetheless, the Cherokee, like all Native peoples, believed their land belonged to the tribe, not the individual. The land was a gift from the Creator and home to their ancestors. In earlier treaties, the Cherokee had already ceded much of Tennessee and *all* of Kentucky. Now, they refused to sell what was left and leave their homeland.

But in 1832 Georgia, emboldened by Jackson's support, initiated a lottery in which Cherokee land was distributed to whites. The new "owners" descended upon Cherokee communities and forced families from their homes. Believing they had no choice, a group of Cherokee leaders, representing no more than 2 percent of the entire tribe, signed the Treaty of New Echota in 1836, in which they agreed to sell the land to the federal government for $5 million. The treaty required the tribe to move across the Mississippi River within two years, to land in present-day northeastern Oklahoma. The vast majority of Cherokees opposed the treaty and begged the federal government to allow them to remain on "the land of our fathers." In 1838, the United States army arrived to remove all Cherokees from their homes and escort them on the 800-mile trek across the Mississippi.

In the next essay, Theda Perdue describes that journey, which came to be called the "Trail of Tears" by the Cherokee. Inclement weather, poor nutrition (the United States government allocated 16 cents per day to feed each Indian, and 40 cents per day to feed each horse), disease, and the grind of traveling (many walked the entire 800 miles) claimed the lives of at least 4,000 of the 16,000 Cherokee. Many of them were children, elderly, or infirm.

Perdue's main focus, however, is on the cultural issues that made the Trail of Tears possible. She shows that for decades before the removal, the Cherokee had changed their way of life in order to placate whites. In the process, traditional gender roles—such as men hunting and women farming—had eroded. Those traditions gave Native women a key role in the Cherokee economy and, to some degree, in political decision making. Perdue suggests that had Cherokee women maintained their traditional gender roles, things may have turned out differently.

Source: Theda Perdue, "Cherokee Women and the Trail of Tears," *The Journal of Women's History* 1, no. 1 (Spring 1989), 14–30. © The Johns Hopkins University Press. Reprinted with permission of The Johns Hopkins University Press.

The Treaty of New Echota by which the Cherokee Nation relinquished its territory in the Southeast was signed by men. Women were present at the rump council that negotiated the treaty, but they did not participate in the proceedings. They may have met in their own council—precedents for women's councils exist—but if they did, no record remains. Instead they possibly cooked meals and cared for children while their husbands discussed treaty terms with the United States commissioner. The failure of women to join in the negotiation and signing of the Treaty of New Echota does not necessarily mean that women were not interested in the disposition of tribal land, but it does indicate that the role of women had changed dramatically in the preceding century.

Traditionally, women had a voice in Cherokee government. They spoke freely in council, and the War Woman (or Beloved Woman) decided the fate of captives. As late as 1787, a Cherokee woman wrote Benjamin Franklin that she had delivered an address to her people urging them to maintain peace with the new American nation. She had filled the peace pipe for the warriors, and she enclosed some of the same tobacco for the United States Congress in order to unite symbolically her people and his in peace. She continued:

> I am in hopes that if you Rightly consider that woman is the mother of All—and the Woman does not pull Children out of Trees or Stumps nor out of old Logs, but out of their Bodies, so they ought to mind what a woman says.

The political influence of women, therefore, rested at least in part on their maternal biological role in procreation and their maternal role in Cherokee society, which assumed particular importance in the Cherokee's matrilineal kinship system. In this way of reckoning kin, children belonged to the clan of their mother and their only relatives were those who could be traced through her.

The Cherokees were not only matrilineal, they were also matrilocal. That is, a man lived with his wife in a house which belonged to her, or perhaps more accurately, to her family. According to the naturalist William Bartram, "Marriage gives no right to the husband over the property of his wife; and when they part she keeps the children and property belonging to them." The "property" that women kept included agricultural produce—corn, squash, beans, sunflowers, and pumpkins—stored in the household's crib. Produce belonged to women because they were the principal farmers. This economic role was ritualized at the Green Corn Ceremony every summer when an old woman presented the new corn crop. Furthermore, eighteenth-century travelers and traders normally purchased corn from women instead of men, and in the 1750s the garrison at Fort Loudoun, in present-day eastern Tennessee, actually employed a female purchasing agent to procure corn. Similarly, the fields belonged to the women who tended them, or rather to the women's lineages. Bartram observed that "their fields are divided by proper marks and their harvest is gathered separately." While the Cherokees technically held land in common and anyone could use unoccupied land, improved fields belonged to specific matrilineal households.

Perhaps this explains why women signed early deeds conveying land titles to the Proprietors of Carolina. Agents who made these transactions offered little explanation for the signatures of women on these documents. In the early twentieth century, a historian speculated that they represented a "renunciation of dower," but it may have been that women were simply parting with what was recognized as theirs, or they may have been representing their lineages in the negotiations.

As late as 1785, women still played some role in the negotiation of land transactions. Nancy Ward, the Beloved Woman of Chota, spoke to the treaty conference held at Hopewell, South Carolina to clarify and extend land cessions stemming from Cherokee support of the British in the American Revolution. She addressed the assembly as the "mother of warriors" and promoted a peaceful resolution to land disputes between the Cherokees and the United States. Under the terms of the Treaty of Hopewell, the Cherokees ceded large tracts of land south of the Cumberland River in Tennessee and Kentucky and west of the Blue Ridge Mountains in North Carolina. Nancy Ward and the other Cherokee delegates to the conference agreed to the cession not because they believed it to be just but because the United States dictated the terms of the treaty.

The conference at Hopewell was the last treaty negotiation in which women played an official role, and Nancy Ward's participation in that conference was somewhat anachronistic. In the eighteenth century, the English as well as other Europeans had dealt politically and commercially with men since men were the hunters and warriors in Cherokee society and Europeans were interested primarily in military alliances and deerskins. As relations with the English grew increasingly important to tribal welfare, women became less significant in the Cherokee economy and government. Conditions in the Cherokee Nation following the American Revolution accelerated the trend. In their defeat, the Cherokees had to cope with the destruction of villages, fields, corn cribs, and orchards which had occurred during the war and the cession of hunting grounds which accompanied the peace. In desperation, they turned to the United States government, which proposed to convert the Cherokees into replicas of white pioneer farmers in the anticipation that they would then cede additional territory (presumably hunting grounds they no longer needed). While the government's so-called "civilization" program brought some economic relief, it also helped produce a transformation of gender roles and social organization. The society envisioned for the Cherokees, one which government agents and Protestant missionaries zealously tried to implement, was one in which a man farmed and headed a household composed only of his wife and children. The men who gained power in eighteenth-century Cherokee society—hunters, warriors, and descendants of traders—took immediate advantage of this program in order to maintain their status in the face of a declining deerskin trade and pacification, and then diverted their energy, ambition, and aggression into economic channels. As agriculture became more commercially viable, these men began to farm or to acquire African slaves to cultivate their fields for them. They also began to dominate Cherokee society, and by example and legislation, they altered fundamental relationships. . . .

The one subject on which women did speak on two occasions was land. In 1817 the United States sought a large cession of Cherokee territory and removal of those who lived on the land in question. A group of Indian women met in their own council, and thirteen of them signed a message which was delivered to the National Council. They advised the Council:

> The Cherokee ladys now being present at the meeting of the Chiefs and warriors in council have thought it their duties as mothers to address their beloved Chiefs and warriors now assembled.
>
> Our beloved children and head men of the Cherokee nation we address you warriors in council[. W]e have raised all of you on the land which we now have, which God gave to us to inhabit and raise provisions[. W]e know that our country has once been extensive but by repeated sales has become circumscribed to a small tract and never have thought it our duty to interfere in the disposition of it till now, if a father or mother was to sell all their lands which they had to depend on[,] which their children had to raise their living on[,] which would be bad indeed and to be removed to another country[. W]e do not wish to go to an unknown country which we have understood some of our children wish to go over the Mississippi but this act of our children would be like destroying your mothers. Your mother and sisters ask and beg of you not to part with any more of our lands.

The next year, the National Council met again to discuss the possibility of allotting Cherokee land to individuals, an action the United States government encouraged as a preliminary step to removal. Once again, Cherokee women reacted:

> We have heard with painful feelings that the bounds of the land we now possess are to be drawn into very narrow limits. This land was given to us by the Great Spirit above as our common right, to raise our children upon, & to make support for our rising generations. We therefore humbly petition our beloved children, the head men and warriors, to hold out to the last in support of our common rights, as the Cherokee nation have been the first settlers of this land; we therefore claim the right of the soil. . . . We therefore unanimously join in our meeting to hold our country in common as hitherto.

Common ownership of land meant in theory that the United States government had to obtain cessions from recognized, elected Cherokee officials who represented the wishes of the people. Many whites favored allotment because private citizens could then obtain individually owned tracts of land through purchase, fraud, or seizure. Most Cherokees recognized this danger and objected to allotment for that reason. The women, however, had an additional incentive for opposing allotment. Under the law of the states in which Cherokees lived and of which they would become citizens if land were allotted, married women had few property rights. A married woman's property, even property she held prior to her marriage, belonged legally to her husband. Cherokee women and matrilineal households would have ceased to be property owners. . . .

The effects of the women's protests in 1817 and 1818 are difficult to determine. In 1817 the Cherokees ceded tracts of land in Georgia, Alabama, and Tennessee, and in 1819 they made an even larger cession. Nevertheless, they rejected individual allotments and strengthened restrictions on alienation of improvements. Furthermore, the Cherokee Nation gave notice that they would negotiate no additional cessions—a resolution so strongly supported that the United States ultimately had to turn to a small unauthorized faction in order to obtain the minority treaty of 1835.

The political organization which existed in the Cherokee Nation in 1817–1818 had made it possible for women to voice their opinion. . . . The protests of the women to the National Council in 1817 and 1818 were, however, the last time women presented a collective position to the Cherokee governing body. Structural changes in Cherokee government more narrowly defined participation in the National Council. In 1820 the Council provided that representatives be chosen from eight districts rather than from traditional towns, and in 1823 the Committee acquired a right of review over acts of the Council. The more formalized political organization made it less likely that a group could make its views known to the national government.

As the Cherokee government became more centralized, political and economic power rested increasingly in the hands of a few elite men who adopted the planter lifestyle of the white antebellum South. A significant part of the ideological basis for this lifestyle was the cult of domesticity in which the ideal woman confined herself to home and hearth while men contended with the corrupt world of government and business. The elite adopted the tenets of the cult of domesticity, particularly after 1817 when the number of Protestant missionaries, major proponents of this feminine ideal, increased significantly and their influence on Cherokee society broadened. . . .

The exclusion of women from politics certainly did not produce the removal crisis, but it did mean that a group traditionally opposed to land cession could no longer be heard on the issue. How women would have voted is also unclear. Certainly by 1835, many Cherokee women, particularly those educated in mission schools, believed that men were better suited to deal with political issues than women, and a number of women voluntarily enrolled their households to go west before the forcible removal of 1838–1839. Even if women had united in active opposition to removal, it is unlikely that the United States and aggressive state governments would have paid any more attention to them than they did to the elected officials of the nation who opposed removal or the 15,000 Cherokees, including women (and perhaps children), who petitioned the United States Senate to reject the Treaty of New Echota. While Cherokee legislation may have made women powerless, federal authority rendered the whole Nation impotent.

In 1828 Georgia had extended state law over the Cherokee Nation, and white intruders who invaded its territory. Georgia law prohibited Indians, both men and women, from testifying in court against white assailants, and so they simply had to endure attacks on person and property. Delegates from the nation complained to Secretary of War John H. Eaton about the lawless behavior of white intruders:

> Too many there who think it a matter of trifling consequence to oust an Indian family from the quiet enjoyment of all the comforts of their own firesides, and to drive off before their faces the stock that gave nourishment to the children and support to the aged, and appropriate it to the satisfaction to avarice.

Elias Boudinot, editor of the bilingual *Cherokee Phoenix*, even accused the government of encouraging the intruders in order to force the Indians off their lands, and he published the following account:

> A few days since two of these white men came to a Cherokee house, for the purpose, they pretended, of buying provisions. There was no person about the house but one old woman of whom they inquired for some corn, beans &c. The woman told them she had nothing to sell. They went off in the direction of the field belonging to this Cherokee family. They had not gone a few minutes when the woman saw a heavy smoke rising from that direction. She immediately hastened to the field and found the villains had set the woods on fire but a few rods from the fences, which she found in a full blaze. There being a very heavy wind that day, the fire spread so fast, that her efforts to extinguish it proved utterly useless. The entire fence was therefore consumed in a short time. It is said that during her efforts to save the fence the men who had done the mischief were within sight, and were laughing heartily at her!

The Georgia Guard, established by the state to enforce its laws in the Cherokee country, offered no protection and, in fact, contributed to the lawlessness. The *Phoenix* printed the following notice under the title "Cherokee Women, Beware":

> It is said that the Georgia Guard have received orders, from the Governor we suppose, to inflict corporeal punishment on such females as shall hereafter be guilty of insulting them. We presume they are to be the judges of what constitutes *insult*.

Despite harassment from intruders and the Guard, most Cherokees had no intention of going west, and in the spring of 1838 they began to plant their crops as usual. Then United States soldiers arrived, began to round up the Cherokees, and imprisoned them in stockades in preparation for deportation. In 1932 Rebecca Neugin, who was nearly one hundred years old, shared her childhood memory and family tradition about removal with historian Grant Foreman:

> When the soldiers came to our house my father wanted to fight, but my mother told him the soldiers would kill him if he did and we surrendered without a fight. They drove us out of our house to join other prisoners in a stockade. After they took us away, my mother begged them to let her go back and get some bedding. So they let her go back and she brought what bedding and a few cooking utensils she could carry and had to leave behind all of our other household possessions.

Rebecca Neugin's family was relatively fortunate. In the process of capture, families were sometimes separated and sufficient food and clothing were often left behind. Over fifty years after removal, John G. Burnett, a soldier who served as an interpreter, reminisced:

> Men working in the fields were arrested and driven to stockades. Women were dragged from their homes by soldiers whose language they could not understand. Children were often separated from their parents and driven into the stockades with the sky for a blanket and the earth for a pillow.

Burnett recalled how one family was forced to leave the body of a child who had just died and how a distraught mother collapsed of heart failure as soldiers evicted her and her three children from their homes. After their capture, many Cherokees had to march miles over rugged mountain terrain to the stockades. Captain L. B. Webster wrote his wife about moving eight hundred Cherokees from North Carolina to the central depot in Tennessee: "We were eight days in making the journey (80 miles), and it was pitiful to behold the women & children, who suffered exceedingly—as they were all obliged to walk, with the exception of the sick."

Originally the government planned to deport all the Cherokees in the summer of 1838, but the mortality rate of the three parties that departed that summer led the commanding officer, General Winfield Scott, to agree to delay the major removal until the fall. In the interval, the Cherokees remained in the stockades where conditions were abysmal. Women in particular, often became individual victims of their captors. The missionary Daniel Butrick recorded the following episode in his journal:

> The poor Cherokees are not only exposed to temporal evils, but also to every species of moral desolation. The other day a gentleman informed me that he saw six soldiers about two Cherokee women. The women stood by a tree, and the soldiers with a bottle of liquor were endeavoring to entice them to drink, though the women, as yet were resisting them. He made this known to the commanding officer but we presume no notice was taken of it, as it was reported that those soldiers had those women with them the whole night afterwards. A young married woman, a member of the Methodist society was at the camp with her friends, though her husband was not there at the time. The soldiers, it is said, caught her, dragged her about at length, either through fear, or otherwise, induced her to drink; and then seduced her away, so that she is now an outcast even among her own relatives. How many of the poor captive women are thus debauched, through terror and seduction, that eye which never sleeps, alone can determine.

When removal finally got underway in October, the Cherokees were in a debilitated and demoralized state. A white minister who saw them as they prepared to embark noted: "The women did not appear to as good advantage as did the men. All, young and old, wore blankets which almost hid them from view." The Cherokees had received permission to manage their own removal, and they divided the people into thirteen detachments of approximately one thousand each. While some had wagons, most walked. Neugin rode in a wagon with other children and some elderly women, but her older brother, mother, and father "walked all the way." One observer reported that "even aged females, apparently nearly ready to drop in the grave, were traveling with heavy burdens attached to the back." Proper conveyance did not spare well-to-do Cherokees the agony of removal, the same observer noted:

> One lady passed on in her hack in company with her husband, apparently with as much refinement and equipage as any of the mothers of New England; and she was a mother too and her youngest child, about three years old, was sick in her arms, and all she could do was to make it comfortable as circumstances

would permit. . . . She could only carry her dying child in her arms a few miles farther, and then she must stop in a stranger-land and consign her much loved babe to the cold ground, and that without any pomp and ceremony, and pass on with the multitude.

This woman was not alone. Journals of the removal are largely a litany of the burial of children, some born "untimely."

Many women gave birth alongside the trail: at least sixty-nine newborns arrived in the West. The Cherokees military escort was often less than sympathetic. Daniel Butrick wrote in his journal that troops frequently forced women in labor to continue until they collapsed and delivered "in the midst of the company of soldiers." One man even stabbed an expectant mother with a bayonet. Obviously, many pregnant women did not survive such treatment. The oral tradition of a family from southern Illinois, through which the Cherokee passed, for example, includes an account of an adopted Cherokee infant whose mother died in childbirth near the family's pioneer cabin. While this story may be apocryphal, the circumstances of Cherokee removal make such traditions believable.

The stress and tension produced by the removal crisis probably accounts for a post-removal increase in domestic violence of which women usually were the victims. Missionaries reported that men, helpless to prevent seizure of their property and assaults on themselves and their families, vented their frustrations by beating wives and children. Some women were treated so badly by their husbands that they left them, and this dislocation contributed to the chaos in the Cherokee Nation in the late 1830s.

Removal divided the Cherokee Nation in a fundamental way, and the Civil War magnified that division. Because most signers of the removal treaty were highly acculturated, many traditionalists resisted more strongly the white man's way of life and distrusted more openly those Cherokees who imitated whites. This split between "conservatives," those who sought to preserve the old ways, and "progressives," those committed to change, extended to women. We know far more, of course, about "progressive" Cherokee women who left letters and diaries which in some ways are quite similar to those of upper-class women in the antebellum South. In letters, they recounted local news such as "they had Elick Cockrel up for stealing horses" and "they have Charles Reese in chains about burning Harnages house" and discussed economic concerns: "I find I cannot get any corn in this neighborhood, so of course I shall be greatly pressed in providing provision for my family." Nevertheless, family life was the focus of most letters: "Major is well and tryes hard to stand alone he will walk soon. I would write more [but] the baby is crying."

Occasionally we even catch a glimpse of conservative women who seem to have retained at least some of their original authority over domestic matters. Red Bird Smith, who led a revitalization movement at the end of the nineteenth century, had considerable difficulty with his first mother-in-law.

She "influenced" her adopted daughter to marry Smith through witchcraft and, as head of the household, meddled rather seriously in the couple's lives. Interestingly, however, the Kee-Too-Wah society which Red Bird Smith headed had little room for women. Although the society had political objectives, women enjoyed no greater participation in this "conservative" organization than they did in the "progressive" republican government of the Cherokee Nation.

Following removal, the emphasis of legislation involving women was on protection rather than participation. In some ways, this legislation did offer women greater opportunities than the law codes of the states. In 1845 the editor of the *Cherokee Advocate* expressed pride that "in this respect the Cherokees have been considerably in advance of many of their white brethren, the rights of their women having been amply secured ever since they had written laws." The Nation also established the Cherokee Female Seminary to provide higher education for women, but like the education women received before removal, students studied only those subjects considered to be appropriate for their sex.

Removal, therefore, changed little in terms of the status of Cherokee women. They had lost political power before the crisis of the 1830s, and events which followed relocation merely confirmed new roles and divisions. Cherokee women originally had been subsistence-level farmers and mothers, and the importance of these roles in traditional society had made it possible for them to exercise political power. Women, however, lacked the economic resources and military might on which political power in the Anglo-American system rested. When the Cherokees adopted the Anglo-American concept of power in the eighteenth and nineteenth centuries, men became dominant. But in the 1830s the chickens came home to roost. Men, who had welcomed the Anglo-American basis for power, now found themselves without power. Nevertheless, they did not question the changes they had fostered. Therefore, the tragedy of the trail of tears lies not only in the suffering and death which the Cherokees experienced but also in the failure of many Cherokees to look critically at the political system which they had adopted—a political system dominated by wealthy, highly acculturated men and supported by an ideology that made women (as well as others defined as "weak" or "inferior") subordinate. In the removal crisis of the 1830s, men learned an important lesson about power: it was a lesson women had learned well before the "trail of tears."

Questions for Discussion

1. What were the motivations behind the federal government's policy of Indian removal? Was Georgia's decision to place the Cherokee nation under its jurisdiction consistent with Indian policy as mandated by the United States Constitution?

2. Why would Cherokee women oppose assimilation to white systems of property ownership and gender relations? Why might Cherokee men feel otherwise? Why did whites push for Native assimilation?
3. It is clear that removal took the Cherokee nation away from its ancestral lands. But according to the author, removal also eroded the very basis for Cherokee culture. How were the two connected?
4. What three things about the removal process strike you most?

For Further Reading

William L. Anderson, *Cherokee Removal: Before and After* (1992); Robert Conley, *The Cherokee Nation: A History* (2005); Arthur H. De Rosier Jr., *The Removal of the Choctaw Indians* (1970); John Ehle, *Trail of Tears: The Rise and Fall of the Cherokee Nation* (1988); John R. Finger, *The Eastern Band of Cherokees, 1819–1900* (1984); Michael Green, *The Politics of Indian Removal: Creek Government and Society in Crisis* (1985); Reginald Horsman, *Expansion and American Indian Policy, 1783–1812* (1967); Wilbur R. Jacobs, *Dispossessing the American Indian* (1972); Theda Perdue, ed., *The Cherokee Removal: A Brief History* (2004), *The Cherokee* (1989), *Slavery and the Evolution of Cherokee Society* (1979); Theda Perdue and Michael Green, *The Cherokee Nation and the Trail of Tears* (2007); Vicki Rozema, ed., *Voices from the Trail of Tears* (2003); Michael Paul Rogin, *Fathers and Children: Andrew Jackson and the Subjugation of the American Indian* (1975); Tom Underwood, *Cherokee Legends and the Trail of Tears* (2002).

CHAPTER

13

After the Gold Rush

The Male World
of California Mining Camps

Malcolm J. Rohrbough

The annexation of Texas in 1845 led to war with Mexico the following year. On the surface, the war erupted over a dispute with Mexico (which had never recognized the independence of Texas to begin with) about the western boundary separating Texas and Mexico. Beneath the surface, the real cause for war was the American desire to possess portions of Mexico that had nothing to do with Texas: the Mexican territories of California and New Mexico. Mexico balked at American pressure to sell this vast territory, and war ensued. Some Americans justifiably believed President James K. Polk had provoked Mexico and lied about events leading up to the war. They included Henry David Thoreau, who wrote *Civil Disobedience* in response to the conflict, and the young Illinois congressman Abraham Lincoln, who opposed the war. Nonetheless, Mexico was handily defeated, and in the treaty of peace in 1848, Mexico ceded New Mexico (encompassing today's states of Colorado, Utah, New Mexico, Arizona, and Nevada) and California to the United States for $15 million.

It may have been the most lucrative real estate "purchase" in history. Before Texas won its independence, Mexico and the United States were approximately the same size. In 1824, the United States of Mexico was 1.7 million square miles in size, while the United States of America encompassed 1.8 million square miles. By the end of the war in 1848, Mexico had lost more than half its country to the United States, approximately 1.1 million square miles. In an earlier settlement with Great Britain, the United States had also

THINGS AS THEY ARE.

In this essay, Malcolm Rohrbough argues that Gold Rush California was a male-dominated culture that reinforced stereotyped gender views of the time. How does this lithograph of 1849 support Rohrbough's view?

added Oregon (to the 49th parallel) and what would become Washington State and parts of Idaho and Montana.

This enormous addition of territory to the United States planted the seeds of both unity and disunity. North and South argued over whether new states carved from the additional territory would be free or slave states. Disputes like this were part of a climate of mistrust and antagonism that eventually pushed the country into civil war. But in 1848, something happened in the sparsely populated territory of California that would eventually help unite—at least physically—the sprawling nation that now stretched from the Atlantic to the Pacific oceans: the discovery of gold.

In 1848, there were approximately 14,000 American citizens living in California, along with about 10,000 *Californios* (Californians of Spanish-Mexican descent) and 150,000 Native Americans. After the Gold Rush, white California's population exploded. By 1852, 250,000 newcomers—the "49ers" who streamed into California from around the globe—swelled the new state's population. (By then, murder, disease, and displacement reduced the Native American population to 25,000, while Californians of Spanish and Mexican descent were desperately scrambling to hold on to their political rights and property.)

The gold would help lay the foundation for the country's future unity and prosperity. More than 81 million ounces of gold were pulled from

California's waterways and soil by 1852. The use of gold in foreign exchange allowed the United States to generate an enormous trade surplus. Among other things, it would trade that precious metal for another, less shiny but equally valuable metal: steel. Steel would tie the country together physically through its role in building the transcontinental railroad. It would bind it economically by its use in the construction of factories and cities. And the Pacific Coast's economic boom, along with its strategic location for trade with Asia, would attract enormous foreign investments to the United States. In short, within two generations after the Gold Rush, the United States would become the world's preeminent economic power.

The Gold Rush itself had an equally dramatic impact on the families who participated in it. The next essay by Malcolm J. Rohrbough describes the Gold Rush as an almost exclusively male undertaking. In the wild, often desperate hunt for quick wealth, tens of thousands of men left their wives and families in the East and traveled to California in (usually disappointing) hopes of striking it rich. The mining camps were an all-male world, and traditional ideas regarding proper gender roles blurred in the absence of women. Men cooked, sewed, cleaned, and otherwise participated in activities that crossed Victorian gender lines. For these and other reasons, married men desperately missed their wives; but, as Rohrbough points out, they also enjoyed the male camaraderie and freedom from family responsibility that life in the camps provided. Many of the "Argonauts" (the mythic Greek term for seafaring adventurers that mid-nineteenth-century Americans used to describe the 49ers) either failed to support their families, returned home to fractured relationships with their wives and children, or simply abandoned them.

The discovery of gold in California helped launch the United States as a world power. It was among the most important public events of the nineteenth century. But it placed enormous stress on the marriages and finances of thousands of families, while it destroyed hundreds of others.

Source: Malcolm J. Rohrbough, *Days of Gold: The California Gold Rush and the American Nation* (Berkeley: University of California Press, 1997), pp. 91–97, 136–140, 243–250, 254–255.

In addition to the other social and economic dislocations brought about by the news of the discovery of gold and the subsequent decisions of tens of thousands of American men to go to California, the Gold Rush plunged the Argonauts into a society that was almost entirely without women. The communities that the Argonauts began to build in the West were as a result defined in many ways by their absence.

The Gold Rush was a search for a scarce and valuable commodity, but the presence of women in California turned out to be, initially at least, even rarer than gold. Indeed, the scarcity of women was one of the most significant shocks that California imposed upon the 49ers. From the bustling streets of San Francisco to the most remote mining towns, the Argonauts commented constantly on the rarity of women. They came from a world in which they had taken for granted the presence of women in their lives, and with their presence, a wide range of services performed for them by the women. A functioning society without women was unthinkable to them. In the gold country, however, men joined into small companies for living and working. When in so doing the 49ers recreated communities and re-forged a number of social bonds, these turned out to be largely all-male.

The lack of female society—as the 49ers referred to the condition—became the object of comment in several contexts. From the beginning of organized companies or chartered ships, the Argonauts remarked on the absence of women in this migration west. They continued to do so across the ocean or across the plains, and their observations extended to the most remote camps of the Sierra. Indeed, the more distant the camp and the scarcer female society, the more it became a central topic of conversation. For some, the absence of women in California became something of an obsession, whether driven by the need for sexual gratification, for intellectual companionship, for domestic services, or for "civilizing" influences. In their private and public thoughts, in their letters home, and in their diaries and journals, the 49ers used the presence or absence of women to measure the transformation of California into what they called a genteel society, and they commented on the many economic opportunities available to women in the context of the Gold Rush. Sometimes they had to deal with requests from women in the East to be allowed to share in this great enterprise.

When the Argonauts of 1849 and subsequent years formed themselves into companies, in the heady business of drawing up constitutions, electing officers, creating committees, and the flurry of activity surrounding departures, they seemed to accept the all-male composition of these groups without question. A few wives accompanied their husbands to California, but in general, only men gathered together to prepare for the greatest adventure of their lifetimes. Thoughts of families and personal attachments were set aside in favor of the pragmatic issues at hand.

Once the Argonauts were embarked on the journey west, whether by land or by sea, the recognition that they had become members of all-male societies evolved in separate stages, marked by time and distance. Married men immediately missed their wives; single men felt the absence of a warm hearth and a mother's presence. Those Argonauts who went to California by sea had little to do except gaze at the horizon and contemplate the growing distance from home. Sometimes new experiences made the absences especially poignant. As he and his companions inhaled the intoxicating scents of the tropics, Rinaldo Taylor of Boston wrote to his wife and his infant daughter: "One of our Californians remarked to his friends, while we were all silently gazing upon the scene, 'John, wouldn't it be nice if our wives were only here?'" Taylor continued, "This was in exact unison with the feelings of us all, I venture to say, although the observation created 'something of a smile' all around. It was the only thing lacking in this intoxication of the sense. By the way I will remark here that almost all of our California passengers have left wives & families at home, & most of them are young men too.". . .

The overland Argonauts experienced the same sense of loss in a different context. In their journals and in long, detailed letters to be sent to their families when they reached California, they wrote of the vast herds of buffalo, the signs of dangerous Indians on the trail, the majesty of the trek westward across the landscape of the expanding American Empire. Other, more practical, considerations, however, soon intruded. From the moment of their departure from home, the 49ers found themselves responsible for all those domestic labors customarily performed for them by wives, sisters, and mothers. One Argonaut from Kentucky confessed to his sister, "I have always been enclined to deride the vocation of ladies until now but must confess it by far the most irksome I have tried & by way of taking lessons in sewing have often examined your stitches in my work bag." Many diarists and letter writers celebrated their first successful home-baked loaf of bread or the first successfully attached button. By the time they reached California, the 49ers who journeyed overland had come to recognize that their new all-male societies had undertaken what previously had been considered women's duties, and indirectly at least, they recognized the skills they had always taken for granted demanded time and competence.

After an initial period of loneliness and longing, 49ers moved on to a second stage: celebration of new adventures and the good fellowship associated with newly adopted companions. When he ventured across the isthmus with his 49er colleagues, Rinaldo Taylor wrote of the trip through the Panama's mud and rain as a kind of adolescent frolic, concluding "I assure you I enjoyed the whole affair mightily. The excitement and novelty of the trip kept my spirits up to the highest point, & I could laugh at the mishaps of the rest, with a relish." However much Taylor and others might lament the absence of their wives, they displayed much enthusiasm for confronting the physical obstacles of the Panamanian jungle and other physical challenges, whether by land or sea.

What emerged were two parallel responses to an increasingly all-male world: the Argonauts of 1849 and subsequent years missed their wives and their families, but they rejoiced in their new adventures and the independence associated with it, far from the mundane duties of farm, shop, and family. Gradually there developed a sense that these expeditions to California were initiation ceremonies for members of a new kind of all-male club. . . .

At the close of 1849, even 49ers in the gold towns of San Francisco, Sacramento, and Stockton lived in largely male worlds. William Prince wrote in the fall of 1849 that Stockton had so "few females that I never yet have seen one in the streets." And a year later, William Brown wrote from the same place, "In fact a woman is a curiosity in this country."

As the Argonauts passed through the towns into the mining country along the ridges of the Sierra, they entered into a thoroughly all-male world. One 49er reflected a common experience when he wrote that he had talked to only two women in his first year in the mines, and another commented in August 1849 that the visit of a Mexican woman to his camp had "created a general sensation." Indeed, many camps and bars were entirely male; the towns and villages only slightly less so. The federal census of 1850 reflected that in California, the male proportion of the entire population was 92.5 percent; for several mining counties, the proportion of women was less than three in a hundred. These figures indicate that the mining camps of the California Sierra were among the most male places in the nation, and for that matter, the world.

The Argonauts now quickly discovered that the search for gold was not a romantic vision but an intensely hard and competitive business, heightened by the strong sense of obligation to those they left behind with such golden visions. In this context of physical labor and aggressive competition, the "feminine" duties of cooking, laundry, sewing, housecleaning, and other such domestic chores were indeed burdensome. Miners did the hardest kind of physical labor, often working in cold, rushing water up to their knees for ten hours a day. To then return to a dirty cabin and prepare an evening meal became one of the hardships with which they saw themselves afflicted.

As they had among the overland Argonauts, in the gold fields these endless chores (which were often costly, as well, for those who hired them done) gave rise to new expressions of respect for women's domestic roles. Men who had rushed to the gold fields left wives, sisters, and mothers with all the responsibilities men were expected to shoulder, wrote to express admiration for their loved ones' domestic abilities. Men had to cook on a continuing basis, and they had to lay in provisions for what they would prepare. They had little choice. With single meals at boardinghouses or roadside eateries at a dollar and a half each, cost was a powerful incentive.

Because domestic service occupations commanded high profits, men hastened to take advantage of occupations formerly exercised by women alone. Epaphroditus Wells wrote to his wife that he and two other men had formed a partnership "to keep an eating house—one of our firm to be Maid of all work." He noted the incongruity of an eating place with a male cook: "I suppose you will think it a singular Tavern where there are none but men to do cooking but I assure you there are scarcely any other Taverns here." He made it clear that where money could be made, men would do women's work. If this work involved cooking for other men, then with meals at twenty-five dollars a week, men would cook.

The absence of women to perform the customary domestic services and the high cost of hiring these services performed by others increased the value of women in the eyes of the 49ers. For most of the 49ers, the need for women was eminently practical, and they tended to speak of the value of women in the unabashed idiom of a society where everything had a price. When William Daingerfield wrote his mother that California was the greatest place in the world to make money, he added that in order to make it a perfect place to live one needed "a woman on the place to keep things neat about the house." And after two years in the gold fields, James Barnes wrote to his brother, "If you send me any thing send me a woman and I never will come home, wimmam command a very good prise out here." Just as their initial scarcity made them immensely valuable, as they increased in numbers, their value was somewhat diminished. Horace Ballew wrote along these lines in early 1851, "Tell the girls that women is not so valuable here as they used to be, because there is too many here now.". . .

As they settled into California in all its varied aspects, the Argonauts saw women as absolutely necessary to the transformation of California from a series of transient, mercenary societies (and recently Mexican and Catholic at that) into something like the orderly communities from which they came. George Raymond wrote his sister: "I like the country much better than formerly and were it not for the want of society (I mean ladies) the Sabbath and the faces of my friends at home, should be content to stay here. There are no women except for a few Spanish.". . .

The 49ers had an almost mystical attachment to the idea of women as civilizers. Yet they also gave the strong impression that however much they sought women to transform California into a moral society, they did not propose to volunteer their wives, fiancées, sisters, female relatives, and friends for the task. As some women made subdued and genteel but persistent entreaties that they be allowed to come to California to join their men, the 49ers responded with horror at the thought. They replied with a continuous litany that they did not want their female companions and relatives to come to California. They preferred to leave them in the states, a perpetual monument to the civilized, orderly, and familiar communities they had left. In part, they saw it as a tribute to their sacrifices for their families that they would endure a lack of female presence and all it implied for months and even years. In part, this was also a declaration of their protective posture in defending the sensibilities of their women against the grossness of this new world. Perhaps also they did not want women to come to California and spoil the campout with their male friends. Whatever the hardships of cooking and sewing, some men clearly enjoyed the conviviality of a male club of like-minded comrades. . . .

THE WORK ROUTINE

To gain access to the gold-bearing streams, the 49ers penetrated into the foothills, canyons, and ravines, and in some cases, into the mountains. These remote locations—ranging from dry and barren in the southern mines [southeast of San Francisco] to steep, timber-covered hillsides in the northern mines [northeast of San Francisco]—forced the Argonauts to take up residence (if that is the term) in remote and often difficult locations.

The first living arrangements were simple campsites—a familiar way of doing things for the 49ers who had come overland over the summer of 1849 and would continue to do in subsequent annual migrations. The seagoing

Argonauts packed tents or purchased them in the cities, towns, or numerous general merchandise stores that . . . quickly sprang up en-route to the diggings. The 49ers established a camp in the closest proximity to their claims to work and protect them most advantageously. A campsite for five to eight men who mined together might be set up in a matter of hours and taken down in even less time. Such a consideration was important for a people constantly on the move. Finally, living in a campsite was inexpensive, and it offered the cheapest way to live while mining.

Work began on the streams at daylight and miners rose in the dark to dress and prepare themselves. The designated cook prepared what passed for breakfast. Standing outside the tents or seated inside on logs or homemade chairs, the miners would eat and smoke, silently preparing themselves for another day of hard labor and high expectations. Within the canyons and ravines of watercourses, the sun appeared late. As the sky began to lighten, the miners put away their tin cups and tin plates, and with their picks and shovels, pans and buckets, advanced on the holes or dams that would provide the daily work. The walk might be brief and direct, down to a nearby watercourse, or long and difficult, to a distant spot at the bottom of a steep canyon.

Once arrived at the claim, the 49ers began a routine of digging, shoveling, carrying, and washing that continued unabated with little variation throughout the day until sunset. In 1849, most companies operated one or more "cradles" [rocking devices worked by four men designed to separate gold from gravel]. In a pattern that stretched from one end of the Mother Lode to the other, one man loosened the "dirt," whether by digging or shoveling; a second carried it to the site of the machine, generally a cradle; there, a third washed the materials. Men rotated the jobs to equalize the work. Fourth or fifth members of the mess might dig or carry. When mining groups reached six or seven or so, they would operate two cradles. . . .

Such machines aside, whatever the greater technical efficiencies in the retrieval of gold, the basic unit of work in the gold mines was the human body. Everywhere across the Mother Lode, in these first years of mining, the dirt had to be loosened and carried to the machine, and the miners performed this labor over and over again, often under unpleasant conditions. Several members of the company (or everyone) might work up to their knees and sometimes higher in swift, ice-cold, moving water. In spite of their determination to present a stoic face to members of their company and their families, 49ers often complained in diaries and letters about the cold and wet. E. T. Sherman wrote to his parents, "You will have to work in water & mud Morning until night [and] it is no boys play."

Contrasting with the icy waters of the snowmelt watercourses was the heat of the California summer. The summer months were crucial for mining because the dry season meant a drop in the water level and, accordingly, exposed bars and riffles that could be dug. So hot were the days that even in the context of the hectic pace of the miners, the company often rested during the heat of the day. For many mining companies, summer hours were from 6:00 to 11:00 in the morning and again from 3:00 to sunset. . . .

During the long workday, a combination of restless energy, hope, self-interest, and group loyalty sustained the labor at a high level. Men drove themselves forward in their routine tasks by the visions of future wealth, encouraged by present small returns and pressed by the need to dig and wash something every day on a continuing basis. Over the first two years of the Gold Rush, the returns of a claim could be calculated by a mathematical formula. A bucket of dirt on an "average" claim in 1849 would produce gold worth about ten cents. Miners need to wash an average of one hundred and sixty or so buckets of dirt a day each—or eight hundred buckets for five men—in order to generate the anticipated one ounce (or sixteen dollars) for each working man. . . .

The intangible compensations—if such existed—lay in the sense of male camaraderie over the evening meal and around the fire as the shadows lengthened. Then, with the day's work behind them and the next one not yet in sight, men relaxed, smoked, and talked. In this male company, the most common topics of conversation were courtships and stories of happy youthful adventures and pranks. Robert Butterfield wrote to his brother this account of how he and his three "chums" relaxed after a long day:

> Thus we lived contently and happy. We worked as usual hard all day and sit around the fire-place with our boots off at night telling stories about what we heard and see, reading papers, re-reading old letters, reading books of whatever kind come our way. Around the cheerful blaze too as we sit drying our feet at night we enjoy the wholesome pipe—occasionally indulging in a cigar. . . .

THE FAMILIES BACK HOME

"How many a happy family has been broken up since the Gold of California has been heard of God only knows," wrote John Slatford's mother to her son in early 1852. From the moment of departure, relationships among 49ers and their families had experienced strains and uncertainties; as these absences lengthened, the anxieties over family relationships increased in like proportion, and these patterns repeated themselves with continuing annual migrations to the gold fields.

Both the men who went to California and the women who stayed behind entered into a new range of experiences, as we have seen. Spousal and family relationships underwent a change unlike any other heretofore seen on such a large scale, as distinct in its numbers and its widespread effect as the mobilization of armies on the opening of the Civil War. . . . [T]he results of these prolonged absences could range from the ideal to the disastrous. As time went on, the effect on families tended toward the disastrous.

Wives increasingly complained to their 49er husbands about what they regarded as negligent treatment. Jane Delano had objected to her husband's voyage to the gold mines in the spring of 1852 from the start, and her anger followed him into the placers. After a long silence, he received a letter from her, and he responded to it with the comment, "Jane I can tell you I dreaded to open it and kept it with me over one hour before I could muster courage to open it." Delano constantly reassured her of his intense devotion to his family. "As for my forsaken family I never shall for I think daily of my wife and children and the thoughts about my family is never one day out of my mind and I can tell you Jane the thoughts of you and the children is ever near and pleasing to me," he wrote. Of course, his spirited defensiveness did not address the central issue of his absence, whether his venture compensated in whatever way for the loss of his presence and affection over a period of years.

Harriet Goff, wife of an absent 49er, laid her husband's departure to a lack of love. To her charges, Goff replied from Hangtown, "I was very Sorry to hear of your feeling so disheartened it made me feel bad to think you had entertained the idea that you was not cared for, &c I think if I know my own feelings, that there is no one cares more or thinks more of their family than I do." He continued, "I hope by the time this Letter reaches you, that you will cast off all those gloomy feelings and Sorrows that you seem to entertain." The evidence of his affection, he argued, was that he missed all the womanly services that she performed for him. His "widower" status was proof that he cared for his family. . . .

Those women left behind in the rush to California became known as "49er widows." The designation "widow" nicely captured the emotional, financial, and legal void into which some wives had descended in the absence of their husbands. Yet unlike real widows, they had no independent legal status. They could not dispose of their husbands' estates as they wished; they could not seek other romantic attachments; they did not have sole legal responsibility for the surviving children. The term long had been in use, but its applicability was especially poignant in the second generation of the Gold Rush because of the lengthening absences. It was already conceivable that some husbands from whom nothing had been heard for months or years might not be intending to return. Their wives lived on in a perpetual condition of emotional and legal uncertainty.

Sometimes under the influence of distance, time, and sense of desertion, spouses sought other relationships. The 49er "widows" and fiancées and the sizable number of people on both sides of the continent who remained less formally committed to each other often lived solitary emotional lives. Aside from the economic difficulties they may have confronted, their letters often testify in endless detail to their loneliness and deprivation. It is not surprising that some sought companionship and even emotional attachment elsewhere. . . .

Sometimes the new relationships were with old friends, perhaps those who had come to offer support and companionship in lonely times. The return of the 49er from the watercourses to the drawing rooms of formal houses might sometimes unleash an emotional storm over endangered affection. When he went to the gold fields in the spring of 1849, Gustavus Swasey left his wife Jane and children in Boston. After mining with success for some months, he lost his money belt, containing fifty-four ounces of gold, to a thief ("I feel like lying face downward and never again attempting to struggle with my sad fate"). At the same time, his creditors would not pay him ("I am so wretched I am determined to go home as soon as I can get enough to pay my passage"). After a brief, unsatisfactory return home, Swasey parted from his wife and set out for California a second time. In Panama, he changed his mind and returned unannounced to his family. There, he made a series of unpleasant discoveries about his wife. Jane used snuff [inhaled tobacco]: "I must confess it was a disagreeable discovery. I express'd my aberrance of the practice. She says Alice Wiley taught her but that it is a filthy practice and she will abandon it, and I believe she will for my sake." But far more disturbing was the disclosure that his wife had been engaged in private correspondence with a mutual friend, William Litton, using her sister Sarah "as a cover for the proceedings." After several unpleasant scenes, Gustavus and Jane Swasey, plus the children, and William Litton went to San Francisco together, where relations between husband and wife further deteriorated. Gustavus Swasey found himself without a wife, family, or business. His search for wealth in the gold fields had become secondary to a series of personal crises. . . .

The stresses and tensions that accompanied the mass migrations to California from families and communities across the eastern half of the nation finally destroyed many families. The failure of 49ers to live up to their promises of support for those back home, let alone to realize their dreams of great wealth, took a toll, but even success could bring division and contention in its wake. So could the division of authority between absent husbands and the wives and other family members left with the responsibilities of raising children, caring for the elderly, and keeping family businesses and farms running. The hardships of the Gold Rush imposed strains and worsened existing tensions within the Argonauts' families, often causing ruptures. And finally, the changes wrought in both the 49ers and those they left behind by the long separation made strangers of them all, those in the East and those in the West each having adapted to ways of life that those on the other side of the country finally could not comprehend.

Problems caused by money began early. Through the wide range of support arrangements the 49ers made for those they left behind ran two common threads. First, from the moment of their initial departure, the Argonauts emphasized that their spouses and immediate families would want for nothing. Everything would be taken care of, they assured them. The

49ers promised to send money as soon as they had begun to claim their share of the fabled riches of the California placers. John Fitch not only sent drafts from the gold fields to his wife with instructions that if troubled by money matters, she would have recourse to his brother, he also remitted funds to his brother George, more than one hundred ounces of gold dust in 1850 alone, with the charge, "I wish you not to fail to see that my wife has money to meet her wants."

This basic assumption of success in the expedition ran parallel to another understanding, that 49ers would share their successes with members of their extended families. When Solomon Gorgas wrote about family sacrifices and dividing up the wealth from his expedition to the gold fields, he mentioned his wife's sister, Mary, and wrote of her and her contributions to the family in his absence, "Sister Mary too, shall not suffer from any debt due her from our dear departed mother, if I am successful—she too shall be remembered." Many Argonauts wrote in grandiose terms, magnanimously dividing up wealth that lay in the future, a fortune so vivid in their minds that they almost considered the Solomon-like judgments they anticipated in its distribution more taxing and awkward than amassing the gold itself. . . .

Of course, some Argonauts simply left their families in perilous financial straits when they departed for the gold fields. That they did so—and admitted at the time and later—reflected a degree of irresponsibility tempered with the knowledge that given their impoverished financial condition, they could justify seizing the opportunity to acquire wealth without the usual prerequisites of name, education, and social standing. That they should wish to participate in order to change the impoverished condition of their families, they reasoned to themselves, was understandable, even if it meant abandoning those same families to that condition.

That some of the well-intentioned Argonauts surely failed, whether from incompetence or bad luck or both, was inevitable. . . . After two years in the gold fields, John Kerr wrote his mother of the condition of his wife. "I have received per last steamer a letter from Elmira. I pity her from the bottom of my heart. She must have a hard time of it. I have not been able to send her any assistance since I have been out here. She represents herself and children as being almost naked. God help them." Kerr wrote constantly of his intentions to bring his wife and children to California, or to return to them in the East. He never made the move, frustrated by indecision and by his uncertain financial prospects. Finally, in 1857, after eight years in California, he asked a friend to prepay postage on a letter to his wife, "for I presume she has no money to pay for anything." . . .

Not the least cause of contention within families, however, was the fact that the 49ers and their families had grown to be strangers to one another. From the mining camps to the towns, cities, and agricultural valleys, the 49ers saw the Gold Rush as unique in ways other than simply the opportunity for wealth it presented. It was also an experience that by its distance from familiar sources of support and comfort, its exposure to different peoples,

customs, and values, and its competitive, all-male character encouraged independence. And as we have already seen, many 49ers found themselves
routinely doing and accepting things that they never would have entertained or countenanced at home, from professionals working at hard labor in
the mines to men of humble origins operating as bankers, and from Sabbath
breaking to gambling and prostitution. Thus, the Argonauts came to regard
themselves as different from the men who had boarded the ships and wagons to head west. They had been tempered by their experiences and their
hardships.

Because of this growing sense of estrangement, many 49ers felt equivo-
cal about returning home. One offered a common observation: "I shudder
when I think of the many trials and temptations to which I have been
subjected," he wrote. "How hard it is for the wanderer to turn his steps
homeward, those who have never been severed from friends, from the asso-
ciations of their childhood, imagine that an absence of a few months would
fill their minds with an unconquerable desire to revisit scenes that were
familiar." Indeed, so powerful was this sense of difference that . . . it constantly informed one of the central topics of the 49ers correspondence with
their families: would the absent one ever return home?

Questions for Discussion

1. What does the Gold Rush experience suggest about the fluidity of gender roles?
2. Why did 49ers view women as "civilizers"? If women were "civilizers," what
   were men?
3. Describe the daily work routine at the mines. How did the California climate
   affect that routine?
4. The Gold Rush made some people rich, and it was a boon to the American
   economy. According to the author, what was its impact on the fortunes and
   families of a majority of 49ers?

For Further Reading

Gail Bederman, *Manliness and Civilization: A Cultural History of Gender and Race in the
United States, 1880–1917* (1995); William A. Bowen, *The Willamette Valley: Migration
and Settlement on the Oregon Frontier* (1978); Gene M. Brack, *Mexico Views Manifest
Destiny: 1821–1846* (1975); John Mack Faragher, *Women and Men on the Overland Trail*
(1979); Marion Goldman, *Gold Diggers and Silver Miners: Prostitution and Social Life on
the Comstock Lode* (1981); William Greever, *Bonanza West: The Story of the Western
Mining Rushes, 1848–1900* (1963); Erwin G. Gudde, *California Gold Camps* (1975);
J. S. Holliday, *The World Rushed In: The California Gold Rush Experience* (1981); Julie Roy
Jeffrey, *Frontier Women: The Trans-Mississippi West, 1840–1880* (1979); Drew Heath
Johnson and Marcia Eymann, eds., *Silver and Gold: Cased Images of the California Gold
Rush* (1998); Susan Lee Johnson, *Roaring Camp: The Social World of the California Gold
Rush* (2000); Rudolph Lapp, *Blacks in Gold Rush California* (1977); Patricia Nelson

Limerick, *The Legacy of Conquest: The Unbroken Past of the American West* (1987); Matt S. Meier and Feliciano Ribera, *Mexican Americans/American Mexicans: From Conquistadors to Chicanos* (1993); Clyde A. Milner II, Carol A. O'Conner, and Martha A. Sandweiss, eds., *The Oxford History of the American West* (1994); Jay Monaghan, *Chile, Peru and the California Gold Rush of 1849* (1973); Leonard Pitt, *The Decline of Californios* (1966); Glenda Riley, *The Female Frontier: A Comparative View of Women on the Prairie and the Plains* (1988); Kevin Starr, *Americans and the California Dream, 1850–1915* (1973); John D. Unruh Jr., *The Plains Across: The Overland Emigrants and the Trans-Mississippi West, 1840–60* (1979); Elliott West, *Growing Up with the Country: Childhood on the Far-Western Frontier* (1989); Stephen Williams, *The Chinese in the California Mines, 1848–1860* (1971); David Wyatt, *Five Fires: Race, Catastrophe, and the Shaping of California* (1997); Mark Wyman, *Hard Rock Epic: Western Miners and Industrial Revolution, 1860–1910* (1979); Judy Yung, *Unbound Feet: A Social History of Chinese Women in San Francisco* (1995).

14

A Religious Challenge to Capitalism

The Oneida Community

Spencer Klaw

By the middle of the nineteenth century, Americans had created the economic and social foundations for a dynamic capitalist society. Their competitive individualism and zest for economic enterprise nourished industrial development. And the rise of the factory system helped swell the population of cities, encourage immigration, and promote territorial expansion.

As we saw in Chapter 10, changes in ideas about gender, marriage, childrearing, and family privacy accompanied these developments. This was especially true within the upwardly mobile, enterprising middle class that lived in cities. It may be useful to quickly review some of the key issues.

By the 1830s and 1840s, the "ideal" middle-class woman was viewed as innately moral, physically fragile, and instinctively nurturing and emotional. She was, therefore, inevitably destined for a life as a wife and mother—and to dwell mostly within the safe confines of the home. At best, she was indifferent to sex except for the purpose of reproduction. By contrast, men were seen as inherently aggressive, ambitious, and even ruthless. They were perfectly suited to compete in the economic and political world outside of the home. Women and men, then, existed in more or less "separate spheres" of social roles, activities, and experiences. Male children should be raised to be self-reliant, self-controlled, honest, and individualistic. These character traits were believed to be essential for success in the business world.

Not all Americans felt comfortable with these economic and social values. From the 1830s to the onset of the Civil War, social reform movements

A mid-1890s gathering of Oneida residents. Were social relations at Oneida as cohesive as this photograph suggests?

challenged various features of the free-wheeling capitalist order. They ranged from demands to end slavery and give women the right to vote, to efforts to prohibit the sale of alcoholic beverages and create utopian experiments in communal living. To one degree or another, all of these movements were inspired by evangelical Protestantism.

One of the most controversial of these efforts was an experiment in communal living founded in 1837 in Putney, Vermont. It was organized by John Humphrey Noyes, a charismatic evangelical clergyman. In 1848 Noyes moved his community of about 200 disciples to Oneida, in upstate New York, where they continued to live as a community until 1881. Noyes believed in the Christian doctrine of "perfectionism." This doctrine held that it was possible for saintly Christians (those convinced their souls were already redeemed) to lead morally perfect lives. In other words, saintly Christians could live "without sin," as though they were already in heaven. And they could live together peacefully, in perfect harmony and equality, without greed, violence, or jealousy.

The economic basis of Oneida was what Noyes called "Bible Communism." It was Noyes's response to what he saw as the egotism and selfishness of capitalism. For Noyes, true Christianity required God's children to share equally in the fruits of their labor. Economic equality paid handsome dividends to members of the Oneida community, who were hardworking, enterprising laborers. In time, the community made significant profits from its many enterprises, including the production of hunting traps and preserved produce. The community's most noteworthy creation was its world-famous Oneida silverware. Profits from these enterprises were shared equally.

As Spencer Klaw shows in the next essay, more than profits were shared at Oneida. Noyes and his followers condemned the ideal of romantic love between two people as selfish and possessive. They believed romantic love, marriage, family privacy, and sexual monogamy were expressions of materialism run amok. Possessing a person in marriage was the same as owning money, land, or cattle. Conventional marriage was a prison for women. And, according to Noyes, it was also sexually boring for wives and husbands.

The Oneida community replaced conventional marriage with what Noyes called "complex marriage." In effect, complex marriage meant that everyone in the community was married to everyone else—and could change sexual partners with regularity. And they did. This was true even of married couples who were deeply attached to one another. As Noyes said in rejecting monogamy: "the fact that a man loves peaches best is no reason why he should not, on suitable occasions, eat apples or cherries." Noyes also rejected the gendered "separate spheres" ideology that dominated American culture by the mid-nineteenth century. Instead, Oneidans believed that women were close to men in intellectual ability and in their capacity for work. As evangelical Christians, however, they did not view women as men's equals. But they did believe women should not be slaves to their husbands' sexual demands, or be the sole caretakers of the home. Children at Oneida were not raised by their parents in isolated households. They were nurtured in a community center, the Children's House, similar in some ways to today's day-care arrangements. Finally, men at Oneida practiced what Noyes called "male continence" during sex: they did not ejaculate. They were supposed to focus on pleasing their female partners. According to Noyes, this approach to sex would elevate women and men beyond self-centered pleasure. Instead, it would transform what in mainstream society was a selfish, merely sensual act, into universal love and closeness to God.

The Oneida experiment is most famous for its unusual sexual arrangements. But as Spencer Klaw demonstrates in the following essay, that is not the only reason for its historical significance. Oneida was important because it emphasized the importance of cooperation and social relationships in an age dominated by "rugged" individualism and family privacy. It was a rebellion against private gain within the marketplace and private domesticity within the middle class. The Oneida experiment also brought to the surface some of mid-nineteenth-century society's most glaring economic and gender inequities. Finally, Oneida is an example of how private religious beliefs, especially those of evangelical Protestants, and public issues have been entwined throughout American history.

Source: Spencer Klaw, *Without Sin: The Life and Death of the Oneida Community* (New York: Penguin, 1993), pp. 104–107, 130–136, 179.

BIBLE COMMUNISM

All work at Oneida was equally rewarded; that is, it was not rewarded at all. All Oneidans, no matter what jobs they did or how well they did them, had an equal claim on the Community for food, clothing, and shelter. For most of the Community's life, members simply applied to a clothing committee when they needed new clothes, or checked off on a printed form the items they would require during the coming year. "If you need a new window curtain, stand-spread, an easy chair, a footstool, a different bedstead, a looking glass, or a larger bureau," the *Circular* [the Community newspaper] explained, "just apply to Mrs. S., who has charge of the furniture, and she will be sure to do her best to accommodate you. When the carpet in your room grows threadbare and shabby, let Miss K. know of it and she will provide you with a better one." It was not until 1862, after a long period when many Oneidans had not handled money from one year to the next, that allowances were instituted: twenty-five cents every three months for each adult, twelve and a half cents for each child. In 1875 the system was changed, each adult being given an annual sum for clothing and incidentals. But everybody got the same amount: that is, the men got $75, while the women, who were expected to make most of their own clothes, got $40.

When visitors were informed of these facts they were often curious to know what was done with people who didn't want to work. The standard reply was a bland assertion that the problem really didn't exist at Oneida because such persons simply "cannot live under our system of religious influence, criticism, and education." Noyes and his followers were not above stretching things a bit when describing their system to outsiders—love and sex were never quite as free of conflict and frustration at Oneida as the world was asked to believe—and now and again someone had to be rebuked for trying to get out of menial jobs. William Inslee, the Community's chief machinist, was once publicly criticized for "daintiness about work," having given the impression that he was too proud to do unskilled work in the trap shop even though more hands were urgently needed there. But, in general, Oneidans willingly took their turns at washing dishes and mucking out the cow barns, and until the very last years, when Noyes and his chief lieutenants worried that the will to work had been sapped by too great a reliance on hired help, laziness was not really a problem. One powerful deterrent to shirking was fear of penalties that could include, besides public criticism, severe restrictions on the shirker's choice of sexual partners. "There is a strong current here which favors activity; and it is easier, I find, to go along with the current than against it," an Oneidan observed mildly. "So if I wanted to be lazy I should choose some other place."

Actually, Noyes worried less about shirkers than about people who worked too hard or in the wrong spirit. In his view, work should develop the worker's understanding and love of God and of his fellows, and he insisted that this was more important than mere efficiency. Work was to be seen as a school in which the young and the spiritually laggard would learn from their elders and betters. Noyes and his lieutenants repeatedly reminded the Oneidans that work was a form of service to God, and that it must not be tainted by the selfishness in which work and business in the world outside were so firmly rooted. In 1856, the foremen of the trap shop were sharply criticized for driving their workers too hard and paying too little attention to their spiritual formation. When the foremen failed to respond to this treatment, a different remedy was prescribed. It was decided to stop the machinery three times a week for shop meetings whose chief object would be "to promote spiritual improvement and the acknowledgement of the presence and spirit of Christ in the business."

* * *

"We believe," the *Circular* proclaimed in 1853, "that the great secret of securing enthusiasm in labor and producing a free, healthy, social equilibrium, is contained in the proposition, 'loving companionship and labor, and especially the mingling of the sexes, makes labor attractive.'" The *Circular*'s message, freely translated, was that mixing up men and women at work not only made work pleasanter, but helped people to find new partners in the dance of complex marriage. Men and women at Oneida worked together not only in doing the laundry, but in getting out the *Circular*, sewing traveling bags, and hoeing corn. In the years when the Oneidans did their housework without hired help, two men were regularly assigned to the kitchen crew, together with five women. Men helped with dishes, men and women both milked cows, and men and women worked together in the Children's House. On occasion men even took a hand in the delivery of babies.

For a long time, women worked alongside men in the trap shop. In a letter written in 1867, not long before she became editor-in-chief of the *Circular*, a young woman named Harriet Worden recalled her days as a trap-shop hand many years before. The letter was addressed to "Father Noyes," as he was often called, who was then living at Wallingford, and it is a declaration of love from a woman who, three years later, was to have a child by Noyes. But it also suggests the loving companionship, to use the *Circular*'s phrase, that would develop when men and women worked together, and when there was a lowering of the barriers that conventionally separated the worlds of work, love, religion, and the nurturing of the young. She wrote:

> Last evening there was a call for volunteers to give a little extra help in the trap shop . . . and as I used to work at that, I thought I would volunteer. . . . My work, the noises and the odors of the shop—everything around me—reminded me of old times; and when not looking up, I could almost imagine that you were standing at the bench with me.
>
> And so my thoughts were gliding down the "gulf of time," and I saw myself at your side, heating springs for you to hammer out, a girl of fifteen just waking up to the idea that this world contained many things not dreamed of at the children's house. Then

I found myself weighing steel for you, and could see your attention to every detail, and myself grown a little older . . . confiding in you for guidance, yet wayward and thoughtless. . . . With every improvement and incident in the trap shop, my own life seemed intertwined, for thinking of one brought up the other; and at this stage, I could see myself with youthful excitement—having seen the end of several youthful flirtations, but under new fascinations, and still clinging to you as my guide and refuge.

Complex Marriage And Women

[Noyes's Bible Communism, the idea that all earthly possessions should be shared equally by all, had a social parallel in his concept of "complex marriage." As Klaw notes in the next section, for Noyes and his followers, emancipation from private property and liberation from monogamous relationships went hand in hand.]

One aim of Bible Communism was to emancipate women from the slavery to which, as Noyes saw it, they were customarily condemned in mid-nineteenth-century America. Looked at from the perspective of late-twentieth-century feminism, the emancipation was far from complete, and the record of how women fared at Oneida is filled with contradictions. But it is clear that they were granted rights, and offered a range of choices as to how they would dispose of their lives, that only the most radical feminists were beginning to claim—and then mainly in private—at the time Oneida was founded.

For one thing, women at Oneida were much freer than they would have been in the outside world to decide for themselves when, how often, and with whom they would have sex. That freedom was not unlimited. The rules of complex marriage did not permit monogamy. Nor did they sanction celibacy, sex being regarded by Noyes as a religious ordinance—an obligatory celebration of the goodness of God. (Christ, he once said, was determined that men and women should "love one another burningly . . . flow into each other's hearts.") Moreover, a woman who violated the rule of ascending fellowship—that is, who persisted in turning down proposals for sex from members of Noyes's inner circle of associates—was inviting public censure. Why, she would be asked, was she stubbornly passing up the opportunity to improve her character by intimate association with her spiritual superiors? But these restrictions were hardly as onerous as those imposed by conventional marriage, in which the wife had virtually no sexual rights at all, her husband being legally and even morally at liberty to use her body for his pleasure at will and on his own terms. At Oneida, by contrast, it was incumbent on men to make sex pleasurable for their partners—the Oneidans emphatically rejected the curious notion, advanced by most medical authorities, that normal women were incapable of enjoying sex—and a man who was sexually awkward or inconsiderate was not only plied with criticism and advice, but might have a hard time persuading anyone to go to bed with him until he had mended his ways.

Another and perhaps more important privilege that Bible Communism conferred on women was the freedom, thanks to male continence, to lead an active sex life without committing themselves to one pregnancy after another. This freedom was also enjoyed by women in the outside world whose husbands practiced coitus interruptus, which, at the time Oneida was founded, was the only reasonably reliable alternative to complete abstinence as a technique for limiting family size. But a husband might refuse to honor his wife's desire to avoid pregnancy. And when this happened she had no recourse other than to leave her husband (which was usually out of the question unless she had relatives willing to take her in) or to take the drastic step of forcing abstinence on him—and herself—by falling, consciously or unconsciously, into invalidism. At Oneida such measures were unnecessary. A man who was unable or unwilling to control his ejaculations could expect to be punished by sexual ostracism or, at least, to be limited in his choice of partners to women past menopause. Under the threat of such sanctions, Oneida men became reasonably skillful at avoiding what Noyes called the "propagative crisis"; in a community of well over two hundred adults, accidental pregnancies occurred at a rate of fewer than one a year.

Women at Oneida were free to have babies, as well as not to have them, provided the Community approved. For more than twenty years pregnancies were discouraged, on the ground that the Community was too poor to support a lot of children. But even then, a woman who had never had a baby, and who was getting up into her thirties, was usually given permission to become pregnant if she wished. And after the general ban on babies was lifted in 1869, when the Community began its ambitious attempt at scientific human breeding, a childless woman who was eager to have a baby was usually told to go ahead even if she did not strike the managers of the experiment as an ideal candidate for motherhood. The theory was that her spiritual or other deficiencies could be offset by choosing an especially well qualified man to be the father of her child.

When a woman at Oneida did have a child, she was relieved of many of the usual burdens of motherhood. For a year or so she was spared from most housekeeping chores so that she could concentrate on caring for her baby. At the end of this period she turned it over to the foster mothers in the Children's House. Mothers were not invariably happy about giving up their children to the care of the Community. But this was thought to be good not only for the children—there was much talk about the harmful effects of "sickly maternal tenderness"—but for the mothers as well. As a Community writer pointed out, "We do not believe that motherhood is the chief end of woman's life; that she was made for the children she can bear. She was made for God and herself." Women at Oneida were also spared much of the domestic drudgery that was the lot of most women in the outside world even when they had domestic help. In part this was because they were under no pressure, as most middle-class Victorian housewives felt they were, to justify their sheltered position in the home by fussing excessively over its furnishings and appointments. By Victorian standards the Mansion House was rather simply and barely furnished, and relatively easy to maintain. Moreover, cooking, housekeeping, and baby tending were far more efficient than in ordinary households. For these reasons—and because men helped out in the kitchen and with heavy cleaning—Community women, even before there were hired girls to do the laundry and certain other domestic chores, had much more time than the great majority of American women to read, study, and invite their souls.

They also had the opportunity, seldom found in the outside world, of living in close association with other women. Many found in long-lasting friendships with other women the emotional security and deep intimacy they were barred from seeking—except for brief periods—in relationships with men. Thus when two friends, Beulah Hendee and Annie Hatch, found themselves falling in love with the same man, Hatch, thanking Hendee for her assurance of "deep sincere love," wrote, "*That* certainly is more gratifying to me than to know that any man loves me, and be assured that Jacques or any other man *shall not* separate our hearts. I prize your friendship and love more than I do Jacques' and you shall have my confidence and the *first love* of my heart—next to God and my superiors."

* * *

But while Oneidans agreed with such militant feminists as Victoria Woodhull and Tennessee Claflin that women in America were cruelly exploited by men, they differed with these and other leaders of the women's rights movement on a fundamental point. Again and again, in the *Circular* and other Community publications, they ridiculed the feminist claim that women were, or should be, the equals of men. "I am a woman, and am in favor of female suffrage, and more than that, of the abolition of marriage-slavery," a Community member observed; "and yet from my very soul I believe in the inherent superiority of man. His essential nature is the noblest. It is not only stronger than woman's, but finer-grained; not only more powerful intellectually, but richest in the affections." Like St. Paul—and like the orthodox Christian theological of his own day—Noyes held that, in the spiritual hierarchy of the universe, God stood above Christ, Christ stood above man, and man stood above woman. It followed that a man who wholeheartedly accepted Christ as his master was entitled, in turn, "to command respect, subordination, and loving receptivity on the part of woman." Women would find happiness and the fulfillment of their destinies in serving such a man as his loving helpmate. "The grand right I ask for women is to love the men and be loved by them," an Oneida woman asserted in the course of an attack on the doctrine of equality. "I want the right of the most intimate partnership with man . . . I would rather be tyrannized over by him, than to be *independent* of him."

Noyes taught his followers that women owed their male masters more than just respect and loving receptivity. They had a further obligation to make men love them—if possible, to love them wildly. Thus, in summing up his criticism of Fanny Leonard, on the occasion when he compared her to a beautiful and fragrant plant, Noyes said enthusiastically, "If a woman has a pure heart, and it will do a man good to love her, I say to her, Come on, I don't care how bewitching you are—the more I am bewitched by real goodness the better." He went on to say that there was even "a sort of sly tact and art" that women could legitimately employ to make themselves bewitching. By contrast, women who were brisk and businesslike in their dealings with men, or who displayed the "self-asserting masculinity" that the Oneidans professed to see in the leaders of the women's rights movement, were likely to be treated harshly by their criticism committees. The ideal woman was, like Mary Cragin [Noyes's favorite lover], one whose "only ambition was to be the servant of love."

In his insistence that women had a sacred duty to make men happy, Noyes was not far out of line with the views held by most contemporary editors of women's magazines and most authors of books on marriage and homemaking. But he differed radically from these authorities in his notions of what kind of helpmate a woman should try to be. The same eulogist who praised Mary Cragin as a servant of love also praised her for her ability as an organizer and leader, and for her "active, powerful intellect." Noyes had no use for the widely held theory that women—middle-class women, that is, not those who worked as kitchen maids or in cotton mills—were by nature too fragile to think hard or work hard, and were therefore unqualified to meddle in the practical affairs of men, or to express strong opinions about anything other than matters of morality and household economy. He assumed that God shared his own preference for women who were lively, frank, firm in their opinions, well informed and well organized, and physically as well as intellectually robust. "The standard of feminine character to which we aspire," Harriet Skinner wrote, "is the acquisition of healthy, vigorous bodies, active, fruitful minds, large hearts, and perfect sincerity of manners." In an age when it was fashionable for women to emphasize how different they were from men by proclaiming their helplessness and dependency, women at Oneida, though they were praised for being bewitching and lovable, were exhorted to "get rid of effeminacy," to cultivate "manliness and robustness of character," and not to shrink from "outdoor manly industry." In the hay fields and the printing shop and the editorial offices of the Community's publications, as well as in the trap shop, Oneida women worked side by side, and on equal terms, with men—a relationship in which a stance of clinging femininity was clearly inappropriate. Women at Oneida were free, too, from the restrictions of Victorian prudery. Writing to Noyes not long after the breakup of the Community, a former member named Gaylord Reeve recalled nostalgically that women who had "not been my especial friends in a sexual sense" at Oneida had nevertheless spoken with him about sexual matters "in a simple manner as they might have done upon any other subject." This struck him, he said, as "something sweeter and purer than I've found in the world in general."

Complex Marriage and Men

[In the previous section, Klaw pointed out that for the most part women at Oneida approved of male continence. For men, however, as he shows in this final section, continence could be problematic.]

But for men, male continence not surprisingly could have an unintended side effect. Coitus interruptus was forbidden at Oneida, Noyes holding that it led a man to concentrate too much on his own physical pleasure and not enough on God and his partner. (He also argued that it wasted a precious fluid that men were better off retaining except when its expenditure was required for procreation.) And while one man at Oneida told Hilda Noyes [Noyes's grandniece] that he himself "never remembered any local congestion following an interview" [i.e., sexual intercourse], he conceded that other men were not invariably immune to the severe pain that can result when prolonged sexual arousal is not relieved by ejaculation. He somewhat improbably insisted, however, that he had never heard of anyone seeking relief from such pain by masturbation—a practice of which Noyes took as dim a view as any conventional moralist or medical authority of his day. At Oneida the only approved remedy for postcoital discomfort was cold water.

In a testimonial written for the Community's first annual report, one man asserted that sex as practiced at Oneida "expands and elevates the heart, roots out and destroys selfishness in its various forms—destroys isolation—unlocks a fountain in the soul unknown before, and leads us to the boundless ocean of God's love." One need not be a cynic to speculate that, under the stern rule of male continence, men may have thought hard about God during sex as a good way to avoid thinking about the exquisite sexual pleasure they were obliged to forgo. But it is likely that the restraint and the quietness imposed by male continence may, in some instances, have transformed sexual intercourse into a quasi-religious experience—an affirmation of the superiority of spiritual to physical love. But this is only guesswork. Such diaries and letters of Oneidans as have survived and are accessible to historians offer few clues as to how men at Oneida really felt about—and coped with—sex without orgasm. All that can be said with confidence is that few of them found it so frustrating that they left the Community. Of the men and boys who were on the Community's rolls in 1853, at the end of its first five years, just under 60 percent were still members a quarter century later when Noyes went off to Canada. [Among other reasons, Noyes fled the United States to avoid prosecution for violating laws against fornication and adultery.]

Questions for Discussion

1. Compare the capitalist system of work and rewards with that of Oneida's. What features of the Oneida labor system would Americans of the time have found attractive or unattractive? Do you agree with Noyes that capitalist materialism and male–female "possessiveness" are related?
2. On balance, did Oneida "liberate" women or confine them by another means?
3. "Complex marriage" and other aspects of the Oneida experiment presented a challenge to mainstream family life in America. In your opinion, why did that challenge fail?

For Further Reading

Ann Braude, *Radical Spirits: Spiritualism and Women's Rights in Nineteenth-Century America* (1992); Maren L. Carden, *Oneida: Utopian Community to Modern Corporation* (1995); Marlyn Dalsimer, "Bible Communists: Female Socialization and Family Life in the Oneida Community," in Mel Albin and Dominick Cavallo, eds., *Family Life in America* (1981); Sterling F. Delano, *Brook Farm: The Dark Side of Utopia* (2005); Barbara Epstein, *The Politics of Domesticity: Women, Evangelism, and Temperance in Nineteenth-Century America* (1980); Lawrence Foster, *Women, Family, and Utopia: Communal Experiments of the Shakers, the Oneida Community, and the Mormons* (1991); Carl J. Guarneri, *The Utopian Alternative: Fourierism in Nineteenth-Century America* (1994); Mark Halloway, *Utopian Communities in America, 1680–1880* (1966); Rosabeth Moss Kanter, *Commitment and Community: Communes and Utopianism in Sociological Perspective* (2005); Louis Kern, *An Ordered Love: Sex Roles and Sexuality in Victorian Utopias—The Shakers, the Mormons, and the Oneida Community* (1981); Robert Allen Parker, *Yankee Spirit: John Humphrey Noyes and the Oneida Community* (1993); Donald E. Pitzer, *America's Communal Utopias* (1997); Constance Noyes Robertson, *Oneida Community: An Autobiography, 1851–1876* (1970); Ronald Walters, *American Reformers, 1815–1860* (1978).

Free Black Women, the Movement to Abolish Slavery, and the Struggle for Women's Rights

Shirley J. Yee

The Oneida experiment was fueled by the religious fervor that swept the country in the first half of the nineteenth century. But the desire for personal and social change ignited by evangelical Protestantism took many forms in those years. And like Oneida, they could be shocking to mainstream notions of respectability, although for different reasons. The most important and controversial of these attempts to transform American society were the anti-slavery and women's rights movements.

By 1804, slavery had been abolished in every northeastern state (the Northwest Ordinance of 1787 prohibited slavery north of the Ohio River and west of Pennsylvania to the Mississippi River). While a handful of individuals, most notably northern Quakers, urged that slavery be ended throughout the United States, few Americans demanded an immediate end to the institution in the early years of the century. In 1817 the American Colonization Society was organized. Its ultimate goals—compensation to slave owners who voluntarily freed their slaves and the deportation of *all* black Americans (free as well as slave) to Africa—were neither practical, nor a serious challenge to the status quo.

This changed in the early 1830s with the development of the abolition-ist movement. Its most important early leader was William Lloyd Garrison.

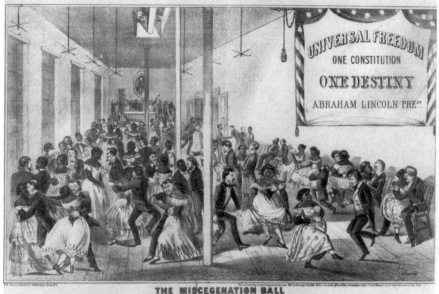

How does this cartoon of 1864 express deeply felt, if seldom expressed, fears raised by northerners opposed to the abolition movement?

Garrison was a New England journalist and fervent evangelical Christian. In 1831 he began publication of *The Liberator*, the first newspaper to call for the immediate, unconditional end to slavery—and without compensation to slave holders. In 1833 Garrison and others founded the American Anti-Slavery Society. Garrison approached slavery from a religious and moral rather than political or economic perspective. For him, slavery was a sin. It stripped slaves of the freedom to choose salvation by making their own moral choices. Garrison quoted from Scripture: "In Jesus Christ, all are one: there is neither Jew nor Greek, there is neither bond nor free, there is neither male nor female." These words had radical implications, because they seemed to require not just the *abolition* of slavery, but *equality* between the races—and the sexes.

Garrison's attack on slavery and racism attracted the support of free black people in the North. Free blacks were the majority of subscribers to *The Liberator* in the 1830s. Frederick Douglass, David Walker, Sojourner Truth, and many other blacks played major roles in the movement. In addition to working with Garrison's group, free black people organized numerous reform societies of their own. Their goal was to improve the condition of free blacks in the North (where more than 90 percent were prevented by law from voting and subjected to segregation in public facilities) as well as to end slavery in the South.

Black and white women also participated in the abolition movement. The participation of women in political movements was previously unheard of; it could potentially undermine what the vast majority of Americans considered women's "proper" place in society. Respectable women were supposed to devote themselves almost entirely to their family and domestic responsibilities. Supposedly, they were neither temperamentally nor intellectually equipped to participate in the male world of economic competition and political conflict.

But women were active in the abolition movement from the start. The first female antislavery society was established in 1832 by black women in Salem, Massachusetts; the following year a group of black and white women founded the Philadelphia Female Anti-Slavery Society, which became one of the most influential antislavery organizations in the country. By the end of the 1830s, women had created thirty-three female abolition organizations.

Most male abolitionists were wary of female participation in the movement or opposed it altogether. Until the late 1830s, however, most were willing to accept women on three conditions: that they remain segregated in their own antislavery societies; that they could not vote or participate in policy-making within the American Anti-Slavery Society; and that they were not permitted to speak before "mixed" audiences of men and women.

By the late 1830s, though, some white female antislavery activists began to see a connection, however vague at first, between the power masters wielded over their slaves and the power fathers and husbands exercised over their daughters and wives. With the support of Garrison and Frederick Douglass, they began as well to exert greater influence within the American Anti-Slavery Society, to speak before mixed audiences at its gatherings, and to vote at its meetings. The struggle against slavery and the idea of women's rights began to merge. As antislavery activist and Garrison ally Angelina Grimké said, "Since I engaged in the investigation of the rights of the slave, I have necessarily been led to a better understanding of my own." Her point, of course, was that slaves had no rights, and to a great extent neither did American women. The women's rights movement that would blossom in the 1840s grew directly from female involvement in the abolition movement. "I feel," said Grimké, "as if it is not the cause of the slave only which we plead but the cause of Woman as a responsible & moral being. . . . What an untrodden path we have entered upon."

As Shirley J. Yee points out in the next essay, by the 1850s free black women also became committed to female rights and laid the foundations for a black feminist sensibility. Former slaves like Sojourner Truth and Ellen Craft and free black women such as Sarah Forten and Mary Ann Shadd Cary attempted to link ending slavery in the South and eliminating racism in the North with enhancing women's rights everywhere in the country. As Yee demonstrates, attempts by black female activists to connect slavery, racism, and women's rights created enormous tensions within the abolitionist movement. White female abolitionists wanted an end to slavery but were often insensitive to the concerns of free black women, or they were racists who believed in black inferiority. Black women committed to women's rights also clashed with black male abolitionists, most of whom wanted their families to emulate the "separate spheres" gender roles of the white middle class. Being both female and black placed these women in extremely difficult circumstances but did not diminish their determination to end slavery and racism as well as fight for women's rights.

Yee's essay has two parts. In the first, she describes the rage aimed at abolitionist women, both white and black, who dared speak in public before mixed audiences. Public speaking at that time was reserved exclusively for men, especially politicians and clergy. Public speakers were expected to be knowledgeable about public issues and possess the power to move and persuade people. In other words, public speakers were figures of authority who could vote. By definition at this time, that meant they were men. For a woman to speak before a male audience was more than "un-feminine." For many Americans, it actually threatened to destroy the private world of the family by blurring gender roles, injecting women into "public" life, and taking women away from their day-to-day supervision of their children and households. This accounts for the verbal and physical violence aimed at women who spoke in public. For example, in 1838, a mob of 10,000 enraged men in Philadelphia hurled stones at the building where a convention of antislavery women activists was being held. The next day the mob burned down the building. And in 1840, Garrison's organization split, mostly over disagreements over the role of women in the movement. In the second part of her essay, Yee describes the development of a black female rights movement and the opposition black female abolitionists encountered from white women and black men in their struggle for women's rights.

Source: Shirley J. Yee, *Black Women Abolitionists: A Study in Activism, 1828–1860* (Knoxville: University of Tennessee Press, 1992), pp. 112–117, 136–153.

WOMEN ABOLITIONISTS AND PUBLIC SPEAKING

For a number of black women, commitment to the movement for racial equality led to participation in activities that challenged nineteenth-century notions of acceptable behavior for women and blacks. When women wrote antislavery poetry and prose, spoke from public platforms, or signed and circulated petitions condemning slavery and northern racism, they defied customary codes of behavior. In the process, they, as individuals and as a group, reconstructed notions of respectability within the free black community regarding black female activism. . . .

In varying degrees, black women's activism challenged prevailing assumptions of black female inferiority. As we know, such images were deeply rooted, complex, and often contradictory. Whites often perceived black women as more docile than black men, simply because they were women, but a "Mammy" stereotype depicting black women as strong and domineering also prevailed among whites, an image that was reinforced when women physically resisted slavery and racism. Black women's activism also carried important implications for sexual dynamics within their communities, defying both racist laws and customs meant to keep blacks illiterate and submissive and gender boundaries helping to define acceptable behavior in nineteenth-century American free society.

With the exception of [former slaves] Sojourner Truth and Ellen Craft, many of the leading black women who engaged in public speaking and writing shared a common background. Margaretta Forten, Sarah Forten, Maria Miller Stewart, Frances Harper, Mary Ann Shadd Cary, and Sarah P. Remond had all been born into free black families in which they enjoyed some measure of economic privilege and formal education. Their background of education, relative economic comfort, and family activism set them apart from both slaves and the majority of free blacks. Their personal and professional connections with abolitionist friends, in addition to their own talents, undoubtedly helped them gain access to abolitionist newspapers and the public platform.

Public speaking and writing had long been acceptable ways for men to engage in intellectual self-expression, but not until the 1940s had women, white or black, begun in any numbers to break the custom barring them from such activities. . . . Proclaiming the evils of slavery and the possibility of racial equality, on the antislavery lecture circuit, was risky for anyone. Like abolitionist writers and editors, who faced the destruction of their presses and physical violence at the hands of anti-abolitionist mobs, antislavery lecturers risked their personal safety in their travels. Black women speakers, like other abolitionist men and women, were often at the mercy of hostile audiences who harassed them physically as well as verbally. Frances Harper, for example, wrote of troubles she and her colleagues encountered when they lectured in small towns in Ohio. At Columbiana they were "interrupted by a manifestation of rowdyism," and when they traveled to Churchill they were met with an attempt at sabotage: "We had some more persons of the same spirit, who made a noise during the time of speaking, and removed some of the linch pins from our wagon. It was, however, discovered in time to prevent any injury to life or limb."

Violence on the lecture tours was an even greater threat for black women than for black men and white abolitionists. Physical and verbal attacks against black women activists could originate at any time or place from crowds motivated by three sources of hostility: anti-black feelings, anti-abolitionist sentiments, and hatred of "public" women. Unlike male abolitionists, women who spoke in public invited criticism from audiences who believed they had violated basic ideals of "proper" behavior for women.

Although black women enjoyed support from the men of their race for their writings and, eventually, for their speeches, they still found themselves bound by codes of proper behavior for women. As in the white community, social custom in the free black community still required women to act like "ladies." Black male leaders applauded black women speakers only so long as they did not criticize black men directly or assume a position of authority in gatherings where men were present. The period between 1830 and the 1860s was one in which female public speakers gradually gained acceptance from both abolitionists leaders and their audiences. . . .

Public speaking, more than any other abolitionist activity, seemed to spark the greatest conflict between the sexes. Public opinion was slow to accept female lecturers, regardless of race, because public speaking was an activity in which an individual assumed a role of authority long the domain of political leaders and a predominantly male clergy and forbidden to women by social and religious custom. . . .

Black and white women speakers drew additional criticism when they spoke to audiences made up of both men and women, in defiance of traditional dictates that male and female audiences be kept separated, sometimes in different rooms. At the World Antislavery Convention in London in 1840, for example, male and female members of the audience sat in separate sections of the hall, with women in the back behind a curtain, where they were not allowed to participate in the proceedings. . . .

For white women, in particular, public speaking posed a threat to domestic tranquility. Writing poetry and essays did not require women to leave their households, and even women who attended local antislavery society meetings or antislavery sewing circles usually did not need to travel outside the neighborhood or town. But delivering speeches was another matter: it required women to leave their homes and towns and, hence, their domestic duties. Men and women who opposed the idea of women speaking in public feared that because it drew women away from their homes and into the political arena with men, they would abandon their domestic responsibilities altogether.

Free blacks may have had similar concerns when they saw women of their race participating in lecture tours. Unlike middle-class white women, black women were often away from their families for most of the day, because most worked outside the home. Although it was clear that black women had not abandoned their family responsibilities when they left home to earn a wage and participate in community activism, some blacks were apprehensive about women who sought to leave their communities to engage in potentially dangerous activity. As a result, black women lecturers received mixed responses. Some black leaders perhaps understood too clearly the damage that racism and economic deprivation had already done to the ideals of manhood and womanhood in the free black community; it was hard enough that black women had to help support their families, and allowing them to draw further from home duties by participating in public-speaking tours might permanently damage the effort to create middle-class gender roles.

FREE BLACK WOMEN AND WOMEN'S RIGHTS

During the 1830s, the "woman question" had opened animated discussion about the possibility of achieving sexual as well as racial equality, given the extensiveness of female activism in the battle against slavery. The abolition movement had provided the setting in which both black and white women challenged their subordinate status as females and campaigned for an equal voice for women in antislavery organizations and in society at large. Black women interested in rights for women continued the struggle against racism, no doubt because experience had made them painfully aware of contradictions between rhetoric and reality in the struggle for equality. White feminist-abolitionists had proclaimed a sisterhood between themselves and black women, likening their own oppression to that of the slave and using as a favorite rhetorical device the image of the black woman as a victim of double oppression—but white women, as a group, could not always be trusted to evaluate their own complicity in racism or even to understand black women's concerns. In fact, only a few white women had publicly addressed the problem of racism among white reformers. . . .

It is well known that white women did create a white women's movement in the 1840s, and that as the campaign developed into an independent movement they paid less and less attention to black women and often discouraged them from joining or participating in predominantly white suffrage organizations. Such attitudes continued throughout the nineteenth century, as white leaders worried that associating with blacks might jeopardize an alliance with southern white women who had not supported abolition. They knew that although abolitionist women were an active and vocal lot, they represented a numerical minority of the American population. Moreover, abolition had been unpopular among many northern as well as southern whites, who feared that ending slavery and promoting racial equality would result in racial amalgamation. But a failure to perceive race and class as essential to women's liberation shaped the agenda of the white women's movement and ultimately prevented the possibility of forging a biracial feminist alliance, a failure of vision that would remain problematic into the twentieth century.

The movement that white women had created, however, was not the only movement, nor the primary one from the perspective of black women. To shift the focus away from middle-class women—to bring women of color in from a marginal position to the center of discussion—opens the possibility of a fuller examination of women's rights. Moreover, such an approach calls into question the existence of a single women's movement, when in fact at least two existed simultaneously. Black women, by virtue of a long history of activism, had also generated a movement for women's rights, one that pursued an even broader agenda than that of white feminists.

White feminists' adoption of overtly racist tactics led black women once again to establish their own pattern of activism by forming black suffrage organizations. When white women fought to dissociate the movement from its abolitionist roots, black women activists recognized the need to maintain black abolitionist goals. Separate participation in the struggle for sexual equality, however, was not simply a response to exclusion by whites; it was a continuation and expansion of a tradition of resistance and protest, in which the terms "liberation" and "equality" included the elimination of racism as well as sexism. Consequently, their agenda was the most dangerous and radical that this generation of reformers could formulate, for it represented the possibility of overturning two of the most firmly entrenched forms of oppression.

Ironically, white and free black women who had participated in reform activities shared similar experiences, because on every level of public activism, sexist conventions had helped define their roles. In their interactions with men, women as a group occupied the "female" role as supporters of male activities. For those women who engaged in antislavery activism, public opinion made them acutely aware of the consequences of engaging in "male" activities. It was in organized abolition that black and white women publicly demanded an equal voice with men in the proceedings of state and national antislavery conventions. . . .

Many white men, including members of the clergy, vigorously opposed women's rights, arguing that political equality for women would eventually draw them away from their domestic responsibilities. But many black male leaders sympathized with the women's rights campaign because they, like all women, had experienced political disfranchisement. These men tended to be more tolerant of equal rights for black women, in particular, because they had suffered race discrimination. To black men, black women's suffrage was a means of achieving racial solidarity through self-improvement and black empowerment, despite tensions between the sexes. Although some black men supported women's rights in principle, leaders such as Frederick Douglass believed it should remain separate from the struggle for racial equality. Others, as illustrated in the black [antislavery] conventions, simply opposed the equal participation of women.

The desire to impose culturally dominant sex roles placed women's rights in direct conflict with the effort to create a self-reliant black community, despite the sense in which women's rights represented another step toward racial equality for black women. In the black conventions, gender ideals were strong enough to prevent some black men from giving full support to women's equality. Although they expressed less opposition to women's rights than did white men, black men were sometimes reluctant to grant women an equal voice in black antislavery and self-help organizations, and by 1869, political expedience had led most of these men to abandon their support for women's rights in favor of universal manhood suffrage.

Efforts by several black and white women to engage in nontraditional antislavery activities during the 1830s produced debate over the extent to which women could participate as public activists without losing their femininity. Within the black community, the issue was particularly sensitive because women's rights seemed to contradict a central goal of black activism, which was to adopt separate sex roles.

Several years before the "woman question" became such a divisive issue, black activist Maria Stewart endured verbal and physical abuse from some of the black men in her audience when she publicly advocated economic independence and education for all women, regardless of race, and criticized the behavior of black men. In an address to the African-American Female Intelligence Society in 1832, Stewart had urged women to save money and build their own businesses, arguing that economic independence would enable them to exercise their capabilities beyond the domestic realm. She advised all women to "unite and build a store of your own. We have never had an opportunity of displaying our talents; therefore the world thinks we know nothing." Although Stewart was unquestionably a strong supporter of women's rights, she, like many others, held forth male standards for behavior: "Possess the spirit of independence. . . . Possess the spirit of men, bold and enterprising, fearless and undaunted. Sue for your rights and privileges. In the same speech, she criticized male social activities such as drinking and gambling. . . .

In the 1850s, the effort by many white feminists to dissociate women's rights from antislavery was self-evident. Discouraging black women from participating with white women in the movement was not difficult, because white feminists had ignored the concerns of black women from the beginning. In 1848, Lucretia Mott and Elizabeth Cady Stanton held the first women's rights convention at Seneca Falls, New York, where they outlined their goals in the Declaration of Sentiments. Motivated by their own experiences as white middle-class women, the framers of the Declaration of Sentiments concentrated on issues such as the oppression of women within the institution of marriage and the family and discrimination in education and the professions. Marriage and family, they argued, denied them the power to control their own finances and prevented them from pursuing other, more worldly, interests. In addition, educational institutions and the professions had excluded women.

No black women attended the Seneca Falls convention. Frederick Douglass, who professed support for women's rights, was reportedly the only black person in attendance. The issues addressed by the delegates held little relevance for most black women's lives. Marriage did not restrict most black women from access to the public domain. Marriage for slaves was, of course, illegal, and unlike middle-class white women, most free black women worked outside the home in low-paying domestic jobs in order to support their families. Many free black women even operated their own businesses. Discrimination against women in higher education and the professions also meant little to most black women, since, as Sojourner Truth later noted, they "go out washing, which is as high as a colored woman gets."

Despite their alienation from white women's-rights organizations, black women fought for female equality either as independent spokeswomen or as participants in black convention movements. All of the black women who supported women's rights before the Civil War, unlike many white women, retained their commitment to abolition. Mary Ann Shadd Cary and Sojourner Truth carried on the tradition of public speaking that Maria Stewart had established twenty years before. Shadd and Truth were two of the most outspoken black female proponents of both women's rights and abolition.

Mary Ann Shadd Cary displayed her willingness to engage in "unfeminine" activities for the sake of abolition by traveling unaccompanied by her husband on lecture tours in order to promote Canadian emigration [of black people] and abolition, and to solicit financial support for the *Provincial Freeman* [her antislavery newspaper] and destitute fugitive slaves in Canada. Her activities as a newspaper publisher and traveling lecturer demonstrated an independence and assertiveness that defied contemporary expectations of black docility and female submissiveness.

Sojourner Truth was one of the only black spokeswomen who attended predominantly white women's-rights meetings before the Civil War and spoke directly to white women about racism in American society and the ways that racism gave white women privileges denied to black women. The predominantly white women's-rights convention in Akron, Ohio, in 1851 revealed the anti-abolitionist and anti-black sentiment of some of the constituents, and Truth's experience as the only black woman in attendance clearly illustrates the attitudes of many of the white delegates toward the presence of black women and their determination to keep women's rights separate from abolition. Despite hisses from the audience, Truth delivered her famous "Ain't I a Woman" speech, in which she pointed out the hypocrisy of "chivalry" and showed how racism had prevented black women from enjoying the respect and deferential treatment that white women received:

> *Nobody ever helps me into carriages, or over mud-puddles, or gives me*
> *Any best place! And ain't I a woman? Look at me! I have ploughed, planted,*
> *and gathered into barns, and no man could head me! And ain't I a woman?*
> *I could work as much and eat as much as a man—when I could get it—and*
> *bear the lash as well! And ain't I a woman? I have born thirteen children and*
> *seen most all sold into slavery, and when I cried out with my mother's grief,*
> *none but Jesus heard me! And ain't I a woman?*

Truth's legendary speech also addressed the racism of the white women in the audience, many of whom expressed discomfort when they saw her at the convention: "The leaders of the movement trembled on seeing a tall, gaunt black woman in a gray dress and white turban, surmounted with an uncouth bonnet, march deliberately into the church, walk with an air of a queen up the aisle, and take her seat upon the pulpit steps. A buzz of disapprobation was heard all over the house." When they saw Truth enter the convention hall, several white observers assumed that the presence of a black woman meant that the women's-rights convention was turning into an antislavery meeting: "there fell on the listening ear, 'An abolition affair!' 'Women's rights and niggers!' 'I told you so!'" Several of the delegates were so determined to dissociate women's rights from abolitionists that they begged Frances Dana Gage, the president of the convention, to stop Truth from delivering her speech: "Again and again, timorous and trembling ones came to me and said, with earnestness 'Don't let her speak, Mrs. Gage, it will ruin us. Every newspaper in the land will have our cause mixed up with abolition & niggers, and we shall be utterly denounced." Gage ignored their requests, despite expressions of disapproval from the audience. . . .

The events of the Akron convention reveal a great deal about the state of the white women's-rights movement in 1851 and the attitudes of many white feminists, who in their attempt to attract a broader constituency, perceived abolition as detrimental to their movement. The attempt to silence Truth, the only black woman at the convention, demonstrates that for many white women, racism ran as deep as their feminist convictions. By entering the convention hall with the "air of a queen" and delivering a public address to whites, Truth defied prevailing expectations of black docility and female submissiveness.

The participation of black women in women's rights also revealed the tensions that existed between themselves and black men, which limited the degree of male-female cooperation in the struggle for freedom. In 1856, Shadd commented on the dearth of women's-rights sentiment in one of the towns she visited on her lecture tour. In her report to the *Provincial Freeman*, she noted that in Geneva, Illinois, "the cause of 'Women's Rights' does not flourish as it should." She also suggested that black men may have helped to undermine women's-rights sentiment in Geneva: "strange enough, the monkey tricks of such colored men are said to injure it. An honest and venerable abolitionist of Geneva was free to express his fears for me and for women generally, because of the many 'failures' of colored men in that region. What absurdity next?" In her speech at the Equal Rights Association meeting in 1867, Sojourner Truth argued that many black women shared with white working-class women the dual burdens of economic and domestic responsibilities and often lacked control over their own wages, for the domestic ideal dictated that men control the family finances: "and when the women come home, they [their husbands] ask for the money and take it all, and then scold you because there is no food. . . . I want women to have their rights."

In addition to articulating their feminist views on lecture tours, in their writings, and at women's-rights meetings, black women also raised the issue of sexual equality at the black conventions. Most black conventions allowed only men to obtain membership, though the delegates usually allowed women to attend and perform "feminine" tasks. Black conventions had been meeting since 1830, functioning simultaneously with Garrisonian abolition but providing an organizational structure through which black men could maintain a distinct black leadership and pursue black abolitionist goals. In 1830, black male leaders organized the first national black convention at Bethel Church in Philadelphia. The following year, fifteen male delegates met in Philadelphia to attend the First Annual Negro Convention, which several leading white abolitionists attended as guests. In addition to condemning slavery, racism, and colonization, delegates promoted both vocational and classical education for blacks, temperance, better employment opportunities for black men, and moral reform. These racially based conventions, though they advocated some of the same goals as the white-dominated antislavery [conventions], also offered black men the chance to formulate their own goals and strategies for the antislavery movement, which they believed was, above all else, a black struggle. . . .

The American Moral Reform Society, which had been born out of the black conventions in 1835, had welcomed women by 1839 to participate as full members. Led by prominent black abolitionist men such as James Forten, Sr., James McCrummell, Robert Purvis, William Watkins, William Whipper, and Jacob C. White, this organization reflected both the broad objectives of radical abolitionism and the radical principle defining slavery as a sin. Moreover, the organizers perceived their role as encompassing moral reform extending even beyond the boundaries of the United States:

> We therefore declare to the world, that our object is to extend the principle of universal peace and good will to all mankind, by promoting sound morality, by the influence of education, temperance, economy, and all those virtues that alone render man acceptable in the eyes of God or the civilized world. . . .

At the third annual meeting in August 1839, held at the Second African Presbyterian Church in Philadelphia, the members resolved to welcome women into the organization on the basis of supposed moral equality that existed between the sexes:

> Resolved: "That what is morally right for a man to do, is morally right for women," therefore, we earnestly and cordially invite women to cooperate with us in carrying out the great principles of moral reform. . . .

Despite official admittance of women, black conventions did not develop consistent policies on the participation of black women; decisions varied from state to state and at individual meetings when the issue arose. While local organizations may have been more welcoming of women's participation in decision-making and recruitment, the state and national conventions, in which hundreds of black male delegates participated, put up stiff resistance to women's equality. . . .

During the 1850s black men in at least two states continued to thwart black women's attempts to obtain an equal voice with men in the conventions on both the state and national level. In 1855, a New York black woman was expelled from a convention "for no other reason than her sex." In Philadelphia that same year, delegates at the National Convention of Coloured Men excluded women from membership when they voted twenty-three to three against admitting Mary Ann Shadd as a member, although they allowed her to deliver an address. Frederick Douglass had been one of the three men who favored admitting Shadd. A male observer at the convention conceded that Shadd had made "one of the best speeches," but noted approvingly that the majority of the men at the convention had separated women's rights from black conventions and denied Shadd membership. He criticized those men who favored her admission: "Great men, however, are not always wise; and Mr. Douglass himself supplied an example, in advocating the Motion, that 'Miss Shadd should be elected a member,' a proposition which was actually entertained, although a few men of sense protested, that 'that was not a Women's Rights Convention.'". . .

In July 1848, Douglass endorsed the Seneca Falls convention: "Our doctrine is that 'right is of no sex.' We therefore bid the women engaged in this movement our humble Godspeed." But Douglass believed that ending slavery was of more immediate concern than achieving female equality, as he told the Rochester Ladies' Anti-Slavery Society in 1855:

> I may say, however, that the first grand division [in abolitionism] took place fourteen years ago, and on the very minor question— Shall a woman be a member of a committee in company with men? The majority said she should be; and the minority seceded. Thus was a grand philanthropic movement rent asunder by a side issue, having nothing, whatever to do with the great object which the American Anti-Slavery Society was organized to carry forward. . . . While I see no objection to my occupying a place on your committee, I can for the slave's sake forgo that privilege. The battle of Women's Rights should be fought on its own ground.

Thus, long before the debate over black male suffrage during Reconstruction, even the most enthusiastic black male supporters of women's rights believed that abolition and women's rights should remain separate, and that women's-rights agitation actually hurt the cause of abolition.

Between 1830 and the 1860s, black women abolitionists had developed a collective feminist consciousness that reflected their particular experiences as black women as well as the aspects of sexism they shared with white women. While white women fought for female equality in predominantly white antislavery organizations, black women abolitionists campaigned for equal rights within the context of organized black abolitionism. But, though both black and white women supported women's rights, their experiences differed in several important ways. First, black women's participation in women's rights reveals the extent to which racism characterized the early stages of the white feminist movement. White feminist leaders had consistently ignored the concerns of black women, and very few black women, notably Truth, [Harriet] Tubman, and Harper, bridged the two movements by attending white feminist meetings.

Second, unlike many white feminists, black feminists continued to support both abolition and women's rights. Their commitment to both movements held important implications for their experience in the struggle for sexual equality. As Sojourner Truth had suggested at the Akron convention, black women brought a perspective on women's rights that clearly differed from that of white women, and for black women, the abolition of slavery and racism were intimately related to women's rights.

This combined commitment to race and gender also affected relationships with black male reformers. Black women's continued participation in the fight to end slavery and racism led them to maintain cooperative ties with black men, unlike many white feminists, who perceived their interests as separate from those of men. Thus, while black women campaigned for women's rights, they also worked with black men in a variety of self-help activities in the black community. On the other hand, as it became evident that many black men had considered racial equality a higher priority than women's rights, black women continued their struggle for women's rights. . . .

Questions for Discussion

1. Why were Americans at the time opposed to women speaking in public? How did attitudes differ toward black and white women who spoke in public?
2. Describe the attitudes of white female activists toward black female abolitionists. How did black men respond to black female activists?
3. Why did some white women separate the causes of women's rights and abolition? What was the response of black female activists?
4. Sojourner Truth delivered her famous "Ain't I a Woman" speech in 1851 before a white female audience. How did the audience respond? Why?

For Further Reading

Robert Abzug, *Cosmos Crumbling: American Reform and the Religious Imagination* (1994); Jim Bearden and Linda Jean Butler, *Shadd: The Life and Times of Mary Shadd Cary* (1977); R. J. M. Blackett, *Building an Antislavery Wall: Black Americans in the Atlantic Abolitionist Movement, 1830–1860* (1983); Richard Carwardine, *Evangelicals and Politics in Antebellum America* (1993); Kenneth Cmiel, *Democratic Eloquence: The Fight over Popular Speech in Nineteenth-Century America* (1990); Clara Merritt De Boer, *Be Jubilant My Feet: African American Abolitionists in the American Missionary Association, 1839–1861* (1994); Ellen Carol DuBois, *Feminism and Suffrage: The Emergence of an Independent Women's Movement in America, 1848–1869* (1978); Paula

Giddings, *When and Where I Enter: The Impact of Black Women on Race and Sex in America* (1984); Debra Hansen, *Strained Sisterhood: Gender and Class in the Boston Female Anti-Slavery Society* (1993); Blanche Glassman Hersh, *The Slavery of Sex: Feminist Abolitionists in America* (1978); Nancy Hewitt, *Women's Activism and Social Change: Rochester, New York, 1822–1872* (1984); Nancy Isenberg, *Sex and Citizenship in Antebellum America* (1998); Donald M. Jacobs, ed., *Courage and Conscience: Black and White Abolitionists in Boston* (1993); Julie Roy Jeffrey, *The Great Silent Army of Abolitionism: Ordinary Women in the Antislavery Movement* (1998); Aileen Kraditor, *Means and Ends in American Abolitionism: Garrison and His Critics on Strategy and Tactics, 1834–1850* (1967); Gerda Lerner, *The Grimké Sisters of North Carolina: Pioneers for Women's Rights and Abolitionism* (1967); John McKivigan and Mitchell Snay, eds., *Religion and the Antebellum Debate over Slavery* (1998); Steven Mintz, *Moralists and Modernizers: America's Pre-Civil War Reformers* (1995); Nell Irvin Painter, *Sojourner Truth: A Life, A Symbol* (1996); Benjamin Quarles, *Black Abolitionists* (1969); Karen Sanchez-Eppler, *Touching Liberty: Abolition, Feminism, and the Politics of the Body* (1993); Kathryn Kish Sklar, *Women's Rights Emerges within the Antislavery Movement, 1830–1870* (2000); Dorothy Sterling, *We Are Your Sisters: Black Women in the Nineteenth Century* (1984); Clare Taylor: *Women of the Anti-Slavery Movement: The Weston Sisters* (1995); Jean Fagan Yellin, *Women and Sisters: The Antislavery Feminists in American Culture* (1989); Jean Fagan Yellin and John C. Van Horne, eds., *The Abolitionist Sisterhood: Women's Political Culture in Antebellum America* (1994); R. J. Young, *Antebellum Black Activists: Race, Gender, and the Self* (1996).

CHAPTER

16

Selling Children
The Domestic Slave Trade

Marie Jenkins Schwartz

Of all the brutalities visited upon slaves, few were as wrenching, painful, or permanent as the forced separation of family members. The legal importation of slaves to the United States from abroad ended in 1808. But a brisk and profitable domestic slave trade developed in the South and thrived until the end of the Civil War. It is difficult to know with precision exactly how many husbands, wives, parents, and children were sold away from one another. Some estimates range as high as one-third. A slave who lived to thirty-five had a 50 percent chance of being sold at least once and would almost certainly have experienced the distress of seeing loved ones sold. Beginning in the 1820s, the settlement of southwestern states ideal for growing cotton, such as Alabama and Mississippi, generated a huge demand for slaves in the lower South. States in the upper southern states, like Virginia, began to export slaves to the lower parts of the region. For example, in the single decade between 1850 and 1860, 269,000 slaves were sold from the upper to the lower South; 111,136 of them were children under nineteen years of age. During the 1850s, perhaps as many as 30 percent of slave children born in the upper South were sold to new owners in the lower South.

Slave families were separated for a variety of reasons. If a slave owner died, his heirs might divide the plantation's slaves among themselves. Or the heirs might have to sell some slaves in order to pay off the estate's debts. To celebrate the birth of a granddaughter, a slave owner might present her with an infant female slave. Slaves were given as gifts to celebrate birthdays, weddings, anniversaries, and Christmas. Some slave children were sold away from their mothers at the insistence of planters' wives. Such women

$200 Reward.

RANAWAY from the subscriber, on the night of Thursday, the 30th of Sepember,

FIVE NEGRO SLAVES,

To-wit : one Negro man, his wife, and three children.

The man is a black negro, full height, very erect, his face a little thin. He is about forty years of age, and calls himself *Washington Reed*, and is known by the name of Washington. He is probably well dressed, possibly takes with him an ivory headed cane, and is of good address. Several of his teeth are gone.

Mary, his wife, is about thirty years of age, a bright mulatto woman, and quite stout and strong.

The oldest of the children is a boy, of the name of FIELDING, twelve years of age, a dark mulatto, with heavy eyelids. He probably wore a new cloth cap.

MATILDA, the second child, is a girl, six years of age, rather a dark mulatto, but a bright and smart looking child.

MALGOLM, the youngest, is a boy, four years old, a lighter mulatto than the last, and about equally as bright. He probably also wore a cloth cap. If examined, he will be found to have a swelling at the navel.

Washington and Mary have lived at or near St. Louis, with the subscriber, for about 15 years.

It is supposed that they are making their way to Chicago, and that a white man accompanies them, that they will travel chiefly at night, and most probably in a covered wagon.

A reward of $150 will be paid for their apprehension, so that I can get them, if taken within one hundred miles of St. Louis, and $200 if taken beyond that, and secured so that I can get them, and other reasonable additional charges, if delivered to the subscriber, or to THOMAS ALLEN, Esq., at St. Louis, Mo. The above negroes, for the last few years, have been in possession of Thomas Allen, Esq., of St. Louis.

WM. RUSSELL.

ST. LOUIS, Oct. 1, 1847.

To avoid sales of children and spouses, slaves might run away. This notice by an owner of slaves does not mention why an African American family ran away, but it goes into detail about individual family members. In what ways do those details reveal important qualities of the institution of slavery?

suspected, all too often correctly, that the children had been fathered by their husbands—or sons. In addition, the sheer desire of slave owners to turn a profit resulted in the sale and separation of tens of thousands of black families. As Thomas Jefferson, owner of hundreds of slaves, noted in another context, "a child raised [born of a slave mother] every 2 years is of more profit than the crop of the best laboring man."

In response to criticisms by northern abolitionists, a few southern states passed laws forbidding the sale of slave children under the age of ten away from their mothers. Only Louisiana's prohibition against such sales appears to have been effective. In any event, most children under ten were usually sold with their mothers. There were some slave owners who thought it cruel to separate children from their parents; they avoided the practice— unless economic necessity dictated otherwise.

Slave children lived precarious lives. Their mortality rate from infancy to early childhood was an astonishing 50 percent (mortality for white southern children that age was under 20 percent). This was due to a variety of factors.

Slave owners often compelled female slaves to continue field work or other strenuous labor deep into their pregnancies; this led to miscarriages or to infants born too weak to survive. The food provided to slave children by masters was both meager and lacking in proper nutrition. Cornmeal and bits of salt pork and bacon were the standard diet for youngsters; on large plantations, the meal was often served to children in a trough. Unsanitary conditions in and around the slave quarters were ripe for the spread of diseases such as hookworm and dysentery.

For slave parents, the heartbreak of a child lost to the slave trade could be as wrenching as that of a child lost to death. In the next essay, Marie Jenkins Schwartz describes the southern trade in African American children. Among other things, Schwartz describes the ways in which slave parents and children resisted these sales, at times successfully. More than anything else, however, the essay paints a distressing portrait of children sold away from their parents, of family members never seeing one another again, and of the irreparable loss experienced by enslaved families.

Source: Reprinted by permission of the publisher of BORN IN BONDAGE: GROWING UP ENSLAVED IN THE ANTEBELLUM SOUTH by Marie Jenkins Schwartz, pp. 156-175, Cambridge, Mass.: Harvard University Press, © 2000 by the President and Fellows of Harvard College.

Slaves and owners viewed the stage of development from the early to mid-teens quite differently. Slaves considered adolescence as a time of sorrow because the likelihood grew as children approached their mid-teens that owners would break the bonds that held families together, wrenching teenagers from their families of origin after they became proficient at adult tasks. Indeed, sales of slaves in the interregional slave trade peaked between the ages of fifteen and twenty-five, and vulnerability to sale began to increase for youths as early as age eight and certainly by the age of ten, when they could work competently with the cotton crop. Owners, in contrast, viewed the maturation of enslaved children as a very positive event. Slaveholders knew that as children reached their teenage years, they would soon prove valuable as "prime hands," as first-rate workers were called, whether they worked at home or were sold at premium prices.

Flush times encouraged the purchase and relocation of slaves. Economic opportunities fueled by the growing textile industries in New England and Europe encouraged slaveholders and would-be slaveholders to move westward into such states as Alabama, newly opened to settlement in the antebellum years. The fertile soil of the southwestern United States promised high yields and profits for planters with enough land and labor to plant and harvest the cotton processed in the mills. Men and women who relocated to frontier areas to grow staple crops often brought bondsmen and women with them, but they also relied on purchasing slaves after they had cleared land and accumulated the capital necessary to commence or increase cotton cultivation. This situation put adolescent, or even prepubescent, slaves at risk for separation from their families. Many were forced to travel to new homes, where they were put to work planting and harvesting the staple crop. Sugar production, limited in the antebellum United States to southern Louisiana, required additional slaves, many of whom were brought to the region from older areas of settlement through slave markets in New Orleans. The transfer of slaves from more established areas of the country to the developing cotton and sugar regions constituted a demographic revolution. Youths old enough to work competently in the cotton fields sold readily, particularly during years when high prices for the crop tempted planters, eager to grow more cotton, to compete for slaves in the open market.

The risk of separation from families through sale was relatively low for very young children, but it increased when children neared the age when they could begin adult work. Between 1820 and 1860, about 10 percent of adolescent slaves living in the upper South were sold in the interregional slave trade. A similar percentage of slaves were sold in their twenties. As slaves moved into their thirties, their chance of sale diminished substantially, but by then many of them had borne children who were or soon would be at risk for sale. . . .

The prices paid for slave children depended on their ability to perform agricultural or household chores, not their age. Planters expected each slave they purchased "to excel at something"—that is, to have been trained to work. Consequently, speculators who purchased children solely to profit from their resale sometimes taught them work skills before putting them up for auction. Generally, the training involved jobs outside the field. According to one informant, girls learned to "do different things such as: weave, cook, sew, and maid service." Few slaves worked in the fields every day, year-round. Most—on some plantations and farms, all—household slaves were assigned to the fields during periods of peak labor demand, and slaves accustomed to work in the fields performed other types of jobs during slack seasons when crops did not demand their attention. Many cotton, tobacco, and grain producers planned for this contingency by purchasing or training house servants who could work in the field periodically and by acquiring field hands who could perform a variety of other chores. Rice planters with large slaveholdings preferred to maintain sharper distinctions between house and field servants than did other planters, but even rice planters expected slaves to work in a variety of occupations. Knowledge of a slave's work skills helped would-be purchasers make decisions about whether to purchase a slave and how much to pay.

Price lists and other records pertaining to sales of slave children frequently classified youths by their physical development, as evidenced by their height or weight. Purchasers relied on such external measurements to gauge whether the child had the strength, dexterity, physical stamina, and good health necessary for completing plantation chores. At times, sellers assigned arbitrarily to a child an age that reflected the youth's physical maturation rather than his or her chronological age. This caused considerable confusion among many slaves as to their exact date of birth. Anna Maria Coffee, traded eleven times in South Carolina and Virginia before she reached her twenties, never knew her true age. In later life, the former slave explained that sellers "made my age jus' what dey wanted it."

Charlotte Thornton's experience selling slaves to an Alabama planter illustrates the principle that physical attributes determined the prices paid for youthful slaves. Payments received by this Virginia piedmont planter for individual boys and girls reflected the perceived physical strengths and weaknesses of each. Columbus, age twelve or thirteen and "well grown," sold for less than Kezia, his seven-year-old sister, because he had once broken his right arm and it had been "badly set." Columbus's younger brother Tom, age eleven, sold for more than his younger sister and considerably more than the older but injured Columbus. John, thirteen years old and apparently unrelated to the other boys, sold for less than Tom: he was "healthy but not well grown for his age." The Alabamian who purchased these four children also bought the unrelated slave girl Milly, described as "healthy and strong, well formed." Her "homely face," also noted, apparently detracted from her value, for her purchaser was able to negotiate her price down to $550 from $650.

For girls, the physical attributes that determined a slave's market value included notions of beauty held by the owning class. Girls reached puberty at about the same time as their physical capacity for work increased sufficiently to make them efficient and effective laborers. Accordingly, they confronted double jeopardy: they were at risk not only for sale but also for sexual exploitation. Some unprincipled men even purchased young female slave expressly for sexual gratification. Eighteen-year-old Rosena Lipscombe's new owner expected her to act as his concubine after he purchased her in Virginia and carried her "down south." Virginian Tom Greene purchased a slave woman named Betty specifically because "he was a bachluh . . . an' he need a 'oman," according to a former slave who lived on an adjoining property. More frequently, masters, masters' sons, and other men who visited or lived in the neighborhood felt themselves entitled to the sexual favors of any female slaves they encountered, pubescent and adolescent girls included. Neither the law nor aggrieved mistresses, who disapproved of sexual relationships between white men and black women, could prevent the practice. Not all white men forced themselves upon enslaved women, but enough did to make a girl's adolescent years a constant source of concern for girls, their parents, and the larger slave community.

Slave girls who were deemed pretty according to slaveholder standards could be sole as prostitutes, or "fancies" in the vernacular of the day. Fredericka Bremer, a Swedish visitor on a tour of the United States, observed "fancy women for fancy purchasers" on display at a Richmond jail. R. M. Owings offered to purchase from his Charleston supplier "all likely and handsome fancy girls" that could be had "at reasonable prices." "Fancies" were generally of lighter skin and sold at higher prices than other slave women. In the Richmond market in 1859, prices paid for fancy women exceeded those paid for prime female field hands by 30 percent or more. An attractive slave woman sold for $1,500 in Columbia, South Carolina, according to Bremer. Relatively few slaves were ever sold as "fancies," but a knowledge of the trade added to the distress of slave girls and their parents as female children approached puberty.

Although would-be purchasers took an interest in the physical attributes of slave women, a desire for economic gain fueled the majority of slave sales. Planters worried about maintaining the best possible balance between the acres of land at their disposal and the number of hands available to work this land. A surplus of labor kept some slaves idle, at least part of the time; a surplus of land represented a lost opportunity for profit. But slaveholders sold and relocated slaves to settle estates and pay debts as well. Many children were purchased as part of a larger group—perhaps the entire population of a plantation, or one heir's portion of the slave population. These groups generally included slaves of different ages, some of whom were related, which eased some of the worry about the fate of children placed on the market. Youngsters sold "in the round" had a chance of remaining with at least some family members and friends. When they contemplated the purchase of a group, planters took into account how many children there were, what proportion of the group they constituted, and what percentage of the children were physically mature or nearly so. The presence of children, particularly those nearing puberty, helped ensure future prosperity, provided they were accompanied by a sufficient number of fully working adult hands. No one wanted to purchase "too many small negroes," but having too few youths was equally undesirable.

Being purchased together did not guarantee that family members would stay together, however—especially if the sale involved a speculator. Families sold to individuals usually went to live with their new owners, but those purchased by speculators who bought and resold slaves for profit could end up scattered. Even slaves belonging to a planter migrating from one region to another might not stay with family members if the slaveholder deemed a sale necessary or desirable. Former slave Tom Morris began the journey south from Virginia with both of his parents. Tom's father and mother had lived on separate plantations in Virginia, but his mother's owner, who planned to relocate to Mississippi, purchased the husband ostensibly to keep the family together. This must have been a ploy to obtain Tom's father for a favorable price or to secure the cooperation of mother and child, because all three family members did not end up in Mississippi. His new owner sold Tom's father before the traveling party reached its destination. Former Virginia slave Susan Keys remembered at age eleven or twelve walking in a drove of slaves, called a coffle, all the way from the District of Columbia to Mississippi, where she was sold to new owners. Some of her companions never made it to Mississippi because they were sold along the way.

Parents who never saw their children again experienced a deep and lasting grief. Those who lost a child through sale occasionally compared their emotional pain to the sorrow associated with a child's death. Aunt Crissy, the mother of seven children, lost two of her older daughters to the slave trade. When her youngest, Hendley, died of illness, she "sorrered much," but found a measure of comfort in her religious faith: "praise gawd, praise gawd, my little chile is gone to Jesus." Turning to her master, she expressed her continuing torment over the sale of her daughters: "Hendley's one chile of mine you never gonna sell." Time assuaged neither the heartache nor the anger associated with her earlier loss.

The disappearance of children represented more than an emotional loss. Sons and daughters made substantial contributions to the slave family's economy. . . . Moreover, the family, backed by the larger slave community, stood as a buffer between the slaveholder and the young slave; members of either or both might act to assuage the child's physical and emotional sufferings under the slave system. Youths torn from families and communities of origin faced an uncertain future, and slave parents were loath to let them go without a struggle or without at least ensuring their ability to cope in new surroundings. . . .

As occurred with other contested conditions of enslavement, slaves whose families were torn apart might refuse to cooperate in completing their owner's work. Fathers were especially likely to bargain with their labor to preserve family relationships. They ran away, and then sent word through other slaves of their willingness to return if an owner called off an impending sale. One Virginia man, sold apart from his wife and children, hid in the woods for twelve months until another planter agreed to purchase him and reunited him with his family. Another father, upon learning he had been sold, threatened to commit suicide rather than leave his family in Georgia, which convinced his buyer to renege on the planned purchase. Still another, who had successfully escaped bondage in Virginia, took the unusual step of volunteering for re-enslavement [in Texas] in order to remain with his young son. . . .

If fathers were more inclined to withdraw or threaten to withdraw from the work site in an attempt to keep their families intact, mothers were more likely to pin their hopes on owners' responding sympathetically to an outpouring of grief. . . . Betty Tolbert of Alabama recalled mothers who would plead: "Don't sell my child, have mercy on me, Lord Jesus." Impassioned protests by parents at the point of sale occasionally elicited the desired reaction from slaveholders. One mother put up such a fit following the sale of her children to slave traders that her Virginia master agreed to let her accompany her daughters to their new home. No doubt her owner worried that she would prove of limited use if left behind, impaired by her grief. He also may have worried that the continued public display of despair by the mother would reveal his identity as a cold and calculating slave trader, rather than a father figure concerned for the welfare of his slaves. . . .

Slaves, desperate to maintain families intact yet with few resources to prevent separations, occasionally employed tactics that included threats of violence or other harm to owners. Unwilling to relocate to Alabama at the insistence of their owner, slaves in North Carolina "took the desperate resolution" of concocting a potion of poison that claimed the lives of two of their owner's daughters. The Baton Rouge *Republic* carried news of this "Shocking Occurrence." Stories of retaliation, including physical confrontations and conjuring, reminded slaveholders to exercise caution in separating slave families. All planters understood the threat to physical safety that violence posed, but they were divided about the ability of slaves to harm through the invocation of a spell, as were the slaves themselves. At least some members of the owning class worried about the supernatural power attributed to certain slaves, and some slaves employed hexes to affect the behavior of owners whose actions they could not otherwise control. Slaves in Amelia County, Virginia, believed they had prevented their relocation to Alabama by employing a conjurer to work his magic power upon their master. It is difficult to know how successful these maneuvers actually were. The large number of slaves traded in the antebellum years suggests that such strategies were generally ineffectual, yet even more slaves might have been relocated if slaves never employed such strategies.

Slave parents through their behavior acknowledged the existence of large-scale family dissolution throughout the South. Even as they resisted separation from their children, parents taught them how to cope if parents were no longer around to care for them. Family stories served to prepare youngsters for what might lie ahead. Parents, grandparents, and other older relatives reminisced about their lives and the lives of ancestors, hoping that treasured memories might remain with children even when parents could not. Many of the narratives provided models for enduring the hardships associated with bondage, including family separation. Eliza Evans, a slave in Alabama, learned the story of her grandmother's capture in Africa, passage across the Atlantic, and sale in America. Her grandmother subsequently ingratiated herself with her owners to such an extent that "they gave her a grand wedding when she was married" and never sold any of her children or grandchildren. Evans came to admire her grandmother's achievements in getting along with her owners, but her family's teachings were not limited to stories of how to accommodate slaveholders. As a girl, Evans often stood guard for the adults when runaway slaves slipped into the slave quarters to get something to eat and to pray with compatriots.

Stories could be sung as well as spoken to prepare children for the emotional trauma of separation. Emma Howard learned as a young child in Virginia to sing this verse:

> Mammy, is Ol' Massa gwine sell us tomorrow?
> Yes, my chile.
> Whah he goin sell us?
> Way down South in Georgia.

Those parents who ignored the subject of sale or other types of separations risked their children's learning of or experiencing the situation unexpectedly. Parents did not wish to worry children unnecessarily, but they wanted all children armed with knowledge that would help them cope with the distress of sudden family partings. Sometimes they delayed discussions too long, and youngsters learned inadvertently of slave sales from older children or by overhearing conversations of adults. In either case, children were frightened and saddened. The song little Emma learned, she later recalled, "always made me cry.". . .

Children had to be polite to everyone, but they had to put their trust in other slaves rather than owners. A common practice whereby children referred to older, unrelated slaves using kinship terms, such as "aunt" and "uncle," reinforced the idea that slaves, rather than owners, would care for children separated from their parents. The language of kinship served to instruct the child in the hierarchy of the slave community and emphasized the child's dependence on and need to obey older slaves. A requirement instituted by some slaveholders that children refer to them in familial terms probably represented their understanding of this use of the language of kinship by the slave population. Owners who adopted the practice must have hoped to insert themselves into the list of people whom young slaves learned to treat with respect and obedience. Hester Hunter, who lived on a rice plantation, was taught to call her mistress "my white mammy." Growing up in Arkansas, Belle Williams learned to call her mistress "Mother Hulsie." Long after slavery ended, George Fleming used the word "daddy" to describe his master.

Parents used given names, as well as kinship titles, to emphasize that individual children belonged to the larger slave community. They were less concerned that children have unique names than that they have names that associated them with other slaves. Parents called children by the names of grandparents, aunts, uncles, dead siblings, other family members, and unrelated slaves, as if to remind everyone that all slaves had a stake in caring for the children. Generally, it was not difficult to find adult slaves willing to accept responsibility for caring for children when parents were unavailable. When the slave woman known as Crecie died in childbirth on the Gowrie rice plantation, the child's grandmother raised the infant for four years and then the boy's great-aunt took over. The elderly slave Molly raised her grandchildren and great-grandchildren on the Butler estate. "Fictive kin" also played a role as the need arose.

Owners objected to the close-knit ties that developed among slaves as reflected in these naming practices. They believed that the slave's most important relationship was with his or her owners. When slaves shared the same name, owners added descriptive terms—"Cook Renty or Old Lucy, or Little Dick"—in an effort to emphasize the individuality of slaves rather than their commonality with one another. Slaveholders might go so far as to insist on naming the children themselves, choosing at times fanciful names drawn from classical mythology or the Bible. Other owners chose diminutives of names held by members of the owning class. One owner named a slave boy after his boat. . . .

Slave parents controlled neither their children's responses to enslavement nor their owners' responses to tactics intended to preserve families. . . . Owners who sold slave youths often made sure to carry out the transaction when parents were not around to raise a storm of protest. One planter simply pulled up to a woman's work station and ordered her into his buggy, explaining "I boughtcha dis mawnin." Other planters practiced various forms of deception for the same purpose. In Scottsville, Virginia, Louis Hughes's owner told the boy's family that he was taking the eleven-year-old slave to Richmond to work on a canal boat operating between that city and Scottsville. Louis and his mother were told that they would see each other periodically when the boat returned home. Instead, the owner turned Louis over to a slave trader, who eventually sold the youth to Mississippi.

Owners who planned to part children from their parents confronted protests by the youths, just as they did from their parents. A slave girl named Nancy Williams yelled "loud's I could" when her master offered her services for hire, then ran home shortly after she arrived at her new residence. She never returned to her would-be employer, probably by the mutual consent of all concerned. . . . Louise Jones also ran away, charging that the Virginia woman who hired her "was de meanes' white 'oman in de world." Like Nancy and other youths who ran away from new masters or mistresses, Louise headed toward home and family. . . .

The sorrow that children felt over permanent separation from their parents lasted a lifetime and heightened appreciation of family ties among youngsters who rightly feared the consequence of losing the love and protection of parents and other relatives. Mariah Bell, many years after the incident, wept at the memory of her mother crying and waving to her as they parted. Her granddaughters shared her anguish as she told the story: "We all used to sit around her and we would all be crying with her when she told that so many, many times." Although slave family ties were often truncated and tenuous, they nevertheless represented a critical source of support—a barrier between slave youths and slaveholders that absorbed some of the harshness of slavery. When the ties were severed, children were pushed toward early adulthood. They were forced not only to shoulder a heavy burden of toil but also to suffer considerable emotional distress.

Slave youths without parents around to protect them could find themselves at high risk for sale in the market or forced to fulfill adult roles in the slave quarter. The slave trade created parentless children, but so did the high rates of mortality among the slave population. A small number of young people were alone because their parents had escaped servitude. Whatever the cause, youths alone might have no one to cook or care for their clothes— particularly boys, who seldom performed these chores for themselves—and owners had few compunctions about selling them when parents were not around to protest. Ella Belle Ramsey at age ten found herself left to cope with a younger brother and sister after her mother ran away from her Virginia home. Adding to her misfortune, both her master and the sheriff believed she knew about her mother's escape and attempted to force her to reveal the details. In her later years, Ramsey explained all she knew: "One night I awoke an' reach out an' my mother wasn't dere. I got up an' look for her an' couldn't find her." Ramsey's owner sold her shortly afterward, and she never heard from her family again. Ramsey's mother left no explanation for her disappearance, which was unusual. Men ran away more often than women. When mothers abandoned children to escape slavery, the most common justification was unrelenting cruel treatment, including sexual abuse, by owners or in some cases by other slaves.

Racial stereotypes of the day encouraged sexual abuse of slave youths parted from parents by allowing white exploiters to blame the black victims for their predicament. Many white southerners considered black women inherently promiscuous because of their supposedly insatiable sexual urges. When asked to recall slavery years after its demise, former Alabama slave-holder M. T. Judge alleged that "young slave girls, as young as 13 or 14 years" commonly solicited "the caresses of men," both "of their own race" but also of "sons of their masters, overseers or any other white men in the neighborhood." Mistresses, too, tried to deny the reality of black women's molestation. Mary Chesnut of South Carolina, who tended to be more honest about slavery than most mistresses, observed that even though "the mulattoes one sees in every family exactly resemble the white children" and every mistress can name "the father of all the mulatto children in everybody's household," those "in her own she seems to think drop from the clouds, or pretends so to think.". . .

Sexual abuse of slave women occurred routinely on many plantations and was not limited to girls separated from their families. But the sale of slaves that broke up families and communities increased the vulnerability of slave girls to sexual exploitation because they lacked family and friends to threaten retaliation for mistreatment. Girls who had been sold, unknown within their new community, could find themselves subject to sexual abuse by other slaves, as well as by members of the owning class. The same held true for girls left in their original communities, if family and friends were no longer around to protect them.

Mothers tried to prepare their daughters as they approached puberty for what might await them. They wanted to forewarn daughters of the potential for sexual exploitation so they could take protective measures, but at the same time, they hoped to prolong childhood for their daughters. Girls who knew a lot about sexuality hardly qualified as children in the minds of their white owners, a fact which caused some parents to wait too long to address the issue. As a result, girls might reach the age of maturity with no clear understanding of the human reproductive cycle. A few even went to their marriage beds without knowing what to expect. Minnie Folkes, who was only fourteen when she married in Virginia, believed that marriage entailed no more than cooking, cleaning, washing, and ironing for a husband. For three months, she and her spouse abstained from sex, because her mother had warned her previously not to engage in the act. At her young husband's urging, the couple visited Minnie's mother to clarify the situation. Only then did Minnie agree to carry out "my duty as a wife."

Folkes's experience suggests that adults somehow managed to keep sexual activities hidden from view, despite the crowded conditions associated with slave cabins and quarters, and to treat the subject as taboo so that children knew not to raise the topic in conversation. To protect children from learning too much, parents sent them out to play or to fetch water from the spring; youngsters who hung around when they were not wanted risked having their legs switched with a nettle brush. One mother apparently kept her son from investigating love-making by telling him the noises he heard in the night—"knockin' and knockin' kinder easy, and [a voice that] sed 'Mary' kinder low"—came from ghosts. . . .

Despite the secrecy surrounding sexual matters, young people eagerly sought to create intimate relationships with one another when they reached their mid- to late teens. For them, as for other youths, the attention of a special boy or girl brought joy and excitement. Because their lives were otherwise more notable for neglect, impoverishment, hard labor, and distress, everyone wanted someone to cherish. In addition, youths who were working as adults and subject to slavery's worst features considered themselves entitled to the privileges of adulthood, including love and its sexual expression.

For young people separated from their families of origin, early marriage offered an emotional and material haven. Marriage could provide assistance in carrying out the tasks of daily living, as well as love and intimacy. For young women, marriage provided a measure of protection from sexual abuse, both from members of the owning class and from other slave. Lizzie Hobbs, long after her father left with his owner for the West, was raped by a white man following her departure from her mother's home in Virginia to work as a house-girl in North Carolina. Carolyn Holland, sold twice as a youth, felt vulnerable to sexual exploitation and married at a young age in Alabama because her seventeen-year-old husband promised her protection from the sexual attentions of another slave man. Of course, slave husbands could not always protect their wives from sexual abuse by others, especially by men of the owning class; but their presence deterred some advances. . . .

Despite the pain associated with previous partings, the overwhelming majority of young adults chose to marry (or remarry if parted from spouses) and have children, whether they went to new homes or stayed behind. "Some uv de time dey'ud sell uh man wife 'way en den he hadder ge' annunder wife," former slave Louisa Collier of South Carolina explained. The desire to create or recreate families occurred even among slaves who did not grow up in family units. Ary and Wilsie Varner met as children in Alabama after each had been sold from their respective families. Too young to remember parents or other relatives, they "grew up together" and married as soon as "they were old enough." Their shared sense of loss and yearning for family must have attracted them to each other and motivated the two to marry.

Questions for Discussion

1. At what age were enslaved children most likely to be sold away from their families? Why?
2. Why did the domestic slave trade flourish in the years leading up to the Civil War? What role did "speculators" play in that trade? Which characteristics of a slave most influenced whether she or he would be purchased?
3. What strategies did slave parents use to resist the sale of their children or spouses?
4. What role did the extended family play in the lives of African American slaves?
5. How would you describe a childhood lived in slavery?

For Further Reading

Ira Berlin, Marc Favreau, and Steven F. Miller, eds., *Remembering Slavery* (1998); John Blasingame, *The Slave Community: Plantation Life in the Antebellum South* (1972); Sylviane A. Diouf, *Growing Up in Slavery* (2001); Stanley Elkins, *Slavery: A Problem in American Institutional and Intellectual Life* (1959); Eugene Genovese, *Roll, Jordan, Roll: The World the Slaves Made* (1974); Herbert G. Gutman, *The Black Family in Slavery and Freedom, 1750–1925* (1976); Jacqueline Jones, *Labor of Love, Labor of Sorrow: Black Women, Work, and the Family, from Slavery to the Present* (1985); Charles Joyner, *Down by the Riverside: A South Carolinian Slave Community* (1984); Wilma King, *Stolen Childhood: Slave Youth in Nineteenth-Century America* (1995); Melton A. McLauren, *Celia: A Slave* (1991); Sally G. McMillen, *Southern Women: Black and White in the Old South* (1992); Todd L. Savitt, *Medicine and Slavery: The Diseases and Health Care of Blacks in Virginia* (1978); Kenneth Stampp, *The Peculiar Institution: Slavery in the Antebellum South* (1956); Brenda Stevenson, *Life in Black and White: Family and Community in the Slave South* (1996); Thomas L. Webber, *Deep Like the Rivers: Education in the Slave Quarter Community, 1831–1865* (1978); Deborah Gray White, *Ar'n't I a Woman?: Female Slaves in the Plantation South* (1985).

17

Divided Houses

Rebel Sons in Union Families

Amy Murrell Taylor

The Civil War was the most catastrophic conflict in American history. Numbers tell part of the story. More than 620,000 Americans died in the four years of the war. More Americans died in the Civil War than in all of the wars fought by the United States *combined* until about 1970, in the middle of the Vietnam conflict. That includes the American Revolution, the War of 1812, numerous Indian wars, the wars with Mexico and Spain, the World Wars I and II, Korea, and most of Vietnam. The South lost 260,000 dead in combat, 5 percent of its white population, one in four of its military-eligible males, *plus* perhaps as many as an additional 50,000 civilian dead, including slaves. About 360,000 northerners fell during the war (including 37,000 African American soldiers). In all, about 2 percent of the nation's *entire* population died in the conflict, a percentage unheard of until the world wars of the twentieth century. Why?

Since the creation of the United States under the Constitution, North and South had moved in dramatically different directions. It can be argued that these regions encompassed at least two distinct cultures, maybe more. Of course, the North and South had much in common, including religious values, language, and a belief in the limited form of government established by the Constitution. They were united in their aversion to black people as well, whether slave or free.

But the South was a slave society with a deep commitment to an agrarian, small town, rural way of life. Although slavery was disappearing in most of the rest of the world, the rural, farming culture that dominated the South was similar to the way most people lived at the time and, for that matter,

Negative by T. H. O'SULLIVAN.   Entered according to act of Congress, in the year 1865, by A. Gardner, in the Clerk's Office of the District Court of the District of Columbia.   Positive by A. GARDNER, 511 7th St., Washington

Incidents of the War.

A HARVEST OF DEATH.

Gettysburg, July, 1863.

The scene at Gettysburg, July 1863. Beneath "Incidents of the War," the caption reads: "A Harvest of Death." More Americans died in the Civil War than any other conflict in the nation's history. Why?

since agriculture had developed thousands of years earlier. Of course, the economic and racial issues bound up with slavery must be placed at the fore-front of the southern situation and the causes for the Civil War. At the same time, however, white southerners were also committed to a way of life that was linked to *both* slavery and to traditional agrarian values. It is important to note that well into the twentieth century, long after the war and the end of slavery, the South would remain predominately small town, rural, and agrarian. Sectional differences did not end with the Civil War.

Meanwhile, during these years the North was leading the way toward modernity. It was entrepreneurial, ethnically diverse, economically competi-tive, open to innovation, and increasingly urban and impersonal. Along with a few western European capitalist countries, the North was a unique and, some would argue, "revolutionary" society in 1860. Even though the South had a few major cities and its share of hard-driving businessmen, it was dominated politically and economically by a slave-owning class of planters, and the majority of its white citizens earned their living in agricultural pursuits. More important, perhaps, the South's leaders saw their region as an agrarian, God-fearing, slave society. And they were convinced their way of life was under assault by what the North represented. It was no accident that defenders of slavery and the southern way of life described the North as a haven for the "money hungry," the "atheistic," and—because of the impersonality of urban life in a free-wheeling capitalist society—the "anarchistic."

Of course, this does not mean that the Civil War was inevitable. Nor does it imply that its immediate causes—territorial expansion, abolitionism, the Fugitive Slave Law, the Dred Scott decision, Lincoln's election as president, and other issues—were unimportant. On the contrary, these issues were crucial to the onset of war. But it may be useful to keep in mind the cultural differences between North and South when thinking about the awesome violence each side perpetrated on the other.

In the next essay, Amy Murrell Taylor describes how the Civil War divided families as well as the nation. According to Taylor, it was not uncommon for sons in border states such as Maryland, Missouri, and Kentucky to defect to the Confederacy while their fathers and these states in general maintained their loyalty to the Union. It is interesting to note that it was not the issue of slavery that divided these fathers and sons. On the contrary, most of these families owned slaves, and both fathers and sons were dedicated to the preservation of the institution. Whatever caused these individuals to wage a family civil war within the national Civil War (Taylor offers a number of astute insights on this question), one thing seems very clear from this essay. At this time, the United States was united in name only.

Source: Amy Murrell Taylor, *The Divided Family in Civil War America* (Chapel Hill: University of North Carolina Press, 2005), pp. 13–27. Used by permission of the publisher. http://www.uncpress.unc.edu

When nineteen-year-old Henry Lane Stone joined the Confederate army, he did not just turn against the Union, or what he called the "cursed dominion of Yankeedom." He also defied his family, especially his father. Stone's parents were natives of Kentucky, but by 1861 they were living in southern Indiana with Henry and his four brothers. They were staunch Unionists, and at least one of Henry's brothers volunteered for the Union army. But in August 1862 Henry, a middle child, felt drawn to fight for the Confederacy. Knowing that his family would try to stop him, he kept his decision secret and departed without even leaving a note. To make his way past Union pickets, he disguised himself as a poor farmer and headed for Kentucky to join the cavalry of John Hunt Morgan. A month later he revealed his whereabouts to this father: "Pap, I do not regret one practical my leaving home and every day convinces me I did right," he explained, yet he realized the personal cost of his actions. "I can imagine how your feelings are, one son in the Northern and another in the Southern Army," he acknowledged. "But so it is. . . . Good times will come again." He signed the letter, "Your rebelling son, Henry."

Stone may have acknowledged that he was "rebelling" when he enlisted in the Confederate army, but he did not say why. Was he, like so many other Confederate soldiers, rebelling against the United States? Or was his a more personal rebellion against his family, especially his Union father? Or both? These questions vexed the Stone family and many other border-state families whose sons enlisted in the Confederate army despite their fathers' Union sympathies. Their division, which mirrored the greater conflict between the long-established Union and the youthful Confederacy, earned the notice of newspapers for its startling frequency across the border states. Few families know how to respond to their sons' departure and spent the early war years trying to sort out the various meanings contained in the word "rebellion."

The personal papers of these border-state families offer few straightforward answers as to why their political allegiances settled along generational fault lines. These families were, like so many others in the border region, landowners who made their living by raising livestock and wheat. They generally lived in the low-lying areas and tended to own fewer than twenty slaves. They did not engage in the large-scale plantation agriculture of the Lower South but were still fairly wealthy, educated, and prominent in their communities. In most cases their nuclear families were intact, with mothers, stepmothers, sisters, and brothers sharing their households and generally working together on the family land. Yet when war came numerous sons, who averaged twenty-two years of age, enthusiastically left home to volunteer for the Confederate service, while their fathers remained Unionist advocates of compromise and moderation.

Fortunately these Union fathers and their rebel sons argued freely on paper during the war, explaining in vivid detail why they believed their loyalties were divided. Even though the sons who split from their fathers in most cases left their siblings and a mother too, it was conflict between father and son that inspired the most introspection. Male kin disagreed in particular how personal their conduct was and to what extent the sons' national loyalties were linked to or contingent on their loyalty to their fathers.

The brewing rebellion of the sons became apparent to border-state observers even before the fall of Fort Sumter. As early as February 1861, twenty-one-year-old Josie Underwood noticed that in her hometown of Bowling Green, Kentucky, "all the men . . . of any position or prominence whatever are Union men—and yet many of these men have wild reckless unthinking inexperienced sons who make so much noise about secession as to almost drown their fathers wiser council." Border-state newspaper editors eventually took note of this family dynamic, including the *Louisville Daily Journal,* which months later declared the father–son conflict an "epidemic" and began writing lengthy essays on its pervasiveness.

What these observers witnessed was the climax of a generational conflict that had been mounting throughout border-state society in the decade prior to 1861. During the secession crisis some of the most vigorous proponents of slavery and states' rights were men born in the 1830s and 1840s. These were young adults who had never known a time without sectional conflict, who had lived through tenuous political compromises in Missouri and violent threats to slavery in "Bleeding Kansas" and in Harpers Ferry, Virginia. What they saw all around them was the elusiveness of a national consensus on slavery and a political landscape where division was the norm. In such an environment it was almost impossible not to take a vigorous stance on the issues of the day. These young border-state advocates of slavery and Southern rights, though not unique, developed a passionate enthusiasm for secession that set them apart from older generations and, in the cases considered here, from their own fathers. . . .

"I would caution you against imbibing all the notions put forth by your advocates for slavery," was how Samuel Halsey responded in 1857 to his son Joseph's blustery anti-abolitionist rant. To make his case, Samuel sent Joseph a "sensible tract" written by a Kentucky minister. Fathers like Halsey detected their sons' radicalism early, but rather than demand outright conformity they generally permitted an open debate on sectional issues. Their letters reveal an energetic but tolerant exchange of ideas throughout the 1850s, as the fathers apparently believed that beneath their sons' political vigor was a deeper agreement on national loyalty.

By 1861, however, the letters of these fathers and sons took on a starkly different tone. Any political difference was no longer something as benign as words on a page; in wartime, it could mean opposing allegiances across a deadly battle. As war seemed imminent, fathers grew less tolerant of their sons' independent political expression. They did not expect their sons to think exactly like themselves, but they did draw a line at specific actions. Service in the Confederate army was unacceptable. "Do not resign under any circumstances without consultation with me," one Kentucky father demanded of his son, whom he feared would leave the U.S. Army for the South. Other fathers struck compromises, even promising to support their rebel sons financially if they did not volunteer for Confederate service. Still others, hopeful that the war would last only a few months, made their sons promise to stay at home for a year before enlisting in the Confederacy.

Union newspapers challenged fathers to prevent their sons from leaving for the Confederacy and to compel them to join the Union forces. "If the young men are slow to enlist in the cause of human freedom," advised the *Louisville Daily Journal*, "let the old men step forward, and by their patriotic example shame their degenerate sons and grandsons." In this paper's view, the mechanism of paternal authority was the most effective deterrent to a young man's military support of the Confederate cause. After all, mid-nineteenth-century society considered it a father's duty to nurture his son's political allegiances. A mother might instill a general sense of civic duty and consciousness, but in matters of partisanship a father's example was to be paramount. Fathers must live up to these expectations, the *Journal* exhorted, and most fathers did in demanding political obedience. Initially, many Confederate-minded sons complied, but over time they found complying with their fathers' wishes intolerable. In the first year of the war the awkward promises of these sons set the stage for the "epidemic" lamented by the *Journal.*

Twenty-three-year-old Matthew Page Andrews of Shepherdstown, Virginia (later West Virginia), promised his father Charles, a pro-Union Episcopal minister, that he would not volunteer for Confederate service and would remain in law school. But this became difficult for him when his classmates began to enlist. "My position is getting more and more embarrassing every day," Matthew wrote his fiancée. "All the young men in town have joined one of the three companies formed here," and they did not understand why Matthew had failed to sign up. Peer pressure was severe; indeed, it had prompted many other young men to fight for the South. Yet Matthew vowed to remain out of service because he did not want to "offend" his father. Meanwhile, Charles Andrews took the opportunity to reinforce his political authority in letters to his son. "I am much more calm than you are, & have a much more intelligent & impartial survey of the whole question," he argued on one occasion and suggested that Matthew would come to share his opinion within weeks. Charles was over confident, for Matthew never accepted his beliefs, although he did not volunteer for Confederate service.

Sons like Matthew Andrews soon faced additional obstacles to obeying their fathers and retaining their civilian status. In 1862 and 1863 both the Union and Confederate governments passed conscription laws that compelled all men between the ages of eighteen and forty-five to serve in the military. For sons in the Union states of Delaware, Kentucky, Maryland, and Missouri, the idea of being forced to join the Union army became an additional inducement to act on their Confederate sympathies and quickly head south. Henry Stone, who opened this chapter, explained to his father that while at home in a Union state he "was in great danger of being drafted where I could not have served." After leaving in 1862 and joining the Confederate army, he wrote, "I'm contented." Sons in the Confederate states of Virginia and Tennessee had the conscription laws on their side, which, in many cases, did encourage a son's enlistment. But even in these regions some fathers stepped in to prevent the laws from affecting their sons. Matthew Andrew's father, for example, used his connections to preempt conscription and to find his son a job in the paymaster's office in Richmond, reasoning that a government job was less odious than service as a combatant against the Union.

Other sons resorted to sneaking away from their fathers when it became too hard to resist the pressure of their peers or the law. The experience of twenty-year-old Ezekiel "Zeke" Clay was fairly common. Before the war, Zeke was schooled by several prominent Unionists. His family, in fact, offered a model of sectional compromise: his father, Brutus Clay, was a Whig member of the Kentucky legislature and a slaveholder, while his paternal uncle, Cassius Clay, was a vigorous abolitionist, and his distant cousin, Henry Clay, was the architect of several plans to prevent slavery from destroying the Union. On the other hand, Zeke had a significant circle of friends his age who attended pro-secession speeches and rallies and encouraged him to join them. His family knew of his dalliance with secession ideas but was openly tolerant of his views, even during the first months of the war. His stepmother, Ann, kept her own Union opinions to herself even while venting to her husband that Zeke talked about secession "like some one crazy." Brutus maintained his silence, apparently confident that his son would uphold his agreement to stay home and mange the family land while Brutus served in the legislature.

Over several weeks in September 1861, however, Zeke secretly plotted his departure. He approached a Confederate officer about obtaining a commission in the army, yet denied having done so when his stepmother heard rumors about the meeting. He also set about making gun cartridges to take with him—working deviously right under his stepmother's nose—but claimed that they were for his father. Then one night the same month, after telling his stepmother that he was going loon hunting, Zeke rode off on his mare, taking along the blanket from his bed, one of his father's rifles, and a small amount of clothing. In a note found in his bedroom, he explained his departure this way: "I leave for the army tonight. I do it for I believe I am doing right. I go of my own free will. If it turns out that I do wrong I beg forgiveness. Good bye. E."

Brutus Clay could hardly contain his anger when he learned what his son had done. Zeke had acted with the same hothead zeal as the South Carolinians whom Clay and other border-state Union men condemned. He had failed to show a moderation in politics that Clay expected of all his sons and, more personally, he had reneged on his promise to remain at home during the war. Zeke evidently preferred to follow the lead of "every scamp in the country" rather than his own father's, Brutus thundered to his wife. Ann agreed with this assessment, having already vowed to find out what it was that had "induced a boy to take sides against a father." To the Clays, this was no ordinary disagreement of two individuals over sectional politics; rather, it was a very personal case of filial defiance.

Other Union fathers had the same angry reaction to the secretive departure of their rebel sons. Although they had given their sons latitude to develop independent political views, few had known how seriously to take their sons' expressions of Southern loyalty; fewer yet expected that their worst fear—Confederate service—would be realized. Union fathers therefore had difficulty knowing how to respond. If they accepted their sons' defection as an independent act of political conscience, then they would be acknowledging the outright rejection of their own political views. But if they attributed it to reckless and defiant behavior, as Brutus Clay seemed to do, it would be much easier to remain secure in their position as fathers. The sons' action would still represent a serious betrayal, but a more familiar and manageable one: it was just another coming-of-age struggle set against the dramatic backdrop of war. . . .

Newspaper observers encouraged Union fathers to view their sons' Confederate service as a deliberate act of filial defiance. In one of the first analyses of divided fathers and sons in 1861, the *Louisville Daily Journal* published a series of articles, entitled "Letters of a Father," elaborating on why the present rebellion of sons was a normal stage in life. The American "political and social system" contained an inherent contradiction, the series argued, one in which sons were required to defer to their fathers while at the same time were instilled with the republican values of liberty. The most readily available expression of that liberty was the rejection of "filial piety" in the home, and for that reason father-and-son conflicts were a natural creation of the republican system. The rebellion of sons in wartime was merely a reflection of this greater flaw in the American "national character"; worse, however, was the Confederacy's exploitation of this phenomenon with "specious appeals to the natural love of liberty."

Indeed, the Confederacy's call for independence meshed well with this younger generation's desire for autonomy. At least one study of secession has found that young men felt a natural affinity for the Southern cause precisely because of the desire for liberty nurtured in their own homes. Fathers, the guardians of their inheritance and future livelihood as the owners of land, slaves, and family businesses, at times posed a substantial obstacle to their sons' transition to adulthood. A father who was unwilling to give up land or otherwise assist his son in building an independent life for himself left him in a dependent position. This aroused a resentment and frustration that made the Confederate rhetoric of "independence" and "liberty" all the more resonant. . . .

Personal liberty may have attracted sons to the Confederacy, but few fathers were willing to view this attraction as a deep ideological commitment. Much more popular was the belief that their sons possessed no ideas at all and were deluded or coerced into the Confederate service. After learning of Zeke's departure, Brutus Clay speculated that his son had been influenced by a "scamp"; other Union fathers similarly directed their frustration toward an anonymous influence. One father complained that "older & more wicked men" had "seduced" his son into service. The *Louisville Daily Journal* concluded that one Unionist's son probably would not have fought for the South "had not poisonous sophistries been poured into his ears by older men who had a design to corrupt his mind and seduce him into the paths of treachery.". . .

No one worked harder to attract their sons' attention, these fathers became convinced, than the leaders of the Confederate cavalry. These men, reputed to be more daring and more talented than their Union counterparts, cut dashing figures and appealed to young men's desire for adventure. One of the most influential in the border region was thirty-six-year-old John

Hunt Morgan of Kentucky. Already legendary among Southern partisans as an embodiment of "chivalry" and "bravery," Morgan and his men swept through Kentucky and Tennessee in July 1862 on a raid that resulted in the imprisonment of 1,200 Union soldiers—with only 95 Confederate casualties. Morgan's words were as bold as his actions. In a circular entitled "Kentuckians!" he made the rousing declaration that he had "come to liberate you from the despotism of a tyrannical faction and to rescue my native State from the hand of your oppressors. Everywhere the cowardly foe has fled from my avenging arms." Crowds gathered along his route to catch a glimpse of the man who would become a folk hero of the Confederacy. His reputation awed young men. "You can't hurt a Morgan man," one Kentucky son boldly concluded after signing on to Morgan's cavalry. At least one hundred men, later referred to as the "sons of our best and strongest Union men," by a Kentucky woman, followed him.

Morgan and his men, according to Union fathers, preyed on their sons to become followers. "My son," as one father described his departure with Morgan, "was seduced into Rebel service by designing men." Also referred to as "Morgan's gang," and "Morgan's guerrilla party," this band of rebel soldiers unnerved Union families. They were persuaded that their sons were too young and too impressionable to resist Morgan's overtures, despite the best efforts of the sons to convince them otherwise. One Kentucky son tried to reassure his family that Morgan's men were "gentlemen of the best families of Ky.," and therefore honorable comrades in battle. But few parents accepted this notion. As one father explained, his son was a "victim" of Morgan's "folly & delusion."

One troubling influence, fathers discovered, lurked within their own homes and were of a decidedly feminine cast. Indeed, in some cases the "scamp" luring their son to the opposite side was none other than his own mother. Union fathers had good reason to suspect their wives: Who else had such close contact with and influence over their sons? While one Virginia father was attempting to dissuade his son for volunteering for the Confederacy, his wife was sending him letters laced with pro-secession sentiment. "What is the benefit of plunging Ben [Matthew] into this certain destruction?" Charles Wesley Andrews asked his wife Sarah, demanding that she protect, rather than endanger, their son. In a Tennessee household, Louisa Brown Pearl chose to remain in the South with her rebel sons rather than follow her Union husband north to escape the hardships of war. Pearl remained in contact with her son throughout the war and effectively condoned his behavior, despite his father's ardent Union stance.

Women like Sarah Andrews and Louisa Brown Pearl occupied an uncomfortable position, caught between the conflicting roles of mother and wife. In accordance with antebellum political culture, they were responsible for their sons' development into moral, civic-minded, and patriotic individuals; many sons also looked to their mothers for guidance in the sectional crisis. At the same time, however, mothers were expected to defer to their husbands on all matters of public affairs. In the two cases cited above, the women put motherhood ahead of wifely duty and thus competed with their husbands in influencing a son's political choices. But, in other cases, the idea that such influence might result in a father and son meeting on a battlefield was agonizing and, as one mother put it, "pursued me like a ghost." For that reason, some mothers chose to suppress their own Confederate sympathies and to seek family unity by urging their sons to uphold their fathers' patriotic legacy. "Your dear Father never took sides either way," wrote one Missouri mother to her son in a plea for neutrality. "Try and follow the bright example your beloved Father has set you."

Whether it was a family member or a cavalryman who deterred a son from that example, Union fathers found a way to explain familial conflict. To blame someone else's influence was to place the blame on the society that produced unscrupulous men (or women) and on sons too young or inexperienced to know better. A son's Confederate service was therefore not an expression of political conscience but instead symptomatic of a separate struggle over a father's paternal authority.

This reading of the son's behavior would seem to explain the common defection of the younger generation to the South, but the sons themselves provided an entirely different perspective. They repeatedly and adamantly denied that taking the Confederate side was in any way a deliberate act of defiance against their fathers. As Henry Stone exclaimed when he heard of his father's anger: "Father, when you look over my career in the past eighteen months, do you feel that I am a traitor? Have I not done my duty, and I have I not followed your teachings of right? Do you feel that I'm unworthy to be your son? God forbid!" While condemning what he called the "despotism" that his father supported, Stone still rejected the notion that he might be "unworthy" as a son. If anything, he believed that, by following the dictates of his conscience, his service to the Confederacy was wholly consistent with his father's teachings.

Obviously, a son would have every reason to deny a personally motivated rebellion against his father. But his denials did indicate a serious disagreement between the generations over the relationship between their family and national loyalties. Whereas fathers saw the two as intertwined—national loyalty was merely a reflection of their personal relationship—sons argued that the two were entirely separate. "I am a secessionist, but that shall not conflict with a duty I owe my father—that of being respectful, and kind," Virginian William Thompson told his father in February 1861. His loyalty to the Confederacy was unconnected to his ties to his father. Dividing his loyalties allowed Thompson and other sons to view their Confederate service more innocently than their fathers did.

Sons accordingly explained their defection as a pure act of political conscience. Zeke Clay seemed to know that his father would attribute his departure to youthful rebellion when he assured his parents in the note explaining his flight south: "I do it for I believe I am doing right." "I know

I am right," wrote another son, though it is impossible to determine how much influence this sense of political "right" actually had on the mobilization of sons. The same question has confronted historians who study why soldiers fought in the Civil War, and it is likely that both ideological convictions and personal considerations motivated most soldiers. But in letters to Union fathers, rebel sons suggested that ideology was *all* that guided them in war. They wrote about fighting "tyranny," "Black Republicanism," and the "despotism of Lincoln," calling on popular political rhetoric to emphasize that their military service was guided only by politics. Their differences with their fathers could be explained simply as the divergent conclusions of two rational, thoughtful men.

Behind these words, however, the political-first principles of the sons did not differ significantly from those of their fathers. On the most crucial and divisive issue of the war—slavery—Union fathers and rebel sons were, for the most part, in striking agreement. Census records show that three-quarters of the fathers were slaveholders themselves, and thus the majority of sons grew up in households in which slavery was openly accepted or tolerated. Rebel sons therefore could associate slavery with their fathers' interests and could see in secession the protection of something on which their fathers depended. Although their fathers, in contrast, may have predicted the eventual "doom of slavery," as one Virginia father put it, or believed that it was best protected in the Union, the sons still could argue that their wartime service realized their fathers' true ideals. The question that divided them was less ideological than practical: How could slavery be best protected—by an independent Confederacy or by the Union?

Such ideological congruence on the issue of slavery may have helped sons downplay any filial rebellion that may have influenced their behavior. William C. P. Breckinridge of Kentucky, for example, had been instructed by his Unionist father, Robert, to remain at home during the war to care for the family's slaves (whom Robert once claimed were "faithful to union Masters"). It hardly seemed a violation of this father's orders, then, to go off and fight to preserve the master–slave relationship. Yet generational tensions may still help explain why common support for slavery gave way to opposing stances in the war. Border-state sons were raised in a white, landowning society that saw slavery as the path to upward mobility, the thing they needed to become independent and achieve manhood. To see a challenge to slavery was to see a challenge to their inheritance, to their future, to their whole way of life; it is understandable, then, that men of this generation would join the Confederate defense of that institution. Meanwhile, their fathers' generation had lived through enough threats to slavery before and had seen compromises worked out between the North and the South. These men had more faith that slavery could be preserved *within* the Union—indeed, some border-state fathers, such as John J. Crittenden, of Kentucky, a slaveholding U.S. congressman, had forged the compromises themselves. Different generational concerns could thus shape divergent outlooks on slavery and the war, suggesting a direct link between family position and wartime politics in the lives of border-state men.

The sons still denied this link, however, and preferred to view their national loyalty separately from their filial relationship. In their letters home, they rarely attacked their fathers' choice to remain in the Union but strongly objected when their fathers tried to punish them for their Confederate service. Union fathers, indeed, considered punishment a necessary response to the personal rebellion they detected in their sons' enlistment. "Just as he has acted, he will be dealt with," was how Brutus Clay furiously explained his decision to withdraw his son Zeke's inheritance after his departure. Since Zeke had denied Brutus his authority as a father, Brutus would reciprocate by refusing what he owed in return: protection. Although disinheritance was rare among divided fathers and sons, fathers like Brutus Clay refused to send the customary aid to their sons, such as clothing or money, or forbade their sons from visiting their homes. These and other punishments served the indirect purpose of restoring the paternal authority that Union father believed was lost when their sons joined the Confederacy. Zeke Clay, however, did not take his father's threat of disinheritance seriously. With humor, he asked his stepmother if he could still keep his wristwatch.

For other sons, punishments were no laughing matter. A father's disapproval was devastating enough, but many sons believed that their fathers' punishments were unwarranted. They saw little purpose in lessons on respect or obedience when they believed that they still upheld these values. One penalty was deemed especially unfair: a father's refusal to correspond with his rebellious offspring. Certainly the wartime security measures of the Union and Confederate governments made it more difficult to communicate frequently, but some fathers deliberately withheld their letters as a form of punishment. After all, in peacetime letter writing was an important means of sustaining a personal relationship. The failure to write regularly had always been a basis for chastisement, and not to write at all was an act of profound significance: the severing of emotional ties. Given the insecurity of wartime, when soldiers found themselves lonely and threatened with death, this punishment could be devastating.

One Virginia father resorted to this step after finding his son's letters "full of the lies [of] Rebel Genl. Bobby Lee." Warner Thompson, a slaveholding farmer trying to maintain a living in the path of war, became fed up with his son's rebel allegiance after his own livelihood was threatened. Thompson suffered financial losses when advancing Confederate troops forced him to flee his Shenandoah Valley home temporarily in 1863. To make matters worse, his secession neighbors—especially the women—had grown increasingly hostile. An outcast, Thompson found it impossible to extend pleasantries to a son who allied himself with the Confederates and opted for silence over false sentiments. His son William, an eighteen-year-old aspiring teacher and a soldier in a Tennessee regiment, recoiled at his father's mindset: "Pa has ceased to think of me as his son," he complained to his stepmother, declaring that his father obviously cared more about Abraham Lincoln than his own son. This was especially traumatic for him when his brother, Jonathan, who also joined the Confederate army, was imprisoned by Union authorities. Without his father to comfort him, William became dependent on the kindness of strangers to help him cope with his brother's incarceration. "For all intents and purposes," William concluded, "I am a lone orphan."

In his father's silence, William detected that he had been consigned to the most desperate position of unwanted child. He saw the worst in the absence of his father's letters, revealing the extent to which he relied on Warner's love. His reaction was yet another reflection of the tension between authority and affection that characterized antebellum families. Whereas Warner, stunned by his son's defection to the Confederacy, chose to reemphasize his parental authority, William found his father's love increasingly important once he endured the foul weather, loneliness, and tainted food of his life in camp. In pleading letters, William accused his father of violating an obligation to extend that goodwill toward his children. "No one is capable of more devotion to a parent than I am," he wrote, "but in order that this feeling have *full* force, there must be a corresponding affection on the part of the parent."

Warner Thompson's silence was not an adequate measure of his true sentiment, however. He was, in fact, more conflicted than his son believed and found it difficult to condemn William outright, even if his cause was "entirely wrong." Warner frequently turned to his diary to wrestle with their relationship. "My natural affection for my sons & love for my country," he once wrote, "cause a struggle in my mind—it is a painful one." Warner had difficulty reconciling his son's act with his own desire to continue as a family. "I feel as if I am committing wrong to allow an active enemy of my country to remain in my house," he wrote of the idea of permitting William to visit, but "than [sic] I am met with the feelings of affection natural to a parent—it is a trial—sore trial." His loyalty to the Union—as well as his own economic security—compelled him to react as a stern patriarch, but deep down he possessed more complicated feelings toward his son. He temporarily resolved this conflict by asking family members for frequent reports on William.

Questions for Discussion

1. How did Union fathers interpret their sons' decision to join the Confederate forces? Did the sons agree?
2. What role did peer pressure play in decisions to disobey one's father and join the "rebels"? According to the author, why were those born in the 1840s more likely to sympathize with the Confederacy than their fathers?
3. How did the slavery issue affect differences between Union fathers and their Rebel sons?

4. Is there evidence to support the idea that sons who joined the Confederacy against their fathers' wishes were rebelling against *both* the Union and paternal authority? What did commentators of the time say about this?

For Further Reading

Stephen Ash, *Middle Tennessee Society Transformed, 1860–1870: War and Peace in the Upper South* (1988); William L. Barney, *The Secessionist Impulse: Alabama and Mississippi in 1860* (1974); Carol Bleser, ed., *In Joy and in Sorrow: Women, Family, and Marriage in the Victorian South* (1991); David W. Blight, *Race and Reunion: The Civil War in American Memory* (2001); Catherine Clinton and Nina Silber, eds., *Divided Houses: Gender and the Civil Warf* (1992); Dudley Cornish, *The Sable Arm: Negro Troops in the Union Army* (1956); David Herbert Donald, *Lincoln* (2000); Drew Gilpin Faust, *Mothers of Invention: Women of the Slaveholding South in the American Civil War* (1996); Don E. Fehrenbacher, *The Dred Scott Case: Its Significance in American Law and Politics* (1978); Michael Fellman, *Inside the War: The Guerrilla Conflict in Missouri during the American Civil War* (1989); William W. Freehling, *The South vs. The South: How Anti-Confederate Southerners Shaped the Course of the War* (2001); William E. Gienapp, *The Origins of the Republican Party, 1852–1856* (1987); Robert E. Griswold, *Fatherhood in America: A History* (1993); Todd Groce, *Mountain Rebels: East Tennessee Confederates and the Civil War, 1860–1870* (1999); Herman Hattaway, *Shades of Blue and Gray* (1997); Michael F. Holt, *The Political Crisis of the 1850s* (1978); John Inscoe and Gordon B. McKinney, *The Heart of Confederate Appalachia: Western North Carolina in the Civil War* (2000); John Inscoe and Robert Kenzer, eds., *Enemies of the Country: New Perspectives on Unionists in the Civil War South* (2001); Gerald F. Linderman, *Embattled Courage: The Experience of Combat in the American Civil War* (1987); John McCardell, *The Idea of a Southern Nation: Southern Nationalists and Southern Nationalism, 1830–1860* (1979); James M. McPherson, *Drawn With the Sword: Reflections on the American Civil War* (1996), *Battle Cry of Freedom: The Civil War Era* (1998), *For Cause and Comrades: Why Men Fought in the Civil War* (1997); Reid Mitchell, *Civil War Soldiers: Their Expectations and Their Experiences* (1988), *The Vacant Chair: The Northern Soldier Leaves Home* (1993); Barrington Moore Jr., *The Social Origins of Dictatorship and Democracy: Lord and Peasant in the Making of the Modern World* (1973); Mark E. Neely Jr., *The Last Best Hope of Earth: Abraham Lincoln and the Promise of America* (1993); E. Anthony Rotundo, *American Manhood: Transformations in Masculinity from the Revolution to the Modern Era* (1993); Glenn Wallach, *Obedient Sons: The Discourse of Youth and Generations in American Culture, 1630–1860* (1997); Eric H. Walther, *The Fire-Eaters* (1992); Russell E. Weigley, *A Great Civil War: A Military and Political History* (2000); Bertram Wyatt-Brown, *Southern Honor: Ethics and Behavior in the Old South* (1982).

18

The Children's Civil War

James Marten

War is more than the sum of its casualties. For both victor and vanquished, it leaves psychological scars that survive long after the fighting is over. This was certainly the case with the Civil War, especially because it was the only modern war fought on American soil. Because Americans experienced the war firsthand, it was not just a soldier's war. It was "total war" and, therefore, a civilian's war as well. Only a thin line separated the civilian home front from the soldier's war front. Very often that line disappeared. This was especially true in the South, where most of the fighting took place. When that happened, and for the only time in their history as a nation, Americans became refugees in their own country; they were prisoners of war in their own land and, at war's end, were occupied by a "foreign" enemy—and "foreign" is exactly how most southerners viewed the triumphant Union and its army.

In the next essay, James Marten shows how the war dragged children into its vortex. They witnessed the battles, heard the thunder of artillery, and saw the mangled and dead bodies. Some youngsters even fought in the war. Perhaps 5 percent of the soldiers on both sides were under eighteen years of age. Drummer boys as young as ten and twelve summoned soldiers to roll call and played taps. President Lincoln issued an order forbidding the enlistment of boys under eighteen, but the staggering casualties made recruiters look the other way. And it was not unusual to find soldiers of fifteen, sixteen, or younger in the Confederate army.

In the South, where most of the war was fought, tens of thousands of women and their children became refugees. The Union army swept through the region destroying towns, torching homes, confiscating food, pulling up railroad tracks, and, most important of all, liberating slaves and their labor. In short, they waged total war. Their goal was to destroy the material basis of the Confederacy's capacity not only to wage war, but to live off the land.

Children, soldiers, and piles of cannon balls amidst the ruins of Richmond, Virginia, in 1865. What might they have been thinking?

Hunger was common; starvation happened. Food riots occurred in many southern towns and cities. Tens of thousands of children, North and South, lost fathers to the war; many were orphaned.

As Marten demonstrates, being part of the war effort was exhilarating for some children (most of this essay deals with male children). They would recall it fondly in later years. For others, it was a terrifying experience that haunted them for the rest of their lives. The greatest impact of the war, however, was on the children of slaves. As the Union army blasted its way through the South, tens of thousands of enslaved children and their parents fled to freedom. In the end, of course, it was the lives of those children and parents that were changed most by the war.

This essay is a classic example of the inherent relationship between public issues and private lives.

Source: James Marten, *The Children's Civil War* (Chapel Hill: University of North Carolina Press, 1998), pp. 101–115, 122–123, 125–131. Used by permission of the publisher. www.uncpress.unc.edu

The war seared images of glory and of tragedy into the memories of Richard Yates Jr., a future governor and congressman from Illinois. He was a well-traveled toddler, for his father served as Illinois war governor and went to the U.S. Senate in 1865. Snatches of music lodged in Richard Jr.'s earliest recollections: a military band, a bugler trumpeting cavalry calls, the refrain "Glory, Glory, Halleluiah!" The first ships he ever saw were gunboats and monitors in the Washington Navy Yard, the first prison he ever saw was the infamous Libby in Richmond, and the first graves he ever saw were in the brand-new cemetery on the grounds of Robert E. Lee's Arlington.

Grief rather than nostalgia framed other children's remembrances, especially in the South. George Donaghey, another future governor whose father spent part of the war in a Union prison camp, claimed that "starvation is one of the sharpest memories of my childhood." The Arkansan recalled going barefoot, even in winter, and wrote that "by the time I was seven or eight years old, I had to work almost like a man, helping mother to keep life in myself and my younger sisters and brothers." For eight-year-old Annie P. Marmion, wartime life in Harpers Ferry was a nightmare in which "the great objects in life were to procure something to eat and to keep yourself out of light by day and your lamps . . . hidden by night" so as not to draw the fire of Union pickets. Life could be cheap in a town that changed hands numerous times during the war. During one siege a shell fragment killed an infant in its mother's arms, and a black women venturing out for water was shot and lay in the street all day.

The death of an anonymous slave woman indicates how tightly African Americans were bound up in the conflict. Since they clung to the bottom rung of the southern socioeconomic ladder, the war had severe ramifications on the lives of enslaved blacks living in the South. Their already stark diet dwindled, thousands endured squalid contraband camps, and hundreds perished from exposure and violence. Yet no other group of war children enjoyed the exhilarating sense of freedom gained by African Americans.

The personal experiences of children during the Civil War ranged from community celebrations to community destruction, from reading war stories to living war adventures. The infinite variety of experiences can be categorized into uniquely northern and southern episodes and circumstances. Early in the war, youngsters shared their parents' rather innocent perception of the conflict as a glamorous adventure. Even as the war turned bloodier, most northern children had to rely on sobering reports from friends and relatives or the stirring accounts in children's magazines and newspapers. Some would learn the hard realities of war through the loss of fathers and brothers. Many southerners—and a few northerners—witnessed battles or their bloody aftermath and submitted to terrifying and sometimes deadly encounters with invading armies. Despite the vast differences in the ways that the war affected northern and southern children, those thrills and tragedies and hardships led youngsters in both sections to respond to the war in very similar ways—as participants, not as bystanders.

Inspired, perhaps, by exciting tales from children's books or magazines, intrigued by letters from brothers and fathers, or merely curious about the noise and commotion created by the huge armies tramping across their land, children all over the United States and the Confederate States dreamt of getting into the action. Although southern children obviously had more opportunities to snoop around army camps and gape at the great and terrible battlefields, whenever Yankee children got the chance, they, too, inched as close to the "real" war as they could. . . .

Opie Read showed . . . boyish adventurousness when he bribed a Confederate bugler with brandy to let him ride with him into a skirmish with Union cavalrymen. "On a beautiful morning," with "shouts and songs of discordant loudness we rode forth to battle." As the long lines of horsemen crossed sabers, "it was beauty and not horror" that impressed Opie; he "saw an iron weed bend its purple head beneath the touch of a lark . . . saw a man with his skull split open, fall to the ground." As the sword fight developed into a decidedly less romantic fire fight, Opie's bugler friend stiffened and leaned back against the boy, nearly unseating him. "I moved to one side, reached around and took hold of the horn of the saddle. Blood spurted from the bugler's breast." Letting the dead Confederate slide to the ground, Opie rode off the battlefield, dismounted, and ran home. . . .

On those few occasions when the shooting war moved into their section, young northerners also dashed into the fray. Residents of northern border towns had, of course, heard rumors of "battles, of town-burnings, or horrible massacres, of treacherous surrenders," according to fifteen-year-old James Sullivan. But it was not until the Army of Northern Virginia invaded Carlisle, Pennsylvania, that James and his friends got a taste of the real war. A few days later, as the Confederates moved into Gettysburg, Charles McCurdy followed Confederate soldiers into the town square, where they showed him "the feeling of protective comradeship that nice men show to little boys." Swallowing their fears, Yankee youths clustered around as Rebel soldiers cooked their suppers, chatting about peace, the causes of the war, and army life. They were surprised to find that these dreaded enemies were "touchingly like our own boys." Others had different images. When Jubal Early's Confederate division stormed into Gettysburg, one ten year old peeked through shutters and thought of "a wild west show."

Once the fighting started, boys scrambled for the best vantage points. Charles McCurdy's parents inexplicably placed "no restrictions . . . on my goings and comings." Neither did Billy Bayly's. He roamed all over the battlefield, watching Federal troops arrive and then climbing Seminary Ridge with his younger brother and a few other friends to pick blackberries. Momentarily forgetting about the imminent bloodletting, the boys were stunned by the concussion of a cannon and a volley of rapid fire, then redeployed to a fence rail near a blacksmith shop. Despite his fright, Billy wrote years later, "to me as a boy it was glorious!" When the main body of Confederates advanced to within a few hundred yards of their position, the boys finally withdrew, "not riotously or in confusion, but decorously and in order." During the battle a group of Gettysburg teenagers forsook their homes, spending a night sleeping fitfully in a storeroom above a shop, listening to Confederate sentries and trying to learn how the battle was going.

Albertus McCreary and a group of friends tagged along after the Eleventh and Twelfth Corps as they formed a line of battle on Seminary Ridge on July 1, but the boys returned when shells began exploding nearby. The next couple of days were a blur of exciting images: ladling water from huge buckets for sweat-drenched Yankees as they retired through the town, an apparently overburdened drummer boy asking him to keep his drum for him, and shadows of "men rushing back and forth . . . fill[ing] us with horror" when the family retreated to the cellar on July 1. As the Confederates settled into the town, Albertus talked with many of them, and the soldiers taught him to distinguish between the sound of minié balls and musket balls and between the various kinds of artillery projectiles. After the battle finally ended, the McCreary household was occupied by wounded Union soldiers for weeks. Albertus and his brothers slept on the floor and ate at the Sanitary Commission headquarters. Dead bodies were everywhere, of course, and "the stench from the battle-field after the fight was so bad that every one went about with a bottle of pennyroyal [aromatic oil] or peppermint oil." Albertus remembered for the rest of his life vast areas strewn with abandoned and broken equipment, bloated horse carcasses, and wrecked fences. From his perch on the back fence he spent hours watching surgeons operating on wounded soldiers. "I must say," he wrote forty years later, "I got pretty well hardened to such sights." Gettysburg children maintained their enthusiasm even after the armies left, eagerly scooping up souvenirs such as rifles, swords, haversacks, cartridges and cartridge boxes, clothing, books, letters, and photographs that littered their streets. Entrepreneurial boys also hunted for bullets to sell for scrap and for keepsakes and sold guidebooks to tourists for years afterward.

Few of the boys seem to have gotten into trouble for flirting with such terrible and unpredictable danger. Perhaps the adults were so relieved when their sons reached home that they suspended their judgment. The reaction of Opie Read's father offered another possibility. Opie Read's horror at the death of his bugler friend was eclipsed by his fear of what his father—who an explicitly ordered him to stay at home—might do to him. "My only hope was to thrill him with my story," and for the first time in his life he "made a clean confession." It worked. His father seemed proud of Opie's courage and the honor it brought to the family name. . . .

Children did not have to travel to Virginia or Louisiana to witness the violence of war. Many children lived through the draft riots that plagued several northern cities in the summer of 1863. The bloodiest, of course, erupted in New York City, where groups of small boys joined the rioters by throwing stones through the windows of the homes of black residents to "mark" them for future attacks. Mobs looting carriages and burning the Colored Orphans Asylum elicited a "mixture of terror and pleasurable excitement" in a boy watching from the roof of his family's home. His most vivid memory was of "a hag with straggling gray hair, howling and brandishing a pitchfork." Eleven-year-old John Bach McMaster saw a black man chased down by a mob and "beaten to death," while Eddie Foy and several friends ventured into the "large colored settlement" near his home, where they also spotted a black lynching victim. "The sight almost turned me sick," he remembered years later, "yet it had a terrible fascination for me," and he repeatedly went back to view the horrible, curious scene. . . .

Of course, many children who did not seek out the war nevertheless came into harm's way. William Wallace of the Third Wisconsin reported that during the Atlanta campaign he saw a woman with two small children dodging shell fire. At each explosion, "she would jump up and the children cling to her dress crying and looking up most pitifully in her face, imploring help from their frightened parent." He also witnessed the Confederates' shelling of Williamsport, Maryland, where "women and children were running screaming and hollering, women barefooted and bareheaded running with their babies in their arms. . . . The soldiers running over every baby that came in their way." Not all children could escape the battles that boiled up and over their lives. Sarah Morgan Dawson reported that during the exodus from Baton Rouge in May 1862, at least two small children drowned, while after a battle in East Louisiana, one former slave remembered that the bodies of little slave children littered the road near a plantation caught in the crossfire.

Children living in or near Vicksburg [Mississippi] suffered particularly harsh and dangerous conditions. The Lanier children, for example, had to subsist for three days on the sugar spilled on the floor after marauding Yankees stripped their farm clean. Many slept or even lived for weeks in caves scooped out of the hills in the town and endured the bombardment from Yankee artillery and gunboats. Arching shells made terrible and beautiful displays during the nightly artillery duels. "Shells were plainly seen," a girl wrote years later, "with their tiny flames of light shooting through the air, making that peculiar scream that the old darkies used to say meant, 'Whar is you? Whar is you?' and when they exploded 'Dar you is.'" Of course, the shells posed a mortal danger to the children of Vicksburg as well as their parents and defenders. Mrs. W. W. Lord described the "horrible shells roaring and bursting all around" her family and neighbors, "the concussion making our heads feel like they would burst." Her own four children were quite young; one of the women with whom she shared a cave had a ten-day-old baby. She proudly reported that her "children bear themselves like little heroes." Every night "when the balls begin to fly like pigeons over our tent and I call them to run to the cave, they spring up . . . like soldiers, slip on their shoes without a word and run up the hill."

And like soldiers, they frequently became casualties. In an extreme example of making the best of a bad situation, after a little girl was struck in the arm by a minié ball, a convalescing Rebel fashioned the soft lead into a tiny set of knives and forks. Most injuries left worse scars. A Unionist woman recorded that a slave child belonging to a neighbor lost an arm and that her own cook's daughter was struck in the head by shrapnel. Another

Vicksburg mother reported the broken arm of a little boy and the deaths of a white and a black child during the bombardment. A series of letters from her sisters to a woman living in San Antonio provided excruciating details of the misery experienced by the besieged residents of Vicksburg, including the diphtheria deaths of four of her youngest siblings just over two months before the city fell to Union forces. The letters reported that at least three women had been decapitated by Union shells, that a little boy had died in a cave, and that the young son of an Irish couple living nearby was killed during the shelling. A neighbor had "heard screams down [in the kitchen] one morning and ran down there. A piece of shell had passed through the bed where the child was laying cutting it in two and its legs were sticking out of the wall where the shell had driven them and still kicking." The horrifying scene had "killed" the sick mother, "and the Father rushed all about town screaming and going on terribly."

The rain of death moved to Atlanta just over a year later. Julia Davidson certainly did not ease her husband's worries when she informed him of a soldier dying in a nearby yard and two wagoneers losing their lives in a street not far from their home. Worse, Davidson wrote her husband, "a little child was killed in its mother's arms," and a week later a shell passed through "the white house on the corner," "killing a man" and "his little daughter Lizzie whom you have seen at our house" as they lay in their beds. Before the Union army had converged on Atlanta, nearly the entire family of a Confederate soldier, including his two children, died even as he defended his own house, when Federal artillery fired at the Confederate flag his wife hung from an upstairs window. . . .

The war brought calamity even to children living outside war zones. Nineteen children at St. Mary's Orphan Home in Natchez died after they contracted smallpox and measles from Union soldiers encamped nearby. All over the United States and the Confederate States, children were killed and wounded in accidental shootings and attacks by soldiers. On one occasion, shells accidentally exploded in Charleston, killing two white and two black boys, while in another incident, a little girl fell into a water-filled entrenchment near Mobile and drowned. Careless soldiers discharged weapons that wounded hapless children, while, inevitably, others were seriously hurt or killed while playing with weapons brought home by furloughed fathers or relatives. According to Albertus McCreary, two Gettysburg boys died when they detonated shells while trying to salvage fuses and powder. Soldiers killed or seriously hurt young boys over the price of a glass of lemonade or for refusing to "hurrah" for Jeff Davis. . . .

Experiencing or even witnessing combat could exhilarate even as it disturbed the sensibilities of children. But the war placed other hard-to-measure pressures on children. One of the most important was the sometimes debilitating fear, loneliness, and weariness that plagued many soldiers' wives, depriving northern and southern children of their attention and guidance and good cheer. Some women lost weight from worry, but more damaging to children were those who fretted over where to take their children after their husbands' departures, who argued with in-laws over everything and nothing, and who succumbed to the depression that forced them to withdraw from the children, to become physically ill, or to crave sleep. . . .

As a classic study of British children during World War II pointed out, the children who stood the best chance of sustaining their emotional health in the face of fear and uncertainty were those whose parents, especially mothers, could manage their own anxiety. However, beset with worry over their husbands' well-being, scrambling to overcome food shortages that reduced their families' status and quality of life, and overcome with feelings of defenselessness and alienation as the war dragged on, many mothers, especially in the South, feared the effects on their children. An Alabama woman knew that her own state of mind affected the young granddaughter who was living with her while her husband and two sons were in the army. In a letter to her husband, she reported that, as usual, she was unhappy and sickly. "Caldonia," she fretted, "ses that hissteria is what ales me about you and I no when I miss getting a letter I feel worse." A difficult pregnancy and a long-standing feud with her landlady sharpened a Texas woman's obsession with her husband's absence; her sad diary barely mentioned her children.

The war could knock an entire household off kilter, especially if the mother in charge was having a hard time grappling with the challenges of war. Even though she maintained a life of relative comfort, Lizzie Neblett, a Crimes County, Texas, plantation wife, was one of the most distraught mothers in the Confederacy. Although her husband Will's post on the Texas coast kept him out of combat, a house full of children, increasingly independent slaves, and a growing sense of despondency about the future nearly overwhelmed her. In long, sometimes angry, and always emotionally demanding letters to Will, she betrayed a deep unhappiness that her children could hardly have missed. Just a month after Will left for the army, Lizzie, whose fifth baby was nearly due, complained, "I do feel so utterly wretched & hopeless at times, when I think that you may never return and my being left a widow with five little helpless dependent children, to raise & educate." She confessed that "if it was not for them, I might end my own life." When her new daughter proved to be a handful, she reported shedding "bitter tears, over the work of last August," the month in which the baby had been conceived. She could "take no pleasure" in little Bettie, "the very sight of her is a pain to me," and "I can't help feeling that her death would be a blessing, to me & her.". . .

Young boys felt constant pressure from worried parents to take advantage of their youth, to learn their lessons quickly, to prepare themselves to fill the gaping holes in society left by the thousands of men lying dead on battlefields around the South. A southern grandmother encouraged her grandchildren to "be diligent in their studies and gain all they can for it is not likely there will be much left to live upon if the war lasts long, and you may all *have to work* for your living." Some parents stressed that the next generation would have to come of age quickly. "The hope of our country for educated men is from boys who are now of your age," wrote Anna Burwell to her twelve-year-old son Edmund. "If this horrid war does not cease all the men who are young & from whom our country expects great things will be killed & you young ones that are coming on must be qualified to take their places." Burwell buried two of her sons during the war—both died in Confederate service—and she wrote Edmund to study hard now, "for if the Yankees come here & our darkies leave . . . you will have to come home to help us work." His education might have to be sacrificed; "you boys that are left will have to do more, will have your part & theirs too to perform in life—be a man 'be of good courage' in everything, do with your might what your hands find to do."

If young southerners had to prepare for a shortened childhood, it was also very apparent that in the future they would enjoy fewer resources. Indeed, the war straitened the circumstances of most southerners, sowing doubt in the minds of many children. Middle- and upper-middle class children saw, perhaps for the first time in their lives, their parents worry about financial matters. When one girl imagined aloud what she would do with $100 in the fall of 1864, her father—frustrated because his work as a railroad superintendent in Georgia kept him from the army—bitterly handed her a Confederate $100 bill and said, "There! Take it down the street and see if it can buy you a stick of candy." Another Confederate father, renowned chemist Joseph Le Conte, lapsed into a deep depression late in the war. His oldest daughter, Emma, described a scene in early 1865. "Poor father! He had Carrie in his arms just now, but her innocent joy and laughter so grated upon him that he had to send her away. It seems dreadful to see anyone smile." After Gen. William T. Sherman ordered the inhabitants of Atlanta to leave the city, "every one," wrote Carrie Berry, including her parents, "seems sad. . . . Mama seems so troubled and she can't do any thing. Papa says he don't know where on earth to go." Among the southerners crowding into the Confederate capital were a number of desperate mothers, many of whom were recently widowed by the war, who applied for jobs in the Confederate Treasury Department. Mrs. F. C. Jones explained in a letter requesting help that "I do not know what will become of us unless some kind friend will lend a helping hand. Certainly," she hoped, "there are some generous hearts in the City, that would not let the widow & orphans of a deceased Chaplain suffer if they knew it."

Northern children were not generally exposed to all of the same pressures and hardships as southern children. But they could also detect a change in their mothers, especially when sons and husbands went away. When little Jeanette Gilder and her sisters dashed into their mother's room to tell her about watching the regiment to which their brother and father belonged march off to war, she "looked at us without seeing us." Mrs. Gilder had shut the windows and closed the shutters to block out the sounds of the regiment's farewell. "The words that were on our lips went unspoken,"

Jeanette remembered, "we turned and went silently down stairs, leaving her alone with her grief." Gilder's father and brother survived the war, but many others were not so lucky. "The war cast a gloom" over McClean County, Illinois, wrote Phoebe Morrison, who clearly recalled the uneasiness and sadness that settled over her farm community when new calls for volunteers came out, when bad news arrived at the tiny local post office, or in the case of her own family, when word of her brother's and cousin's deaths arrived. "Wherever we went or whoever came to our house we heard dreadful things talked about." George Norris, the future senator from Nebraska, was only three when his father and brother both died in the army. Brother John had entered the army against his mother's wishes—but she tied up his treasured letters with expensive red ribbon. It seemed to George that, when word arrived of John's death, the spirit went out of his mother. He wrote that he "never heard a song upon the lips of my mother. I never even heard her hum a tune. . . . The war ended, and the young men came back, but John slept in a soldier's grave in the blackened southern countryside. There were times when it seemed that her heartache over her son would never pass.". . .

As Union pressure on the Confederate homeland mounted, untold thousands of southerners fled their homes. The population of Augusta, Georgia, doubled during the war, in large measure because of refugees from the path of Sherman's armies. Many newcomers joined longtime residents in war-induced poverty; by early 1865, 1,500 families lived on the pittance provided by local relief agencies. Confederate sources described the pitiful cabins and shelters in which Fredericksburg women and their children shivered during the late winter of 1862, while a large portion of their more affluent neighbors arrived in Petersburg a few weeks later were reportedly children. After Atlanta fell, perhaps 200 families with 1,000 children fled to Macon, where they lived in railroad cars and clustered at the mayor's office to beg for food. In Nashville in the summer of 1864, hundreds of women and children languished in stark, filthy refugee camps, suffering and dying from typhoid and other diseases. Administrators of orphanages in Charleston and Natchez scrambled to find refuge for their young charges. Over 130 orphans received absolution from the bishop under a Yankee bombardment before escaping to a rat-infested, abandoned plantation house outside Natchez. At least some of the women and children among the 400 mill workers expelled from Roswell, Georgia, by Gen. William T. Sherman ended up in a Louisville military prison or in an Indiana refugee camp. The *Baltimore Daily Gazette* reported indignantly that some of them had been hired out as servants in Louisville. . . .

* * *

An orphaned free black named Jim Limber lived the last year of the war with the Jefferson Davis family. He participated in family outings and holidays, became an inseparable playmate of Joe and Jeff Davis Jr., joined the little boys' gang that clambered through the neighborhood near the Confederate White House, and accompanied the Davises when they fled

Richmond. He was eventually taken from them and sent, almost literally kicking and screaming, into Union lines by the soldiers who captured the Confederacy's first family in Georgia.

Jim Limber shared his white benefactors' fortunes and disasters. Yet black children generally experienced a war very different from that known by white northern and even southern children, facing the most dramatic changes, as well as the most difficult conditions, confronted by Civil War children. They were exposed to soldiers and other northern whites, who treated them differently from, if not always better than, their masters. Those who became refugees—contrabands in wartime lingo—were thrust into unnerving, harsh, deadly situations. By the same token, the upheaval opened up new worlds of education and opportunity that they could not possibly have anticipated.

The war saturated the lives of many slave children, who like their white counterparts, eagerly sought news about the progress of the war or about the well-being of family members living near the fighting and of masters or masters' sons serving in the Confederate army. Many young blacks watched the drills and maneuvers of southern militias and army units and overheard war news from the gossiping soldiers. Booker T. Washington, who was only nine when the war ended, often fanned the flies away from his master's family during mealtime. "Naturally," he wrote in his famous memoir, "much of the conversation of the white people turned upon the subject of freedom and the war." The little boy "absorbed a good deal of it" and no doubt reported it to his elders back in the quarters. Even the youngest slaves on his Virginia farm knew what was at stake in the great war. As a result, "every success of the Federal armies and every defeat of the Confederate forces was watched with the keenest and most intense interest." Washington believed that slaves often acquired the latest intelligence before the whites, usually from slaves who fetched the mail from their unsuspecting owners. As a slave who frequently worked in the big house, young Booker was part of what he called the "grape-vine telegraph" that alerted slaves to events and incidents of the war.

But the most basic experience for southern black children was hunger. Supplies of clothing and shoes declined quickly in the South, and when salt reserves disappeared, so did meat from the diets of masters and slaves. As southern whites found themselves tightening their own belts, their much-vaunted paternalism withered, causing shortages and hardships to be passed on to slaves already living on the margin of survival. The war "sho' did mess us up," said one former slave, as the food and clothing and shoes they would normally have received went instead to the army. Slaves substituted parched potatoes for coffee and poke berries for greens and went without salt and sugar. Even a prewar staple like peas vanished from one South Carolina plantation, where the slaves ate only "corn-bread, mush, 'taters and buttermilk." After Union troops had swept through the neighboring countryside, burning or confiscating any foodstuffs they found, George King and his six siblings had to "search 'round the barns" hoping to find kernels of corn in the manure left in abandoned livestock pens. According to former slaves, many children and older people starved during the war.

Other facts of life also changed. Slave children learned to fear the beefed-up slave patrols as well as deserters from either army, who, according to Booker T. Washington, would cut off the ears of any "Negro boy" they found in the woods. When fugitives near Magnolia Springs, Texas, found black children near their hiding places, they would "ketch dem an' whip dem an' scare dem an' sen' dem home so dey wouldn' came back no mo!" Other young blacks were afraid of being kidnapped by strangers roaming the countryside looking for slave children to steal and sell.

Slaveowners reserved particularly harsh treatment for the families of African American men who ran away to join the Union army. Angry masters took out their frustration in physical abuse, deprived them of food and clothing, or sold them off to plantations far from husbands and fathers. Other planters simply drove the families of African American soldiers away, condemning them to destitution and homelessness. Black soldiers bitterly resented the abuse their families endured. A white colonel testified to the African American Freedman's Inquiry Commission that one of his African American soldiers had enlisted for the sole purpose of freeing his wife and three children; he paid the ultimate price for their freedom at the battle of Pascagoula. Another insisted that the colonel retrieve his children from his former mistress. "I am in your service," he declared, "wear military clothes; I have been in three battles; I was in the assault at Port Hudson; *I want those children.*" In some parts of Kentucky, according to a Freedman's Bureau agent, family members of black soldiers could not be buried. . . .

The impressments of male slaves by the Confederate government to work on fortifications and of slave women to work in hospitals and factories separated thousands of families and forced children into adult jobs. Even within Union lines, as black men went into the Federal army, their wives and sons and daughters had to take over work on the small farms the army gave them to manage. A more dramatic uprooting of slave children occurred when masters hustled their bondsmen and -women out of the paths of advancing Union armies or when their own parents exploited the chaos of invasion to flee. At least 30,000 and perhaps more than 100,000 slaves ended up in the relative safety of Texas, working on rented plantations or hired out to other whites. Masters left some of the youngest and least valuable slaves behind. When Union troops threatened Rosa Green's East Louisiana plantation, her owner collected his best slaves and headed for Texas. He "lef us little ones; say de Yankees could git us effen dey wan' to." Allen Manning was only a child when his master packed up his Mississippi plantation and moved to Louisiana, where after only a year he relocated once again to Texas. "About that time it look like everybody in the world was going to Texas," Allen remembered. He and his siblings often had to get off the road to let wagons "all loaded with folks going to Texas" pass by. Allen and the other slaves moved at least twice more in Texas before the end of the war finally freed them. . . .

Like their white counterparts, refugee slave children faced unfamiliar scenes, encountered white people different from any they had ever known, and endured greater hardships than they probably expected. Children comprised a significant percentage of refugee blacks. In the "contraband camps" that sprang up wherever Union armies established posts, women and children dominated the population because so many men were absent as workers or soldiers. Army posts and occupied territories naturally became magnets for African American refugees, with over 10,000 streaming into the lower four counties of the Virginia peninsula. Fifteen thousand sheltered on South Carolina's Sea Islands even before the arrival of the additional thousands trailing Sherman's troops in the spring of 1865, and over 50,000 refugees lived in enclaves along the Mississippi River from Cairo all the way south past Vicksburg. Nearly half of the 2,000 residents of a camp near Murfreesboro, Tennessee, were children, while 2,500 women and children— the families of a regiment of black soldiers—clustered around Clarksville, Tennessee. . . .

Some of the camps took on the aspect of rustic villages, with schools, churches, and shops lining bustling streets. A former slave who spent part of his childhood on a "government farm" in wartime Alabama remembered that "dey treated us all mighty good. We had plenty of good food and clothes." However, most occupants of the camps bore severe deprivations, caused at least partly by army quartermasters who sold their rations and supplies on the black market. Medical care in the camps was sporadic at best, and in 1864 Congress eliminated funds for treatment of contrabands, leaving overworked and under-trained army surgeons with woefully inadequate resources to care for the seriously ill. The "contraband hospital" in Washington was only a collection of "rough wooden barracks" planted "in an open, muddy mire." A white nurse reported that dozens of refugees arrived daily suffering from malnutrition, exposure, smallpox, frozen limbs, hernias, and injuries sustained on their hard journeys to freedom. Cornelia Hancock reported that two little boys each lost a leg after falling from the wagon transporting them to the hospital. Sometimes grinding poverty forced parents to give up their children. . . .

The quality of housing in the camps varied greatly, although many refugees lived in primitive conditions. As military governor of Tennessee, Andrew Johnson refused even to issue tents to contrabands during the winter of 1863, claming that it would make them too dependent on the government. . . . Other freedmen, -women, and -children occupied old packing crates, tobacco barns, sod huts, and if they were lucky, abandoned houses. In some places single rooms housed six families. The crowding took a heavy toll, particularly on children. Even those youngsters who survived witnessed heartrending and health-breaking conditions that rivaled and probably exceeded anything they had experienced before. Of the 4,000 black refugees in Helena, Arkansas in 1863–64, about 1,100 died. In Memphis, 1,200 of the 4,000 contrabands died in only three months, while the camp at Natchez, also holding 4,000 refugees, suffered a nearly 50 percent mortality rate in 1863. Many of the children living near Memphis had no shoes or "suitable underclothing" during an abnormally cold winter in which five soldiers had frozen to death. At another camp, 600 or 700 "poor creatures" huddled in tents and leaky, smoke-filled cabins. One report from Vicksburg in the summer of 1863 called the camp at Young's Point "a vast charnel house" with "thousands of people dying without well ones enough to inter the dead." According to one horrified visitor the extraordinary hardships had crushed the energy and motivation of the freedmen. "They had become so completely broken down in spirit through suffering," wrote a Yankee minister, "that it was almost impossible to arouse them." A white nurse in Arkansas wrote that the freedmen were so demoralized by the squalor of their lives that "any idea of change for the better seems utterly impossible" to them. To make matters worse, Confederate guerillas frequently attacked isolated and defenseless contraband settlements, sometimes kidnapping and selling men, women, and children, who fetched $100 each on the slave market.

Questions for Discussion

1. Describe the Civil War experiences of white children from the North and South. How did they differ from each other? How did experiences of black children differ from both?
2. Within a generation following the Civil War, many portrayed it as a "family" disagreement between "brothers." In light of the violence described in this essay, do you agree?
3. How did parents respond to the eagerness of their male children to expose themselves to danger during the Civil War? What does this tell you, if anything, about the experience of violence in American culture? Do you think violence had a different impact on Civil War children—who *directly witnessed* it—than it does on children today, who usually experience violence in the *virtual* world of video games, the Internet, and television?

For Further Reading

Stephen Ash, *When the Yankees Came: Conflict and Chaos in the Occupied South, 1861–1865* (1995); John Blassingame, *The Slave Community: Plantation Life in the Antebellum South* (1979); Jane Turner Censer, *North Carolina Planters and Their Children, 1800–1860* (1984); John Cimprich, *Slavery's End in Tennessee, 1861–1865* (1985); Marilyn Mayer Culpepper, *Trials and Triumphs: Women of the American Civil War* (1991); E. L. Doctorow, *The March: A Novel* (2005); Drew Gilpin Faust, *Mothers of Invention: Women of the Slaveholding South in the American Civil War* (1996); Randall Jimerson, *The Private Civil War: Popular Thought During the Sectional Conflict* (1988); Lee Kennett, *Marching through Georgia: The Story of Soldiers and Civilians during*

Sherman's Campaign (1995); Wilma King, *Stolen Childhood: Slave Youth in the Nineteenth Century* (1995); Francis Lord, *Bands and Drummer Boys of the Civil War* (1966); Steven Mintz, *Huck's Raft: A History of American Childhood* (2004); Reid Mitchell, *The Vacant Chair: The Northern Soldier Leaves Home* (1993); Jim Murphy, *The Boys' War: Confederate and Union Soldiers Talk about the Civil War* (1990); William B. Styple, *The Little Bugle: The True Story of a Twelve-Year-Old Boy in the Civil War* (1998); Emmy E. Werner, *Reluctant Witnesses: Children's Voices from the Civil War* (1998); G. Clifton Wisler, *When Johnny Went Marching: Young Americans Fight the Civil War* (2001).

Freedom?
After the Civil War

Black Women and Their Families during Reconstruction

Noralee Frankel

In 1865, with the war winding down, a former slave, now a soldier in the Union army, ran across his old master, now a prisoner of war. "Hello, massa," said the black soldier in the dialect of the time, "bottom rail on top dis time." Amid the chaos and destruction of the defeated South, there was some justification for this free man's optimism. Four million slaves had been emancipated after 250 years of bondage. The political and economic power of their former masters was broken. The freed slaves believed the triumphant North would confiscate the plantations they had toiled on for generations without compensation and distribute them to emancipated slaves. After all, as one former slave rightly said, the property owned by their former masters "was nearly all earned by the sweat of *our* brows." Black people would not only become property owners, but would enjoy the full rights and privileges of citizenship, including the right to vote.

None of this happened. In the end, the Reconstruction era, which lasted until 1877, was a bitterly disappointing experience for black Americans. There were moments during the post-war years when former slaves enjoyed the basic rights of citizenship. But they were short-lived. Nothing could compensate black people for the horrors they had endured during slavery. But Reconstruction was an opportunity to provide black citizens with a measure of equity and justice. It failed. Why?

There are a number of issues raised by this 1874 depiction of life in the South after the Civil War. What do you think are the three most important?

For one thing, it is important to keep in mind President Lincoln's goal in fighting the Civil War. Lincoln's aim in the early years of the conflict was to save the Union, not to free the slaves, much less provide free black people with political rights equal to those of whites. Although personally opposed to slavery, Lincoln was a reluctant emancipator. As he put it, "If I could save the Union without freeing any slave I would do it, and if I could save it by freeing all the slaves I would do it; and if I could save it by freeing some and leaving others alone I would also do that." In other words, emancipation was a war measure and ending slavery a means toward achieving victory. Anything approaching racial equality was never part of this equation. This was evident in Lincoln's plan for Reconstruction—for bringing the South back into the Union after the war. His initial proposal limited voting rights and office holding to white southerners. The slaves would be "free," but would lack basic political rights. A few days before he was assassinated,

Lincoln softened this stance somewhat by advocating the vote for educated black men and those who were veterans of the Union army.

For another thing, in order for Reconstruction to work, the South would have had to be economically "reconstructed." The former slaves possessed neither land nor the money to purchase it. How were they to survive, much less prosper, after the war? They were also educationally disadvantaged. Most could not read or write. Prior to the Civil War, every slave state except Tennessee prohibited teaching slaves to read and write. Under these circumstances, the only way to ensure their economic viability would have been to provide the tens of thousands of emancipated black families with land. That meant either giving them land owned by the federal government or confiscating the property of their former masters (who, after all, were viewed as traitors by the North), or both. Most freed black people expected this to happen. It did not, and instead they were left to fend for themselves. In the end, as the next essay by Noralee Frankel makes clear, the majority of black families eventually became sharecroppers on land owned by former slave holders. They were no longer slaves, but the system of sharecropping placed the economic destinies of most southern blacks in the hands of wealthy white planters who had the power to exploit them.

Finally, in order for the South to be "reconstructed" racially, its tradition of white domination had to be challenged. For a time it was—especially during the period when Reconstruction was controlled by the "radical" Republicans in Congress. Among other laws, Congress passed the Fourteenth Amendment to the Constitution (approved in 1868) that prohibited states from denying "equal protection of the laws" to any citizen. In 1870 the Fifteenth Amendment went into effect; it prohibited the state and federal governments from depriving any male citizen of the right to vote because of race. (It should be noted that the South did not have a monopoly on preventing blacks from voting; more than 90 percent of black men residing in northern states were prohibited from voting as well.) The Civil Rights Act of 1866 outlawed the infamous "Black Codes," laws passed by southern states restricting the freedom of black Americans (they are described in Frankel's essay). And in 1867 Congress passed the Reconstruction Act, which divided the conquered South into five military districts, prohibited former Confederates from voting or holding office, and guaranteed the rights of black people to vote and hold office.

At first, this worked. Black men voted in huge numbers, and more than 1,500 of them held a variety of political offices in the South. One became governor of Louisiana, fourteen were elected to the House of Representatives, and two were sent to the United States Senate from Mississippi. Hundreds of former slaves became policemen, sheriffs, postal workers, justices of the peace, and state legislators. In other words, Reconstruction could have been effective in undermining the southern tradition of white domination.

But most northerners did not care about the destinies of black people and were tired of the financial and political costs of occupying the South. In

1877, Reconstruction officially ended. The South, left to its own devices, began the process of reasserting the domination of whites over blacks. Over the next twenty years, it passed laws that deprived black people of the basic rights of citizenship, including voting and holding office. Laws were passed mandating racial segregation in public accommodations and education. And where the law fell short in ensuring white domination, terrorist groups like the Ku Klux Klan took over.

Noralee Frankel describes the Reconstruction era in Mississippi in the next essay. Although Frankel's work is focused on the post–Civil War black experience in Mississippi, her discussion is relevant to other southern states as well. The Black Codes, Klan violence, sharecropping, and the desperate efforts of black parents to create a decent life for themselves and their children occurred across the South.

It is hard to imagine a "public moment" in American history that had more of an impact on "private lives" than the emancipation of 4 million slaves. It is equally hard to imagine the disappointment and disillusion felt by black people as the promise of Reconstruction turned into the bitter reality of poverty, violence, and second-class citizenship.

Source: Noralee Frankel, *Freedom's Women: Black Women and Families in Civil War Era Mississippi* (Bloomington: University of Indiana Press, 1999), pp. 56–59, 66–70, 70–72, 76–78, 111–112, 127–131, 138–141. Reprinted with permission of Indiana University Press.

Although most African Americans in Mississippi continued to be agricultural workers, emancipation encouraged them to challenge the conditions under which they worked. Freedwomen performed the same type of work as they had when they were slaves, but freedpeople and former slave owners held conflicting views about the definition of non-slave labor. For African Americans, free labor meant adequate compensation and less white supervision. Blacks contested the insistence of white planters that they make all their labor decisions and their continued use of force.

As 1865 ended, freedpeople were reluctant to enter into year-long contracts as wage laborers because they expected to receive their own land. They also concluded that the labor contracts would limit their control over their own labor. They resisted the insistence of northern and southern whites that they become laborers for whites. Blacks wanted to work for themselves. They preferred to set their own work schedules and construct a greater distinction between public and private life, which laboring for whites permitted.

Employers expected their workforce to continue to labor the same number of hours each day and under many of the same restrictions as slavery. Many former slave owners relied on the threat of violence as a means of controlling workers. Whites even found it hard to adjust to new terminology for their employees. The word "slaves" was erased from W. S. Noble's labor contract of July 11, 1865, and "servants" written in its place.

The agricultural and domestic work of blacks set the scene for struggles with employers, but labor disputes must also be viewed in the context of the larger political struggle for race equity. Historian John Hope Franklin refers to this period (1865 and 1866) as Confederate Reconstruction, a particularly apt phrase for Mississippi. In Mississippi, whites elected former Confederates to office, such as Governor Benjamin Humphrey, a general in the Confederate army. In the fall of 1865, the Mississippi legislature passed restrictive legislation collectively known as the Black Codes. The codes were so named because almost all the provisions applied solely to African Americans. The legislation included restrictions on owning or renting rural land in the state by newly freed African Americans.

These laws reflected the attitude of the majority of white planters toward free labor. Although planters accepted the demise of slavery, they rejected the concept of free labor for African Americans by which laborers freely sold their labor and worked without coercion. This lack of faith in free labor, combined with their need for racial domination, led the Mississippi legislature in 1865 to approve strict vagrancy laws as part of the Black Codes in order to force African Americans to work on plantations. The laws were aimed at African Americans who resisted working for former slave masters.

The vagrancy laws defined African Americans solely in terms of laborers and more specifically in terms of their employment to whites. Targeting African American women as well as men, the vagrancy laws ensured that any African American who left an employer for any reason without permission could be arrested as a vagrant. These laws, reinforced by year-long labor contracts that were strictly enforced, vastly decreased the ability of African Americans to gain higher wages when they signed contracts. Such conditions made African Americans leery of signing labor contracts.

Most freedpeople anticipated that freedwomen would work with their husbands on their own land safe from sexually harassing or violent overseers or employers. The failure to divide and distribute the land of former owners bitterly disappointed freedpeople and forced them to seek employment with former masters. Nevertheless, African Americans continued to petition the government for land "for every man and woman" and they remained reluctant about working for white planters. . . .

During Confederate Reconstruction and for a few years after, the federal government through the Freedman's Bureau . . . continued to supervise free labor and legal marriages of former slaves. Although Congress established the Bureau, in part, to oversee the distribution of land taken from the Confederates, this program ended quickly with [President Andrew] Johnson's restoration of plantations to southern owners. Bureau agents attempted to dissuade African Americans from the tenaciously held belief that the plantations of former slave owners would be divided by the government and that the former slaves were entitled to it.

Bureau agents encouraged the planters to offer higher wages or a greater share of the crops, while agents grimly informed former slaves that the federal government was not giving them their forty acres. Samuel Thomas, the first Freedman's Bureau assistant commissioner in Mississippi, wrote a stern letter on January 2, 1866, "To the Colored People of Mississippi." He explained, "some of you have the absurd notion that if you put your hands to a contract you will somehow be made slaves. This is all nonsense, made up by some foolish or wicked person." He added, "I hope you are all convinced that you are not to receive property of any kind from the government and that you must labor for what you get, like other people." Additionally, he reminded them that "the time has arrived for you to contract for another year's labor, I wish to impress upon you the importance of doing this at once. . . . You cannot live without work of some kind. Your houses and lands belong to the white people, and you cannot expect that they will allow you to live on them in idleness." A combination of remonstrations by Freeman's Bureau officials, strict vagrancy laws, and restrictions on available land pushed reluctant African Americans toward contract labor by early 1866. . . .

The factors that influenced the evolution of sharecropping included the failure of land to be distributed, disputes over nonpayment of monetary wages, white supervision and intervention both in labor and family life, and the fundamental nature of the meaning of freedom. The northern concept of wage labor did not work successfully in the south. Freedpeople and planters defined free labor differently. Slavery shaped the responses of both freedpeople and former masters. Planters expected freedpeople to behave with the deference and obedience of slaves. Former slave owners anticipated that they would rule their laborers with absolute authority and reacted vehemently and sometimes violently to any challenge. In contrast, workers separated their lives from those of their employers whenever they could in ways that had been impossible during slavery.

Labor contracts and vagrancy laws kept freed men and women from using market forces to barter for better wages in spite of labor shortages. For example, [Freedman's Bureau] agent John Sunderland reminded freedwomen who worked for Charles Gordon that, under the stringent laws known as the Black Codes passed by Mississippi legislators in 1865, they could be incarcerated as vagrants if they left Gordon without due cause. Bureau agent John Knox dispatched a man to force African American laborers "Betsey and family" to return to their place of employment. Knox believed that workers needed to demonstrate strict obedience to their employers. When workers refused to "obey" a planter's "lawful orders," they failed to live up to "their contract and ought to be discharged," often without payment.

Nonpayment of wages to freedmen and women kept wage labor from becoming the success northerners wanted it to be. According to Freedman's Bureau documents, including complaint books, the largest area of conflict between African American men and women and plantation owners was the unwillingness of planters to pay wages to their workers. . . .

To freedpeople, wage labor seemed too reminiscent of slavery. Male and female workers complained that planters found trivial excuses to dismiss workers after the harvest to avoid paying them. This caused hardships for employees both because they failed to receive wages and because employers forced them to leave their homes on the plantations where they worked and lived. Although workers could be forced off plantations, workers could not leave when they wanted to hire for better wages.

Employers countered the complaints of workers. They justified their refusal to pay wages at the end of the year by arguing that they merely withheld accumulated debts from the pay of workers. Restrictive mobility clauses in the labor contracts as well as the inability or refusal of employers to pay in cash often forced freedpeople to buy from their employers and kept laborers from better priced goods available elsewhere. Planters charged at least 20 percent over cost for these products, although some added as much as 50 to 100 percent. Although these are not unreasonable amounts for modern retailers, the prices were expensive for African Americans. For example, a fifty-cent bar of soap became a relatively expensive luxury for a freedwoman who earned a maximum of $10 a month. . . .

In addition to difficulties over the payment of wages, conflicts between freedpeople and planters erupted over what kind of labor would be performed, when, how, and for whom. These disputes pushed both freedpeople and planters toward sharecropping. Former slave owners tried to continue to organize their workers in gangs, having successfully relied on them during slavery. Laborers resisted the supervision of a gang system. They preferred to contract in smaller units on a certain number of acres of land, sometimes with family members working in squads.

In addition to resisting work gangs as a method to organize and control their labor, African American men and women also vigorously protested the use of force. Although labor contracts forbade physical punishment, white Mississippi employers believed that only force made African Americans obey them. Planters occasionally used it as a punitive measure as well as a warning to other workers. Although some whites used violence more readily than others, former slave owners and overseers (after the war referred to as agents) in Mississippi generally considered physical coercion a permissible way to resolve labor disputes with workers. . . .

According to Freedmen's Bureau complaint records, although freedmen received physical punishment more than female workers, a woman's sex, as in slavery, failed to protect her from physical abuse. Freedwoman Mary Connor's employer struck her because she "did not know how to plough." Naomi Smith's employer kicked her for "not washing the clothes clean." When her former master ordered her to build a fire, Harriet Kilgore told him that she "had backache and was not in any hurry to get up there." Outraged by her defiance, Kilgore beat her. He later justified his action by explaining, with unconscious irony, that she acted as if she "was free and would do nothing he told [her] to." Another former master beat a woman for attempting to leave his plantation, explaining that he had "a right to beat her for she is his slave." In the first two examples, employers beat freedwomen for incompetence, just as they would have during slavery. In the last two examples, employers physically abused their former slaves for asserting themselves as free laborers: One woman set her own slower work pace and showed, in her employer's mind, disrespect and the other woman decided to exercise her right to leave.

In actions that were reminiscent of slavery, employers hit freedwomen with their fists, kicked them, and whipped them with horsewhips and switches. Southern white gentlemen pistol-whipped freedwomen and struck them with canes. From the violent legacy of slave discipline, whites set dogs on disobedient freedwomen. One employer forced a freedwoman to labor in the fields while wearing a chain. The bodily harm inflicted on freedwomen was sometimes grievous. One woman died from "250 lashes." The records are unclear about the punishment of the men who were accused of the whipping. During these violent episodes, southern men insulted African American women with epithets that were theoretically inapplicable to white women of their own class such as "black bitch." The literal reduction of African American women to animals exemplified the desire of whites to demean African American women. Their race, poverty, and class exempted them from southern male chivalry.

White women also resorted to violence against women workers. When white women physically attacked their female employees, they often used household articles. One woman attacked a freedwoman with a pair of scissors, and another "imprinted a hot flat iron" on a freedwoman's face. When a freedwoman was "insulting" to her white female employer whom she felt had cheated her out of part of her wages, her employer hit her with a fire shovel. African American women retaliated when possible. When her employer, Mrs. Scarborough, hit her with a brush broom, Laura Sloan fought back and tossed "a bucket of water on her." Such actions by employers strengthened the desire of African American women to remove themselves as much as possible from working directly for whites. . . .

When freedwomen complained to the Freedman's Bureau about sexual assaults, they most often accused their employers of making unwarranted advances or attempting rape. Ann Woodson accused both her employer and his son of pursuing her. Women and their men both protested such attacks. They pleaded for release of the women from their labor contracts with pay and without penalty.

Although sexual harassment by white men often occurred in a work context, freedwomen were subject to assault from white men other than their employers. White violence toward African American men and women enforced racial domination. Vigilante groups such as the Ku Klux Klan that were formed to repress black equality used gang rape as an instrument of terror and racial control. Although these groups murdered more African American men than women, freedwomen were vulnerable to sexual assault. While in disguise "with their faces blackened," white men whipped an African American man and his wife and then raped her "three times after they beat her."

Such events acted as powerful reminders of the continuation of southern white domination after the war and the fragility of African American women's protection from white assault. Freedwoman Laura Sanders stated that six white men "broke into her house" and three "ravished her and otherwise mistreated her." The attackers picked some of their victims because of their links to political activists. Ellen Parton testified in the early 1870s before the United States Congress Joint Select Committee to investigate the Ku Klux Klan that eight men broke into her home looking for Republican activists, and one "committed rape upon me." She explained, "I yielded to him because he had a pistol drawn, when he took me down he hurt me of course." In addition to being devastating for women, rape served as a surrogate attack on African American manhood, because it reinforced an image of the powerless African American man. Men could not protect their women in spite of emancipation and the women could not protect themselves. In cases such as Ellen Parton's, the assaults also reminded African American men that their support of the Republican party endangered the entire community. . . .

Regardless of whether or not they involved violence, labor disputes were tied to the definitions of former slaves of the concept of freedom in terms of who controlled African American labor, leisure, and time within the family. Freed men and women were interested in the fundamental question of how emancipation would differ from slavery and how freedom was going to change their work. Disagreements between employers and employees developed over the intention of freedpeople to work fewer hours than they had as slaves. After the war, freedpeople strove to minimize the interference of former slave owners in the domestic and family portion of their lives. Although planters opposed any changes from slavery, freedpeople expected that the needs of African American families would be important components in decisions about how much time freedwomen and their children devoted to outside employment. African American parents wanted to send their children to school rather than to the fields. African American women, who assumed most of the domestic responsibility for their households, needed more time for their families.

Freedwomen wanted their agricultural work to be performed for the benefit of their family and perceived field work, just as much as washing or cooking, to be part of their labor for their family. They did not want to work only for the material betterment of white people but also for their own households. After the war, the link between labor and family strengthened for women as decisions about one had the capacity to influence the other. Ultimately, the desire of freedwomen to set their own schedules for domestic tasks caused men and women alike to resist gang labor and become sharecroppers.

Freedwomen needed more time for their families in part because their private domestic responsibilities increased after the Civil War. Cooking and clothes-making often ceased to be communal activities as they had been under slavery. . . . After emancipation, freedwomen prepared more meals for themselves and their families. When employers gave their workers patches of land, African American women planted gardens and raised produce, including potatoes, squash, and peas, for sale. Although male farm workers on J. G. Colbert's place received pay of one-third of the crop, Colbert gave their wives "three acres of land" for their own use. African American women also raised animals for their families, such as hogs and chickens for food, while men tended to the draft animals. Pigs proved to have the added advantage of being as loyal and affectionate as dogs. (One freedwoman described a sow that she raised "just like one of her children.") In addition to cooking, washing, sewing and gardening, freedwomen took charge of caring for their own children. . . .

As husband and father, a freedman assumed the role of legal head of the family and maintained guardianship of his children. Symbolic of the transfer of family power from slaveholder to father was the universal acceptance of the father's surname by former slave wives and children. Widowed Jane Kendrick explained that "the reason I changed my name to Jane Reece was my husband's father was named Reece and directly after the war every slave had the privilege of choosing their sir names and I chose the name of my husband's father who had chosen the name of Reece."

After emancipation, as freedmen gained the responsibilities of citizens, the male head of household became the family's legal representative and protector. When necessary, African American men went to court on behalf of their families, acting for their wives and siblings as well as their extended kin. When employers refused to pay both husband and wife their wages, or drove families off their plantations, the husband spoke for the family before the Freedman's Bureau agent. . . .

African American men attempted to act as intermediaries between their families and employers. They tried to protect their families against violence. When Richard Bryant's wife's employer severely whipped her, Bryant demanded an explanation. For his efforts, Richard Bryant barely escaped death from an attack with an iron bar. Peter Robinson complained to the Bureau that Gill Gordon struck Robinson's wife to the ground and kicked her. When J. Monroe Palmer beat Abner Abraham's wife, Abraham protested. In retaliation, Palmer "beat him." Men also objected to other injustices, such as when whites insulted their wives. When a Justice of the Peace called William Davis's wife a "damn black bitch," Davis threatened to report him to the federal military officer stationed in the town. African American husbands also resorted to violence to protect their wives. One African American man defended his shooting of a white man, explaining that the man had "abused [his] wife."

Wives rarely voiced complaints on behalf of their husbands in a public forum such as the Freedman's Bureau. African American women represented their husbands only when circumstances kept men from speaking for themselves, for example, in cases when their men were unfairly jailed or very infirm. Instead, women defended their husbands in more informal ways. When necessary, wives refused to reveal the hiding places of their husbands, thereby shielding their men from the Ku Klux Klan. Fearing death at the hands of the Klan, men ran for safety, leaving their wives because, as one man explained, the Klan "don't hurt women unless some of the women is sassy to some of their wives, or speak like a white woman, and they call that sass; then they go and nearly whip them to death." This man felt comfortable leaving his wife because he knew she "wouldn't say nothing; she says nothing, or only so little that you can't take no offense at it—can't get mad." Such loyalty incurred risk. A Klansman hit Ann Burris with his gun when she refused to divulge where her husband had fled, and Klansmen threatened to kill Hester Buford for withholding her husband's location from them. Women left behind were also vulnerable to rape.

In addition to assuming responsibilities as head of the family, African American men exercised certain familial prerogatives. White employers and Freedman's Bureau agents encouraged freedmen to control freedwomen's labor when such behavior reinforced the sanctity of the labor contract or ensured the women's continued participation in the labor force. Thus, employers and the Freedman's Bureau supported a dominant role for African American males when it promoted their own interests. . . .

Although the male head of the African American family maintained legal rights such as custody and right of contract over other family members, his power was less than the law implied. The legacy of the slave experience and racial animosity from whites undermined the authority of the father within the family. Southern whites generally refused to acknowledge the African American man's newly acquired legal privileges over members of his family, especially when the father's rights interfered with the labor supply of white employers or with white male sexual access to African American women. As Thomas C. Holt has argued, "there was a blatant contradiction between the notion that workers would imitate the bourgeois private sphere and the planters' demand that they control the labor of whole families."

The Black Codes that were passed in 1865 in Mississippi in part denied African American men privileges associated with manhood, including land ownership, possession of a weapon, and "civil responsibilities and rights." These policies helped to keep African Americans in an economically and racially subordinate status to white men. Southern whites refused to defer to African American men regarding their families. White expectations of African American subservience also included a concept of work which required African Americans to labor for whites. White belief in African American inferiority ill-prepared whites to accept the creation of an African American patriarchy. According to one Freedman's Bureau agent, Mississippi whites wanted "to establish some relation which evades the simple recognition of the freedom and manhood of the Negro."

The ability of white southerners to dictate labor terms, and, by extension, the structure of the family, to freedpeople was a prominent feature of the postwar labor economy. It was inconceivable to white employers that any African American father or husband would challenge their will. As one Freedman's Bureau agent noted, "The marital relations of the freedpeople is anything but pleasing. Nothing is more surprising that the disregard . . . by the whites in their dealings with them." He elaborated, "If it suits the white man's or woman's convenience to discharge the husband . . . and retain the wife . . . they will." A perplexed Mississippi planter requested that the Freedman's Bureau help him regain a freedwoman employee who left once her husband brought an order from a Bureau agent that authorized the husband to remove her without penalty from the plantation. The employer expressed puzzlement about the freedwoman's action in joining her husband because the woman never "expressed a desire to leave." Similarly, A. F. Mount pleaded with the Bureau to force the spouse of a former hand to return to his place. Mount state simply, "I do not want him. I only want his wife and children." He saw no inherent problem even though his request, if granted, separated the wife and children from their husband and father. . . .

After the war, one of the greatest threats to the African American family and African American parental authority over their own children was the apprenticing of African American children by white planters. The majority of disputes concerning children that freedpeople brought to the Freedman's Bureau involved attempts by southern whites to retain or apprentice African American children. These conflicts combined the issues of African American control over their families and the labor of freedpeople. Special laws passed in 1865 as part of the Black Codes authorized Mississippi officials, which included "sheriffs, [and] justices of the peace" to report African American (defined as "freedmen, free negroes and mulattos") orphans and impoverished children to local authorities so that the probate court could apprentice them. The law also specified "that the former owner of said minors shall have the preference when, in the opinion of the court, he or she shall be a suitable person for that purpose." Former slave owners paid a bond in probate court for the child after following legal procedures that required "due notice" to the parents (if living) "by posting notices in five public places, and by calling [the parent's name] three times at the court house door." Such legal gestures did not protect African American parents from losing their children, especially given the high rate of illiteracy among freedpeople and their unfamiliarity with the law. One woman who swore that she could support her daughter lost her case because she "was ignorant of the requirement of law regarding witnesses" that she needed to fulfill to prove that she could support the child. Apprenticed children remained with the white family until they reached 21 years of age, if male, or 18 years, if female. Immediately after the war if the court declared African American parents destitute or vagrants, it apprenticed the children without parental consent. The courts justified their decisions on the grounds that un-apprenticed, orphaned, or destitute children needed private support to prevent them from becoming a financial burden to the local government. Children were apprenticed in significant numbers during Presidential Reconstruction. According to one historian, "the probate court at Calhoun City apprenticed two hundred and twenty at one term."

In disputed cases between parents and former owners, the Mississippi local courts usually gave the children to whites. In 1865 and 1866, the local government, controlled by Democrats and still sympathetic to the interests of planters, supported the apprentice system as a form of race and labor control. In contrast, the federal government, usually represented by Freedman's Bureau agents in Mississippi, generally sided with freed families who were trying to regain their children if the families could support them. Although it was committed to keeping former slave families together, the Bureau also wanted to prevent African American children from becoming financially dependent on the federal government. Because the apprentice law allowed whites to break up families and gave them the virtual slave labor of children, Freedman's Bureau agents protested the widespread abuse. As Samuel Thomas [a white Union officer] wrote the head of the Freedman's Bureau, Oliver Otis Howard, the apprentice law "is capable of being made an instrument of oppression to the colored people and is being so used." Former slave masters swore that children who were bonded to them were orphans and tried to convince the courts that parents who claimed them were frauds. Others falsely accused parents of destitution even in those cases where such claims proved highly questionable. J. H. Grace testified in civil court that the mother of the children he wanted to apprentice, all of whom were his former slaves, was mentally deficient and incapable of caring for her children. The court granted him the apprenticeship. When the mother sought aid from a Freedman's Bureau agent, he found her completely competent and bitterly complained to his superior, "better would it have been for them to remain in slavery if they are to be dragged up and apprenticed in violation of law, and against their will and common sense.". . .

To counteract such as the apprenticeship legislation that discriminated against African Americans, the United States Congress passed the Civil Rights Act in 1866 over Andrew Johnson's presidential veto. The act stated that "citizens, of every race and color, without regard to any previous condition of slavery or involuntary servitude . . . shall have the same right[s] . . . as . . . enjoyed by white citizens." Because the special apprentice laws passed in Mississippi as part of the Black Codes applied only to African American children, the Civil Rights Act effectively nullified the law. Some Bureau agents interpreted the Civil Rights Act as requiring parental consent prior to the apprenticeship of children. To regain custody of their children under the Civil Rights Act, African American parents needed to obtain a writ of habeas corpus in Circuit Court and file it with the probate court. Even with a writ, the courts required parents to prove their ability to support their children. Although the use of habeas corpus expanded after the Civil War, African Americans discovered that the legal system was expensive, slow, and governed by incomprehensible court procedures. . . .

* * *

As historian W. E. B. DuBois pointed out, "Mississippi was the place where first and last Negroes were largely deprived of any opportunity for landownership." Because of the inability of freedmen to obtain land and the unwillingness of former slave owners to pay monetary wages, African American women and their men became sharecroppers as a way to support themselves. When a family worked as a labor unit in the fields, rather than as gangs of men and women, it often received a share of the crop. This system, along with factors such as who provided the tools and draft animals, evolved into the sharecropping system. Sharecropping gradually became the fate of freed men and women, although it developed more slowly in some areas of Mississippi than in others. African Americans were sharecropping as early as 1867, when sharecropping coexisted with monetary and share wages.

Ultimately, sharecropping returned African Americans to a new reliance on whites and crippled them economically by keeping them indebted. The federal government's refusal to give land to freedmen had a profound impact on the extent to which African Americans could be self-employed. Because they could not acquire land, freedpeople expected wages; when they became disillusioned with monetary wages, they negotiated for a share of the crop. The failure of employers to pay monetary wages, and the desire of freedpeople for less white supervision in the fields all led to sharecropping. Sharecropping developed as cotton prices declined and white landowners in Mississippi made little effort to shift to mixed agriculture. It emerged despite the political change from Democratic to short-lived moderate Republican control of the state. Even under the civil rights reforms of the late 1860s and early 1870s in Mississippi that outlawed the Black Codes, African Americans continued to work for whites. Freedwoman Rina Brown recalled that "every thing we got we had to buy it on credit an' den de white man got whut we made."

The inability of Reconstruction to bring about a radical change in the economic lives of the former slaves represented one of the most acute failures of emancipation for African Americans. The lack of economic opportunities ensured that freedpeople remained laborers for whites, unable to achieve upward mobility. To that extent, they felt that freedom had failed them. As one Mississippi woman bitterly stated, "Is I free? Hasn't I got to get up before daylight and go into the field to work?" As the quote points out, formerly enslaved women worked as field hands or domestic workers who performed the same work that they had as slave women. With more resignation, another freedwoman explained, "[D]ere wasn't no difference in freedom cause I went right on working for Miss."

Although sharecropping was far less than what African Americans wanted, the labor system did change from slavery. Although sharecropping did not permit economic self-sufficiency and economic mobility, it allowed more flexibility than gang labor. The use of overseers decreased and workers determined more of their own work schedules.

After emancipation the rural African American family became a stronger unit than it had been under slavery. Black women controlled more of their private domestic lives but they had more familial labor to perform as well as the need to work for wages (in money or shares). . . .

In one sense work and family were more strongly tied together under sharecropping because families often worked in the fields together. But sharecropping was also part of the separation between family and labor as freedpeople removed their family concerns away from white interference. Women's familial concerns informed the labor choices of freedpeople as they tried to separate reproductive from productive work in their dealings with whites. Although they wanted the end of white supervision of both types of labor, they were never totally successful in their attempts to gain control of these two spheres.

Questions for Discussion

1. Why did former African American slaves expect to receive land—"40 acres and a mule"—after Emancipation? Were their expectations justified?
2. What methods did southern whites use to reassert their control over the lives and labor of newly emancipated black people? How effective were they? On balance, was the federal government's response to this situation more supportive of southern whites or of southern blacks?
3. What was sharecropping? Why did it evolve? Did it help or hinder black families in their quest for economic security?
4. How did black family life develop after slavery? Why did southern whites oppose powerful family ties among former slaves? What did they do to prevent them?

For Further Reading

Cindy Barden, *The Reconstruction Era* (2002); William L. Barney, *Battlefield for the Union: The Era of the Civil War and Reconstruction, 1848–1877* (1989); W. E. B. DuBois, *Black Reconstruction in America* (1935); La Wanda Cox, *Lincoln and Black Freedom: A Study in Presidential Leadership* (1981); Jane Dailey, *Before Jim Crow: The Politics of Race in Postemancipation Virginia* (2000); Eric Foner, *Reconstruction: America's Unfinished Revolution, 1863–1877* (1988); John Hope Franklin, *Reconstruction after the Civil War* (1960); Chungchan Gao, *African Americans in the Reconstruction Era* (2000); Jacqueline Jones, *Labor of Love, Labor of Sorrow: Black Women, Work and the Family, from Slavery to the Present* (1985); Kenneth Kusmer, *The Civil War and Reconstruction Era, 1861–1877* (1991); Leon F. Litwack, *Been in the Storm So Long: The Aftermath of Slavery* (1979); John Solomon Otto, *Southern Agriculture during the Reconstruction Era, 1860–1880* (1994); George C. Rable, *But There Was No Peace: The Role of Violence in the Politics of Reconstruction* (1984); James L. Roark, *Masters without Slaves: Southern Planters in the Civil War and Reconstruction* (1977); Willie Lee Rose, *Rehearsal for Reconstruction: The Port Royal Experiment* (1964); Nina Silber, *The Romance of Reunion: Northerners and the South, 1865–1900* (1993); Mitchell Snay, *Finians, Freedmen and Southern Whites: Race and Nationality in the Era of Reconstruction* (2007); Kenneth Stampp, *The Reconstruction Era* (1967); Betty Stroud and Virginia Schomp, *The Reconstruction Era* (2006); Allen W. Trelease, *White Terror: The Ku Klux Klan Conspiracy and Southern Reconstruction* (1971); Rick Warwick, *Freedom and Work in the Reconstruction Era: The Freedman's Bureau Labor Contracts of Williamson County, Tennessee* (2006); C. Vann Woodward, *Origins of the New South, 1877–1913* (1951); Richard Zuczek, *Encyclopedia of the Reconstruction Era* (2006).